Three Art Assessments

◇ ◇ ◇

Three Art Assessments

The Silver Drawing Test of Cognition and Emotion;
Draw a Story: Screening for Depression;
and Stimulus Drawings and Techniques

◇ ◇ ◇

Rawley Silver, EdD, ATR, HLM

Brunner-Routledge
New York   London

Published in 2002 by
Brunner-Routledge
29 West 35th Street
New York, NY 10001

Published in Great Britain by
Brunner-Routledge
27 Church Road
Hove, East Sussex, BN3 2FA

Brunner-Routledge is an imprint of the Taylor & Francis Group.

10 9 8 7 6 5 4 3 2 1

Library of Congress Cataloging-in-Publication Data

Silver, Rawley A.
    Three art assessments : the Silver drawing test of cognition and emotion ; Draw a story : screening for depression ; and Stimulus drawings and techniques / Rawley A. Silver.
        p. cm.
    Includes bibliographical references and index.
    ISBN 1–58391-352-1 (pbk.)
    1. Psychological tests for children. I. Silver, Rawley A. Silver drawing test of cognition and emotion. II. Silver, Rawley A. Draw a story. III. Silver, Rawley A. Stimulus drawing techniques. IV. Title.
        BF722.3 .S55 2002
        155.4'028'7—dc21
                                                            2001052522

For my husband, Ed, and our sons, Paul and Jon

The scientific search for truth and the human search for
understanding belong together.

—Jacob Bronowski

Contents

◇ ◇ ◇

List of Figures   xiii
Foreword by Christine Turner   xix
Acknowledgments   xxiii

Introduction and Theoretical Background   1
Introducing This Book   5
Drawing from Imagination   6
Cognitive Skills   7
How the Assessments Evolved   8
Studies of Individuals and Groups   9
How the Book Is Organized   9

Section I The Silver Drawing Test of Cognition and Emotion (SDT)

Chapter 1 How the SDT Was Developed and Field-Tested   13
The Drawing from Imagination Subtest   14
The Predictive Drawing Subtest   16
The Drawing from Observation Subtest   18
Why the SDT Was Developed and How It Evolved   19
Doctoral Project   19
A Demonstation Project for Children and Adults with Hearing Impairment   20

Three Art Assessments

First Pilot Study   20
Second Pilot Study   21
State Urban Education Project   22
National Institute of Education Project   22

Chapter 2 Administering and Scoring the SDT   25
The Predictive Drawing Task   26
The Drawing from Observation Task   36
Examples of Scored Responses   39
The Drawing from Imagination Task   44
Draw What You Imagine   45
Examples of Scored Responses to the Drawing from Imagination Task   51
Humorous Responses to the Drawing Tasks   64

Chapter 3 Reliability and Validity of the SDT   65
Scorer Reliability   65
Judges with No Special Training   67
Retest Reliability   69
Correlations Between the SDT and Traditional Tests   70

Chapter 4 Normative Data   79
Previous Norms and Case Studies   79
Expanded Norms   84
Scores of Adolescents, Young Adults, and Senior Adults   85

Chapter 5 Outcome Studies: Using the SDT as a Pre–Posttest to Assess Programs   97
State Urban Education Project for Children with Auditory–Language Disorders   97
Children with Visual–Motor Disorders   104
National Institute of Education Project for Children Performing Below Grade Level   106
Marshall's Study of Children with Learning Disabilities   109
Dhanachitsiriphong's Study of Incarcerated Adolescents in Thailand   109
Henn's Study of Adolescents with Multiple Handicaps   110

Chapter 6 Assessing Age and Gender Differences and Similarities in Attitudes and Cognition   111
Attitudes Toward Food or Eating   111
Attitudes Toward the Opposite Sex   114
Gender Differences in Self-Images, Autonomous Subjects, and Relationships   118
Age and Gender Differences in Attitudes Toward Self and Others   118
Attitudes of Older Adults   119
Attitudes and Spatial Skills of Aging and Young Adults   119
Comparing Spatial Skills of Male and Female Adolescents   122
Comparing Spatial Skills of Adults, as Well as Adolescents   122
Comparing SDT Scores of Hearing Girls and Boys and Those Who Are Deaf   123

Comparing SDT Scores of Hearing Girls and Boys and Those Who Are Deaf   123
Comparing SDT Scores of Girls and Boys with Learning Disabilities,
     Deafness, and No Known Impairments   128
The Hiscox Study of Children with Learning Disabilities, Dyslexia,
     and No Known Disabilities   128

Section II Draw a Story: Screening for Depression (DAS)

Chapter 7 Introducing the Draw-a-Story Assessment   133
The DAS Instrument   133
Administering and Scoring the DAS Task   134
Examples of Scored Response Drawings   141

Chapter 8 Reliability and Validity of the Draw-a-Story Assessment   161
Diagnostic Criteria of Depressive Illness   161
Reliability   162
Screening Children and Adolescents for Depression   164
Second Study of Depression   164
Third Study of Depression   168
The Self-Report and Masked Depression   169

Chapter 9 Using DAS with Clinical and Nonclinical Populations   171
Adolescents with and without Emotional Disturbances   171
Age and Gender Differences in Attitudes Toward Self and Others   173
Ellison and Silver's Study of Adolescents Who Are Delinquents   176
Gender Differences in the Fantasies of Adolescents Who Are
     Delinquent and Those of Nondelinquent Adolescents   178
Turner's Use of DAS with Adolescents Who Have Experienced Abuse   180
Wilson's Use of DAS with Patients Who Had Brain Injuries   181
Wilson's Use of DAS with Adolescents Who Had Contemplated
     or Attempted Suicide   182
Dunn-Snow's Use of DAS with Children and Adolescents
     Experiencing Emotional Disturbances   182
Coffey's Use of DAS in a Psychiatric Hospital   182
Brandt's Comparison of Adolescents with Depression and Those
     Who Committed Sex Offenses to Typical Adolescents   183

Section III Stimulus Drawing Techniques in Therapy, Development, and Assessment

Chapter 10 Introducing the Stimulus Drawing Techniques Assessment   187
Objectives and Procedures of the SD Techniques   188

Chapter 11 Reliability and Validity   197

Three Art Assessments

Mike   198

Andy   202

Sam   203

Chapter 12 Using the Stimulus Drawing Assessments with Clinical
          and Nonclinical Children, Adolescents, and Adults   205

Burt: A Child with Auditory and Language Impairments   205

Mrs. M   209

Mr. O   211

Senior Adults in Community Recreational Programs   213

Joey: A Child with Learning Disabilities   213

Vilstrup's Study of Adolescents in a Psychiatric Hospital   216

Sandburg's Study of Adults with Chronic Schizophrenia   217

White-Wolff's Study of Twins   217

Malchiodi's Use of Stimulus Drawings with a Child Who Had
          Experienced Sexual Abuse   217

Couch's Use of Stimulus Drawings for Patients with Dementia   218

Age and Gender Differences Among Groups of Unimpaired
          Children and Adults   218

Section IV: Correlations Between Assessments, the Use of Humor, and Cross-Cultural Studies

Chapter 13 Correlations Between the Silver Drawing Test,
          Draw a Story, and Stimulus Drawings and Techniques   223

Relationships Between the SDT Drawing from Imagination
          Subtest and Stimulus Drawings and Techniques   223

Relationships Between Draw a Story and Stimulus Drawing and Techniques   224

Relationships Between Draw a Story and the SDT Drawing from Imagination Subtest 224

Comparing the Negativity of Responses to the SDT and DAS Tasks   228

Comparing Emotional and Cognitive Constructs   228

Chapter 14 The Uses of Humor   231

Background Literature   231

Lethal Humor   232

Disparaging Humor   234

Resilient Humor   237

Ambivalent or Ambiguous Humor   236

Playful Humor   240

A Study of the Uses of Humor   242

Chapter 15 Cross-Cultural Studies   247

Use of the SDT in Brazil   247

Use of the SDT in Australia   249

Use of the SDT in Thailand   250
Use of the SDT in Russia   252
Use of the SDT with Hispanic Students in the United States   253
Observations   257

Chapter 16 Concluding Observations   259

Section V Appendices

Appendix A The Silver Drawing Test of Cognition and Emotion   263
Drawing What You Predict, What You See, and What You Imagine   265
SDT Predictive Drawing   266
SDT Drawing from Observation   267
Drawing What You Imagine, Form A, Silver Drawing Test   268
Drawing What You Imagine, Form B, Silver Drawing Test   270
SDT Layout Sheet   272
SDT Drawing from Imagination   274
SDT Classroom Record Sheet   275
Record Sheet for Response Drawings   276
Forms for Assessing Individual Responses to the Silver Drawing Test   277

Appendix B Draw a Story   281
Draw a Story Drawing Page   283
Draw a Story, Form A   284
Draw a Story, Form B   286
Form for Assessing the Story Content of Responses to the Draw-a-Story Task   288

Appendix C Stimulus Drawings and Techniques   289
Form for Assessing the Emotional Content of Principal Subjects and Environments   290
Drawing Page   291
56 Stimulus Drawing Cards   292

References   303
Index   311

List of Figures

◇ ◇ ◇

Fig. i.1.	"Shout in silence," by Charlie, age 11	2
Fig. i.2.	"Shout in silence," by Charlie, age 14	2
Fig. i.3.	"Landscape," by Charlie, age 11	2
Fig. i.4.	"Landscape," by Charlie, age 14	3
Fig. i.5.	Charlie's Adult Drawing from Imagination	4
Fig. i.6.	Charlie's Adult Drawing from Observation	4
Fig. i.7.	Charlie's Adult Predictive Drawing	4
Fig. 2.1.	The SDT Predictive Drawing Task	27
Fig. 2.2.	Predicting a Sequence	29
Fig. 2.3.	Predicting Horizontality	31
Fig. 2.4.	Predicting Verticality	32
Fig. 2.5.	Predictive Drawing by Tania, age 9	34
Fig. 2.6.	Predictive Drawing by an adult in a university audience	35
Fig. 2.7.	Predictive Drawing by George, expressive and receptive language impairments	35
Fig. 2.8.	Predictive Drawing by Caroline, age 3 years, 8 months	36
Fig. 2.9.	The SDT Drawing from Observation Task	39
Fig. 2.10.	Example of Drawing from Observation	40
Fig. 2.11.	Example of Drawing from Observation	41

Fig. 2.12.	Example of Drawing from Observation	42
Fig. 2.13.	Drawing from Observation by an art teacher	43
Fig. 2.14.	Drawing from Observation by a social worker	43
Fig. 2.15a.	Form A, Stimulus Drawings	45
Fig. 2.15b.	Form B, Stimulus Drawings	46
Fig. 2.16.	Drawing from Imagination Page	47
Fig. 2.17.	"Muscle boy having a snack after school," by Mack, age 12, no impairments	51
Fig. 2.18.	Untitled drawing, by Dan, age 15, language-impaired	52
Fig. 2.19.	"The bride and the mouse," by Jody, age 11	53
Fig. 2.20.	"The dying bride," by Connie, age 14, no impairments	54
Fig. 2.21.	"Victims of death," by John, age 8, no impairments	55
Fig. 2.22.	Untitled, by Betty, age 13, severe sensori-neural and receptive language disabilities; hearing loss 78dB in her better ear	56
Fig. 2.23.	"N–N–N–Nice Doggie," by Bill, age 14, no impairments	57
Fig. 2.24.	"Going to the Malt Shop," by Sara, age 14	58
Fig. 2.25.	"The dog is chasing the cat," dictated by Caroline, age 3 years, 9 months	59
Fig. 2.26.	"The Great Mouse Murder," by Roy, age 17, no impairments	60
Fig. 2.27.	"Mister Man Siting (sic) on a chair," by Teddy, age 9, no impairments	61
Fig. 2.28.	"The Great Escape," by Bruce, age 16, no impairments	62
Fig. 2.29.	"Jig-a-dig-dig, 2 kids on a pig," by Max, age 13, no impairments	63
Fig. 4.1.	"The Girl Who Never Stops Crying"	81
Fig. 4.2.	"A Lifetime of Growth"	83
Fig. 4.3.	"Hedges May Hide Surprises"	83
Fig. 4.4.	Predictive Drawing and Drawing from Observation by Mr. O	83
Fig. 6.1.	"I tell her not to eat sugar, then I do," by a young woman	112
Fig. 6.2.	"A Sneaky Snacker," by Charlotte, age 9	112
Fig. 6.3.	"The mouse really wanted the drink," by Charlene, age 9	113
Fig. 6.4.	"The Bride," by a girl, age 7	115
Fig. 6.5.	"The Lady Getting Married to a Dog"	115
Fig. 6.6.	"Woman sees mouse," by a man	116
Fig. 6.7.	"Fat couch potato," by a woman	116
Fig. 6.8.	Responses to the Verticality Task by Senior Adults	121
Fig. 7.1.	Rating Scale for Assessing the Story Content of Responses	135
Fig. 7.2.	Draw a Story, Form A	136

Fig. 7.3.	Draw a Story, Form B	138
Fig. 7.4.	DAS, Drawing Page	140
Fig. 7.5.	"The Man Jumps"	141
Fig. 7.6.	"Mr. Henderson"	142
Fig. 7.7.	"The Sleeping Bride"	143
Fig. 7.8.	"Help!" "No Escape!"	144
Fig. 7.9.	"My ex-husband wanting to kill me"	145
Fig. 7.10.	"The Left-Out Mouse"	146
Fig. 7.11.	"How much she wish the apple"	147
Fig. 7.12.	"One day there was a girl standing by a tree and she was scared because it was moving like a person"	148
Fig. 7.13.	"The boy is making fun of the duck"	149
Fig. 7.14.	"The Evil Deprived Young Man"	150
Fig. 7.15.	"Oops! this isn't the spot they promised me I'd land. a hot seat! pow! zing! zap! yike! hey! i'm outta here!"	151
Fig. 7.16.	"The cat who tried to save the rat."	152
Fig. 7.17.	"Why do tornados hate me?"	153
Fig. 7.18.	"Mice on a dead branch."	154
Fig. 7.19.	"There is no story. He's gonna go take a fly that's all"	155
Fig. 7.20.	"Meeting. Hi! Hellow"	156
Fig. 7.21.	"Mouse and baby chick"	157
Fig. 7.22.	"When birthday balloon took me back in time, I saved my ancestors' castle"	158
Fig. 7.23.	"Walking My Dog"	159
Fig. 7.24.	"The bride and the prince are getting married"	160
Fig. 8.1.	DAS Responses by Depressed and Nondepressed Subjects	165
Fig. 8.2.	Rating Scales for Assessing the Use of Space, the Use of Detail, and the Self-Report, Later Eliminated	166
Fig. 9.1.	Distribution of DAS Scores of Normal Adolescents Who Have Emotional Disturbances and Learning Disabilities (ED/LD)	172
Fig. 10.1.	Untitled drawing by an 8-year-old boy	193
Fig. 10.2.	"The Desert Man," by another 8-year-old boy	193
Fig. 10.3.	Untitled Drawing About a Chick	194
Fig. 10.4.	"What goes up must come down," by an older woman	194
Fig. 10.5.	"Return from outer space," by another older woman	195
Fig. 10.6.	"Rappin Saurus," by an 18-year-old boy	195
Fig. 10.7.	"Midnight Break," by a young man	196

Fig. 11.1.	"Why do you bother me?"	199
Fig. 11.2.	"The bear was going to eat the little bird"	199
Fig. 11.3a.	"Wach it (sic). How's ther (sic)?"	200
Fig. 11.3b.	"The Killer"	200
Fig. 11.3c.	"The mouse is schocked (sic)"	201
Fig. 11.4.	"The man in the gabich (sic) can"	201
Fig. 11.5.	"The sword was on a ladder"	202
Fig. 11.6.	"The sword hit the man's butt"	202
Fig. 11.7.	"A strange kill"	203
Fig. 11.8.	"To kill"	203
Fig. 11.9.	"The dinosaur was going to eat the bird"	204
Fig. 11.10.	"The fight"	204
Fig. 12.1.	Sketch of Burt	206
Fig. 12.2.	Burt's Sketch	207
Fig. 12.3.	"Planes Dropping Bombs"	208
Fig. 12.4.	"Nurse on crutches"	208
Fig. 12.5.	Burt's Drawing from Observation	209
Fig. 12.6.	Mrs. M's First Drawing from Imagination	210
Fig. 12.7.	Mrs. M's Second Drawing from Imagination	210
Fig. 12.8.	Mrs. M's Third Drawing from Imagination	211
Fig. 12.9.	Mrs. M's Fourth Drawing from Imagination	211
Fig. 12.10.	"Come home quick there's a whale in sight"	212
Fig. 12.11.	"Gathering magic herbs"	213
Fig. 12.12.	"The Killier (sic)"	214
Fig. 12.13.	"The elephant's journey"	214
Fig. 12.14.	"The Bear Chased Them Amay (sic)"	215
Fig. 12.15.	"Seeing an Elephant in the Woods"	216
Fig. 12.16.	Age and Gender differences in Emotional Content of Response Drawings	220
Figure 13.1.	"I'm in an airplane without fuel headed downward to the sea. I can't imagine what I'd be thinking so I can't draw it." DAS response by a woman, age 83	229
Figure 13.2.	"I was on a sailboat wrecked in a storm. I was washed overboard. I can only imagine sinking wondering what. . . . No way to draw that because I don't have any image of dark space." Her SDT response	230
Fig. 14.1.	"GODZILLA VS. MIGHTY MOUSE"	233
Fig. 14.2.	"Ouch"	233
Fig. 14.3.	"Survival of the Fittest," by Walter, age 17	234

Fig. 14.4.   "The Scared Dragon"   235
Fig. 14.5.   "Panic in a Church"   235
Fig. 14.6.   "I Think I'm in trouble"   236
Fig. 14.7.   "I am a Pisces, so where is the other fish?"   236
Fig. 14.8.   "Gid a yup, bronco. Says who?" by an older man   237
Fig. 14.9.   "In this country a worm has to fly"   238
Fig. 14.10.   "Untitled"   238
Fig. 14.11.   "Help!"   239
Fig. 14.12.   "The snake and the Mouse"   239
Fig. 14.13.   "Lyin' in the Livingroom"   240
Fig. 14.14.   "Cat sip or cat-a-tonic"   240

Foreword

◇ ◇ ◇

It is a great pleasure to introduce the reader to this remarkable book by one of the most highly respected authors in the profession of art therapy. Dr. Rawley Silver's career has been a long and distinguished one. Her commitment and seemingly boundless energy are inspiring to those who have followed her work for many years. Thanks to her keen, inquiring mind and dedication to ethical research, her contributions to art therapy assessment methods are among the finest.

Characteristically, as Dr. Silver entered her eighth decade of life, she was busy preparing a series of publications. They include a synthesis of her life's work as both therapist and researcher. This is the third of those publications. *Three Art Assessments* is a great gift to art therapists and other mental health practitioners who are seeking thoroughly researched, theoretically grounded ways of integrating visual art with their practices. It is the companion volume to an earlier book, *Art as Language: Access to Thoughts and Feelings Through Stimulus Drawings*, in which the assessment methods designed by Dr. Silver are introduced. *Three Art Assessments* goes on to present the reader with more specific information on the interesting tests Dr. Silver developed over the course of her professional career. In one neat volume, the reader is provided with test materials and procedures for administering and scoring tests that have been used for decades with diverse populations within the United States and abroad. The scope and depth of Dr. Silver's research is impressive. She enlists the cooperation of therapists worldwide, incorporating their findings and constantly updating her work based on recent research. Consequently, the information in this book on reliability and validity is of the 21st century, but it draws on a body of work of more than 40 years. Dr. Silver's contributions to research have been well received by the art therapy community. She has been the recipient of the Research Award of the American Art Therapy Association four times. Experienced therapists use these tests with confidence.

Therapists who are new to these tests may be pleasantly surprised by the positive responses the stimulus drawings elicit from many clients. Simple, nonthreatening, and stimulating to the imagination, the tests are usually well received, even by highly resistant individuals. The stimulus drawings inspire metaphorical art, and the accompanying stories often yield a wealth of material to explore with clients. Many interesting examples of drawings and stories are included in this book.

To fully understand and appreciate Dr. Silver's work, one must consider the context in which it was developed, as well as the person who created it. Dr. Silver's first book, *Developing Cognitive and Creative Skills Through Art*, contains some of the foundations for her later work. The book is replete with examples of children's art that demonstrate Dr. Silver's ability to inspire her young clients' trust and artistic creativity. Theory is presented clearly, and Dr. Silver unfailingly supports her contentions with data. The book was personally inspiring to many of us who used it as a text in our studies of art therapy decades ago. Dr. Silver's publications date back to 1962, when she was working with children who were deaf and those with less severe hearing impairments in New York City. Even then her interests were clear. An article from that year addressed art as communication, art and intellectual growth, and art and adjustment. Fortunately for those interested in Dr. Silver's journal articles, a collection has been published recently, "Studies in Art Therapy 1962–2000." Rawley Silver's work with persons who are deaf extended beyond direct services, research, and writing. She organized two traveling exhibitions of the art of children with deafness, circulated by the Smithsonian Institution. Illustrated catalogs—"Shout in Silence" and "Art and Language"—were created for the exhibitions. Her work had a significant influence in helping those who work with individuals who are deaf to appreciate the creativity and intelligence present in children who have other limits. Stemming from this work, Dr. Silver went on to create the "Silver Drawing Test of Cognition and Emotion," "Draw a Story," and "Stimulus Drawing Techniques." These tests comprise this book and, as the reader will see, they are used with many different client populations.

For those of us exploring the art therapy field over 20 years ago, the collection of literature was spare. Margaret Naumburg, Edith Kramer, Janie Rhyne, and Rawley Silver were the pioneers whose approaches to art therapy shared some common bonds: their love of art and their ability to facilitate creative experiences for clients. One might assume that all art therapists share such values and skills; however, that is not always the case. Today, art therapists bring a variety of beliefs and skills to the work, and stimulating clients' creative, artistic expression has become less important for many. For Rawley Silver, and for the other women who created this professional practice, art is at the heart of art therapy. An accomplished artist herself, Rawley Silver continues to paint, draw, and exhibit her work. She provides us with an example of the artist–scientist practitioner, attesting to the fact that one does not have to sacrifice the "art part" of the practice of art therapy in order to take a scientific approach. This integration is as much a part of who she is as of what she writes.

A few years ago I had the privilege of making a film about Dr. Silver's work, *Rawley Silver: Art Therapist and Artist.* A small collection of her drawings and paintings is shown in the film, as she discusses the evolution of her career and the concurrent development of the profession of art therapy. Dr. Silver's confidence in the profession is summarized in her remarks:

> Art therapists bring something no other group can bring and that is the perception, sensitivity, and empathy that comes with understanding drawings. Art therapy has a future and a valuable contribution to make. I'd like to see it continue to draw on both the scientific community and the art community as only art therapy can. That's the way I hope it will go.

With the publication of this book, Dr. Silver has once again contributed to the likelihood of just that. Readers seeking a balanced perspective that integrates creativity and research can feel confident that Rawley Silver speaks with great integrity and with authority derived from many years of experience. I expect that this book will be welcomed and appreciated by both students and faculty in graduate programs, as well as by experienced practitioners. It will join Dr. Silver's earlier works as an enduring classic in the art therapy literature.

—Christine Turner, ATR–BC LPC NCC
Chairperson, Graduate Program in Art Therapy
Marylhurst University, Marylhurst, Oregon

Acknowledgments

◇　◇　◇

The studies reviewed in this book could not have been carried out without the help of many art therapists and teachers who volunteered to administer the drawing tasks or score responses, as well as psychologists who performed the statistical analyses. Their assistance and my appreciation are gratefully acknowledged. They include:

Georgette d'Amelio, MS; Doris Arrington, ATR-BC; Allison Berman, ATR; Andrea Bianco-Riete, ATR-BC; Janice Bell, MA; Nancy Benson, MS; Eldora Boeve, MA; Hope Larris Carroll, ATR; Sherry Carrigan, ATR-BC; Lin Carte, ATR-BC; Felix Carrion, ATR; Fran Chapman, MA; Linda Chilton, ATR; Bette Conley, ATR; Sylvia Corwin, MA; Mariann Demasi; Peggy Dunn-Snow, PhD, ATR-BC; Cheryl Earwood, ATR; Joanne Ellison, ATR-BC; Patricia English, ATR; Cyrilla Foster, ATR; Betty Foster, MA; Phyllis Frame, ATR; Elizabeth Gayda, MA; Madeline Ginsberg, ATR-BC; Maryanne Hamilton, ATR-BC; Robin Hanes, ATR; Karen Hayes, MA; David Henley, ATR-BC; Eileen McCormick Holzman, ATR-BC; Ellen Horovitz-Darby, PhD, ATR-BC; Judith Itzler, ATR; Lynn Jamison, ATR; Beth Kean, MA; Jared Massanari, PhD; Maggie McCready, MA; Kate McPhillips, MA, OTR; Janeen Lewis, ATR; Madeline Masiero, ATR-BC; Eva Mayro, ATR; Carol McCarthy, ATR; Sally McKeever, MA; Dorothy McLaughlin, ATR-BC; Christine Mercier-Ossorio, ATR; Yetta Miller, ATR; Constance Naitove, ATR; Ruth Obernbreit, ATR; JoAnne O'Brien, ATR; Bernice Osborne, MA; Norma Ott, MA; Carol Paiken, MA; Sara Jacobs Perkins, MA; Marcia Purdy, ATR;

Lillian Resnick, ATR–BC; Michelle Rippey, ATR–BC; Kimberly Sue Roberts, ATR; Patricia Schachner, MS; Beverly Schmidt; Joan Swanson, MA; Andrea Seepo, ATR; Louise Sandburg, ATR; Miriam Saumweber, ATR; Patricia Schachner, MA; Niru Terner, ATR; Mary Tousley, ATR; Christine Turner, ATR–BC; Kristen Vilstrup, ATR–BC; Robert Vislosky, PhD, ATR; Mary Waterfield, ATR; Jules C. Weiss, ATR–BC; Kay Weiss; Simon Willoughby–Booth; Phyllis Wohlberg, ATR; and Shelley Zimmerman, ATR–BC.

I also want to thank the psychologists who provided the statistical analyses. They include Madeline Altabe, PhD, who performed the analyses during the past 6 years; John L. Kleinhans, PhD (New York State Urban Education Project No. 147 232 101); Claire Lavin, PhD (National Institute of Education Project No. G 79 008); and Beatrice J. Krauss, PhD (1983 and 1990 editions of the *Silver Drawing Test*).

Finally, I want to thank the children, adolescents, and adults who created the drawings and stories reprinted here. Although their names have been changed to protect their privacy, I am deeply grateful to all of them for responding to the drawing tasks.

Introduction and Theoretical Background

◇　　◇　　◇

The art assessments presented here evolved from a belief that we tend to underestimate the intelligence of inarticulate children and adults. For example, Charlie (not his real name) quickly learned art techniques, even though, at age 11, he could not lip-read or speak. He was among the children in my art class during the 1960s, when manual language was forbidden in schools for children with auditory or language disorders. We communicated by gesturing. When Charlie was pleased, he would kiss his fingertips in salute and often saluted the brushes and paints.

Three years later, when Charlie and I met again in an art class elsewhere, his drawings and paintings had changed dramatically (Silver, 1966, 1967). Consider the portraits he drew at age 11 and at age 14 (figures i.1 and i.2) and the change in his landscapes from leafy to leafless, broken trees (i.3 and i.4). His sister told me he was in a class for slow learners in another school, that he "came home wild" and refused to do his homework.

I made an appointment with the school's psychologist to share what I knew about Charlie. For example, when our art class visited a museum, Charlie led the way because he read the museum's diagram quickly, even when it was upside down in my hand as we walked. I was unable to interest her in testing Charlie, so I asked some psychologists for guidance, one of whom, E. Paul Torrance, sent a copy of his test and offered to score the results.

Charlie's scores on the Torrance Test of Creative Thinking, a test of creative intelligence, exceeded the scores of most hearing children. He scored in the upper 5% in Originality, the upper 3% in Fluency, the upper 10% in Flexibility, and in the final category, Elaboration, his score was "almost unexcelled." Dr. Torrance described his performance as "truly outstanding," reflecting "a high order of ability to acquire information, form relationships, and in general, to think."

Figure i.1. "Shout in silence," by Charlie, age 11

Figure i.2. "Shout in silence," by Charlie, age 14

Figure i.3. "Landscape," by Charlie, age 11

Figure i.4 "Landscape," by Charlie, age 14

The school psychologist was not impressed. As she explained, Charlie's scores "change nothing because language comes first, and there's a limit to what you can do without language."

What are the limits? If hearing children use words to express their thoughts and feelings, can children like Charlie use drawings? These questions led to further questions and, eventually, to the assessments on the pages that follow.

Several years later, four of Charlie's drawings and paintings were included in an exhibition of drawings and paintings by children and adults with deafness. The Smithsonian Institution circulated the exhibition, *Shout in Silence*, from 1969 to 1976. When the tour ended, it was shown at the Metropolitan Museum of Art, which not only published a catalogue (Silver, 1976a), but also invited the exhibitors to a party.

After the party, Charlie, now a young man, agreed to respond to the three drawing tasks that eventually became the Silver Drawing Test (SDT). When his cognitive scores were compared with the scores of typical, unimpaired adults, Charlie scored 15 points, above the adult average of 12.64 points and the maximum possible score, as shown in figure i.5 (normative data for the SDT may be found in chapter 4). In Drawing from Observation, he also scored 15 points, above the adult mean score of 13.88 points (figure i.6). His scores in Predictive Drawing cannot be compared with typical scores because at the time, only two of its three tasks had been developed when he took the test. Nevertheless, Charlie received the maximum possible scores on the two tasks as well (figure i.7).

On the other hand, in expressing emotions, Charlie's Drawing from Imagination was below average, more negative (see figure i.5). It scored 2 points on the emotional content scale, below the average of 2.94 for young men; and in self-image, 3 points, below the average of 3.61, suggesting that Charlie's outlook was less cheerful and self-confident than typical young men of his age.

Figure i.5. Charlie's Adult Drawing from Imagination

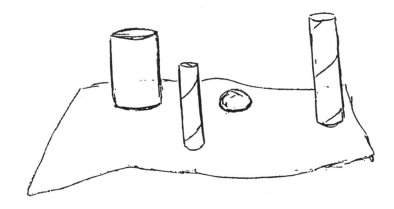

Figure i.6. Charlie's Adult Drawing from Observation

Figure i.7. Charlie's Adult Predictive Drawing

Introducing This Book

This book is a compilation of three art assessments that use stimulus drawing to elicit response drawings, as the primary channel for receiving and expressing ideas. The assessments are based on the premises that drawings can bypass verbal deficiencies and serve as a language parallel to the spoken or written word; that cognitive and affective information can be evident in visual, as well as verbal, conventions; and that even though traditionally identified and assessed through words, they can also be identified and assessed through images. The assessments include the Silver Drawing Test of Cognition and Emotion (1983b–1996a); Draw a Story: Screening for Depression (1988b–1993a); and Stimulus Drawings & Techniques in Therapy, Development, and Assessment (1982a, 1997b).

The assessments began in an attempt to communicate with children like Charlie, who had difficulty talking or understanding what was said. I had volunteered to teach art in his school after being deafened (temporarily) in an accident. Previously, painting had been my vocation, and I wanted to introduce students to the pleasures and challenges of drawing, painting, and modeling clay. I learned that studio art experiences can compensate for verbal deficiencies in many ways, as well as express thoughts and feelings simultaneously.

I soon became aware that my art students were as quick to learn as any I had known, perhaps because, "in large measure, the function of art and the function of the visual brain are one and the same," as observed by neurobiologist Semir Zeki (1999, p. 1). As Zeki explains, the pre-eminent function of the visual brain is to acquire knowledge about the world by representing the constant, essential features of objects, situations, and so forth. This function is less concerned with particular objects than with generalizing from them to obtain knowledge about categories. Knowledge is achieved by selecting essentials and discarding much that is superfluous. He also describes a second function— abstraction, subordinating the particular to the general—noting that discovering how the brain forms abstractions is a central problem in neurobiology (Zeki, 2001).

Zeki may be unaware that a 10th century Chinese painter, Ching Hao, expressed similar ideas about the essence of painting, namely, "one should disregard the varying minor details, but grasp their essential features" (p. 92, 1948). According to Ching Hao, the purpose of painting is not to obtain likenesses or create beautiful things, "but to fathom the significance of things and to grasp reality" (p. 84, 1948).

My students with hearing impairments also seemed to express feelings as well as thoughts in their drawings and paintings, an observation that seems to be supported by cognitive scientists today. Emotions may be inextricably linked to cognition, according to cognitive neuroscientists Richard Lane and Lynn Nadel (2000); and the neurologist Antonio Damasio (1994) has proposed that human reasoning consists of several brain systems working in concert, that emotions are one of the components, and contrary to traditional opinion, that emotions are involved in decision making and are just as cognitive as other percepts.

For more than 50 years, psychologists have used drawings to assess emotional indicators, and measure intellectual maturity. The House, Tree, Person Test (Buck, 1948) and Kinetic Family Drawings (Burns & Kaufman, 1972) assess emotional indicators. The Draw-a-Man test (Goodenough-Harris, 1963) measures intellectual maturity by requesting drawings of a man, a woman, and a self-portrait. The Human Figure Drawing Test (Koppitz, 1968) assesses level of intellectual development, as well as emotional indicators. The Torrance Test of Creative Thinking (Torrance, 1984) measures fluency, flexibility, originality, and elaboration.

For more than 30 years, art therapists have demonstrated ways of using drawing tasks to assess and enhance emotional well-being. Some present unstructured tasks to encourage spontaneity, whereas others specify what to draw (Cohen, B. M., 1986; Gantt, L. & Tabone, C., 1988; Kramer, 1993; Lachman-Chapin, 1987; Levick, 1989; Malchiodi, 1997, 1998; Rubin, 1987, 1999; Ulman, 1987).

In this book, art assessments are based on the observation that limiting choices can stimulate creativity and that structuring need not inhibit spontaneity. If respondents are offered choices within boundaries and are free to make final decisions, a structured task can provide support, particularly when drawing or painting are novel experiences.

The assessments present a variety of images and are concerned with the cognitive and emotional content of responses to stimulus drawing tasks, rather than with the physical attributes of drawings, such as color, shape, or line quality.

Drawing from Imagination

The aims of the task are to provide access to fantasies and to screen for emotional needs and cognitive skills. Each assessment includes a Drawing from Imagination task, asking respondents to choose two or three stimulus drawings, imagine something happening between the subjects they choose, and then show what is happening in drawings of their own. They are encouraged to alter the stimulus drawings and add their own subjects and ideas. As they finish drawing, they are asked to provide titles or stories and, finally, to discuss their drawings, whenever possible, so that meanings can be clarified.

Each assessment presents a different set of stimulus drawings—line drawings of people, animals, places, and things. Although the stimulus drawings call attention to the external world, they tend to elicit subjective responses expressed indirectly. Some are explicit, others ambiguous, to encourage associations. They are presented in appendices A, B, and C, together with the testing materials of each assessment.

Respondents tend to perceive the same drawings differently, based on past experiences. They also tend to alter the stimulus drawings, often in subtle ways. Some choose subjects that represent themselves or others in disguise, to fulfill wishes vicariously, or to express fears or frustrations indirectly through visual symbols and metaphors.

To quantify responses, the assessments provide 5-point rating scales that range from strongly negative to strongly positive themes, as discussed in the sections that follow. The Emotional Projection Scale ranges from fantasies about murder or suicide to fantasies about loving relationships or achieving goals. The Self-Image Scale also ranges from negative to positive self-images. A third scale, ranging from negative to positive humor, is discussed in chapter 14.

Cognitive skills also are assessed on 5-point rating scales, based in part on experiments by Piaget (1967), Bruner (1966), and others who have traced the development of cognition through successive stages. Although their tasks tended to be verbal, their stages of development serve as paradigms for assessing cognitive skills expressed through drawings. The Silver Drawing Test presents two additional cognitive tasks, Predictive Drawing and Drawing from Observation, as discussed in chapter 1.

Cognitive Skills

The cognitive components evolved from the belief that concepts can develop without words, if need be. This belief has support in the writings of linguist Sinclair de-Zwart (1969), who proposed that language follows, rather than precedes, logical thinking. Originally, she had believed that language produced thought, but, after several experiments, she concluded that language is structured by logic, not the other way around.

In addition, Jean Piaget (1970) observed that language and thought develop independently, and that children are capable of generalizing from their actions even before acquiring language. For example, if they have learned to pull a blanket to reach a toy, they are capable of pulling the blanket to reach other objects.

The views of Witkin (1962) suggested that preferred modes of thinking are established early in life, and that imagery is the preferred mode for some individuals. Arnheim (1969) supported this view with questions that reveal preferred modes of thinking. For example, if it is now 3:40 P.M., what time will it be in half an hour? Some individuals use arithmetic to determine the answer, whereas others visualize the face of a clock, its minute hand advancing halfway around.

It would seem to follow that imagery can be more than a matter of preference for children with hearing impairments, and that the traditional assumption of causal relationships could be reversed. Linguists could consider the possibility that higher levels of thinking might be the cause, as well as the consequence, of improved language skills, and nonverbal procedures might cause levels of language to rise.

Philosopher Suzanne Langer (1957, 1958) described art as a way of articulating thoughts and expressing experiences that cannot be put into words. Although the most universal form of expression is verbal, speech is only one kind of symbolic process and, even with speech, "when we want to convey a new experience or a direct sensation, we turn to the imagery of art, to metaphor" (1957, p. 23).

Cognitive science provides further evidence. Donald Hoffman (1998), noted that visual intelligence occupies nearly half the brain's cortex, and, like Zeki, finds that vision is not passive perception but an active, intelligent process, performed the way that scientists develop theories, through experimental evidence. The principal difference is that scientific constructions are performed consciously, whereas visual constructions are often unconscious. Hoffman also observed that we are complex beings with visual, emotional, and rational facets. Understanding how these facets interact is a key to understanding who we are as a species and what we might become (Hoffman, 1998, p. 202).

It seems to be generally agreed that the two lobes of the human brain serve different functions. According to Schlain (1998), the function of the right lobe is to perceive space, recognize images, and integrate feelings. Although nonverbal, the right lobe deciphers nonverbal language and generates metaphors, intuitive insights, feeling-states, and humor. The left lobe is associated with speech, numbers, logical analysis, and abstract thinking; describing and measuring objects; and processing information without images.

Art therapist Frances Kaplan (2000) reviewed the findings of neuroscientists who suggest that graphic representation is a complex activity, involving areas of the brain associated with language. For example, Restak (1994) reported that more brain neurons are devoted to vision than to the other senses. Kaplan suggested that studio art can facilitate problem-solving abilities, stimulate pleasure and self-esteem, and provide opportunities for successful functioning by children and adults with cognitive impairments.

How the Assessments Evolved

My two vocations, painting and social work, converged during the 1960s. After attending Smith College School of Social Work, I was employed as a medical social worker for several years, then returned to painting and exhibited work in individual and group shows during the 1950s. After volunteering to teach in Charlie's school, which did not have an art teacher, I enrolled for master's and doctoral degrees in fine arts and fine arts education at Teachers College, Columbia University. Subsequently, I worked with children and adults who had other disabilities, attempting to meet their cognitive and emotional needs through drawing from imagination and observation, painting, modeling clay, producing sequences of shapes and color, and manipulating objects such as plumb lines, to test out predictions. The original assessments were developed in one of those programs, a state urban education project, when I was asked to devise an assessment to determine whether the art experiences had been useful, as reported in chapter 1.

The Stimulus Drawings

In trying to communicate with Charlie and others who had language disorders, I learned that a quick sketch could take the place of talk. For example, a quick sketch of my family prompted sketches of their families, drawings that revealed feelings, such as drawing themselves larger or smaller than other family members, or isolated by a tree (Silver, 1976b, 2001). To encourage those who were shy or reluctant, I sketched animals, people, places, and things, some of which prompted expressive responses from stroke patients and others. Eventually, my sketches became stimulus drawings in the assessments.

Studies of Individuals and Groups

This book presents its findings in two forms: studies based on responses to the drawing tasks by groups of children, adolescents, or adults large enough for statistical analyses and studies based on responses by individuals or small groups that were unexpected or surprising. To find out whether they were unique, I presented the drawing tasks to larger and larger groups in order to determine mean scores, percentages, and, when appropriate, statistical analyses.

I believe both forms are valuable. Without both, the information that is evident in the behavior of individuals or small groups may disappear within the group large enough for statistical analysis and generalizing. On the other hand, without quantified, objective facts, theories remain speculations.

This book is addressed to readers interested in administering and scoring the assessments. It presents new studies published for the first time, and reviews studies published before and after the test manuals were last published. It also updates previous editions with additional normative data and new forms for recording the scores of individuals and groups. A previous book, *Art as Language* (Silver, 2001), has presented the procedures that were used to develop cognitive skills and additional studies of particular individuals.

How the Book Is Organized

The three assessments have been combined in this book, for the convenience of readers and to avoid redundancy. Section I presents the Silver Drawing Test (SDT): how it was developed and field-tested, guidelines for administering and scoring, and examples of scored responses (chapters 1 and 2). It also presents studies of reliability and validity (chapter 3); and normative data (chapter 4). Chapter 5 reviews outcome studies that used the SDT as a pretest–posttest measure to determine whether therapeutic or developmental programs were effective. Chapter 6 reviews studies of gender and other differences in spatial skills and attitudes toward self, others, the opposite sex, and food or eating. The respondents included children, adolescents, young adults, and senior adults who had learning disabilities or auditory, visual–motor, or language disorders. They also included those with no known impairments, incarcerated adolescents, and students performing below grade level.

Section II presents similar information about the Draw-a-Story assessment (chapters 7 to 9); section III, Stimulus Drawings & Techniques (chapters 10 to 12). Section IV presents correlations between the three assessments (chapter 13); various kinds of humor conveyed in responses to the drawing tasks (chapter 14), cross-cultural studies of respondents in Brazil, Australia, Thailand, and Russia as well as Hispanic and non-Hispanic students in the United States (chapter 15); and concludes with final observations (chapter 16). Section V, appendices A, B, and C, presents testing materials for the three assessments.

Section I

The Silver Drawing Test of Cognition and Emotion (SDT)

◇   ◇   ◇

Chapter 1

How the SDT Was Developed and Field-Tested

◇   ◇   ◇

This chapter begins with an overview of the SDT, proceeds to why it was developed and how it evolved, and concludes with the field trials undertaken before it was first published in 1983. The SDT has cognitive, as well as emotional, components and includes three subtests: Drawing from Imagination, Predictive Drawing, and Drawing from Observation.

Each subtest was designed to assess one of the three concepts said to be fundamental in mathematics and reading. There are three basic concepts from which all branches of knowledge can be generated, according to Jean Piaget (1970). The first is based on the concept of a group and applies to classes and numbers. The second is based on the idea of sequential order and applies to relationships. The third is based on ideas of space and applies to neighborhoods, points of view, and frames of reference. Although these ideas may seem highly abstract, Piaget observed similar ideas in the thinking of children as young as 6 or 7, and although the concepts are usually associated with language, they can also be perceived and expressed visually.

The same concepts seem to be fundamental in reading. In examining the performances of children with dyslexia on the Wechsler Intelligence Scale for Children (WISC; 1971–1991), Bannatyne (1971) noted that they performed well on WISC subtests involving spatial ability, moderately well on subtests of conceptual ability, and poorly on subtests of sequential ability. He also observed that these children had intellectual abilities of a visual–spatial nature that are seldom recognized or trained. Other investigators also found that readers with disabilities scored highest in the spatial category and lowest in the sequential category (Rugel, 1974; Smith et al., 1977).

The subtests are also based on the ability to conserve, to recognize that an object remains the same in spite of transformations in its appearance. Most rational thought depends on conservation, according to Piaget (1970), and Jerome Bruner (1966) noted that the ability to recognize equivalence under different guises is a powerful idea not only in science but in everyday life. Up to the age of about 7, children typically are unable to conserve a quantity of liquid over alterations in its appearance.

The Drawing from Imagination Subtest

As discussed in the introduction, respondents are asked to select stimulus drawings, imagine something happening between them, and then draw what they imagine. As they finish drawing, they are asked to add titles or stories and, finally, to discuss their responses whenever possible. The task is based on the observations that different individuals perceive the same stimulus drawing differently, that past experiences influence perceptions, and that responses reflect facets of personality and cognitive skills in ways that can be quantified.

This SDT task provides two sets of stimulus drawings. Form A includes 15 stimulus drawings reserved for pretesting and posttesting only. Responses to Form A were used in the studies of reliability and validity presented in chapter 3 and to collect the normative data presented in chapter 4. Form B is provided for use in therapeutic and developmental programs. Both forms are reproduced in appendix A. Responses are assessed for emotional and cognitive content, based on rating scales ranging from 1 to 5 points.

Emotional Content

Responses to the Drawing from Imagination task often reflect wishes, fears, frustrations, and conflicts, as well as inner resources such as resilience and self-disparaging humor. Strongly negative themes, such as fantasies about murderous relationships or sad solitary subjects, score 1 point. Moderately negative themes, such as fantasies about stressful relationships or frightened solitary subjects, score 2 points. The 3-point, intermediate score is used for themes that are ambivalent (both negative and positive), ambiguous (unclear), or unemotional. The 4-point score is used to characterize moderately positive themes, such as friendly relationships or fortunate solitary subjects; and 5 points is used for strongly positive themes, such as loving relationships or powerful solitary subjects. Guidelines for scoring are presented in chapter 2, together with examples of scored responses.

Because the emotional projection scale does not distinguish between self-images and fantasies about others (which may conflict), a 5-point self-image scale also is provided. Respondents who seem to identify with subjects portrayed as sad, isolated, or in mortal danger score 1 point; 2 points when their protagonists are frustrated, frightened, or unfortunate. Fortunate protagonists score 4 points; powerful, effective, or beloved protagonists score 5 points. Self-images that are ambivalent, ambiguous, unemotional, or invisible (such as the narrator) score 3 points.

Cognitive Content

Selecting, combining, and representing seem to be fundamental not only in cognition but also in the visual arts, neurobiology, and linguistics. Painters, for example, select and combine colors or shapes, and if their work is representational, they select and combine images as well. The neurobiologist Semir Zeki (1999) observes that visual art contributes to our understanding of the visual brain because it explores and reveals the brain's perceptual capabilities (2001). This brain continually searches for constancies, distilling from successive views the essential characters of objects and situations (1999). It is a collection of many different anatomical areas and individual cells, which are not only highly selective for particular attributes, such as straight lines, but also indifferent to other lines. By selecting and rejecting, the brain forms categories that integrate, represent, and apply to many objects and many situations. He notes that visual art also seeks constancies and contributes to understanding because it explores and reveals the brain's perceptual capabilities.

The linguist Ramon Jakobson (1964) identified selecting and combining as the two basic verbal operations. The ability to produce language starts with selecting words, then combines words into sentences. The ability to comprehend language proceeds in the reverse order. Jakobson defined expressive language disorders as a disturbance in the ability to combine parts into wholes and receptive language disorders as a disturbance in the ability to select.

Ability to Select

Hornsby, a psychologist, found three levels of ability to select (see Bruner, 1966). The lowest level is perceptual; the intermediate level, functional; and the highest level, abstract. In her experiments, Hornsby asked children to select objects that were alike in some way and then to explain why they were alike. The children progressed from grouping objects based on perceptual attributes, such as color or shape, to grouping based on function—what they do or what is done to them. She found that grouping based on perceptual attributes declined steadily from 47% at age 6 to 20% at age 11, whereas functional grouping increased from 30% at age 6 to 47% at age 11, and that adolescents developed true conceptual grouping based on abstract, invisible attributes, such as the concept of class inclusion.

The Drawing from Imagination task is based on the premises that respondents who imply more than is visible in their drawings, or who use abstract words in their titles or stories, have developed the ability to select at the abstract level (5 points), and that lower levels, based on perceptual attributes or functional grouping also can be inferred and scored. Responses that simply show what subjects do or what can be done to them score 3 points, reflecting ability to select at the functional level, and responses with a single subject or several subjects unrelated in size or placement score 1 point, reflecting ability to select at the perceptual level. Responses at intermediate levels score 2 or 4 points.

Ability to Combine

The importance of being able to integrate or combine the subjects of a drawing meaningfully becomes evident when the ability is lost as a consequence of lesions in particular areas of the brain (Zeki, 1999, p. 74). Some patients can recognize the details of a face, such as eyes or nose, but cannot combine the information sufficiently to recognize the face of a friend or close relative. The failure is one of binding the elements together, then registering them with the brain's stored memory for that face.

Piaget and Inhelder (1967) have observed that the most rudimentary spatial relationships are based on proximity. Before the age of 7, children typically regard objects in isolation rather than as part of a comprehensive system. Gradually, they consider objects in relation to neighboring objects and to external frames of reference, such as the ground. Children tend to represent the ground by drawing or implying a base line parallel to the bottom of the paper, relating objects to one another along this line, but, as they mature, become aware of distances and proportions.

In the Drawing from Imagination task, scoring is based on the premise that responses that depict depth or take into account the whole drawing area reflect high levels of ability to combine (5 points). Responses that relate subjects to one another along a base line reflect moderate levels of ability (3 points), and those that relate subjects on the basis of proximity reflect low levels of ability (1 point).

Ability to Represent (Creativity)

Drawing and painting, whether narrative or abstract, have tended to represent objects, throughout history and around the world. Children can recognize a circle long before they can draw one, as Piaget and Inhelder have pointed out. To draw a circle, a child must be able to visualize it when it is out of sight.

The ability to represent is imitative and passive at first, then intellectually active. Highly creative representations show originality, independence, and the ability to toy with ideas (Rogers, 1962; Torrance, 1980) and Torrance has cautioned against trying to separate creativity from intelligence because they interact and overlap. He also observed that highly creative children often have inferior verbal skills.

In the SDT, scoring for the Ability to Represent is based on the premise that respondents whose drawings *transform* the stimulus drawing they select by being highly original, expressive, playful, or suggestive score 5 points. Responses that reveal ability to *restructure*, by changing or elaborating on stimulus drawings or stereotypes, score 3 points; and responses that are *imitative*—that is, simply copy stimulus drawings or use stereotypes such as stick figures—score 1 point.

The Predictive Drawing Subtest

In this subtest, respondents are asked to predict changes in the appearance of objects by adding lines to outline drawings. The ability to recognize that an object remains the same in spite of changes in its appearance—the ability to conserve—is basic in logical thinking (Bruner, 1966; Piaget, 1967). Until the age of about 7, children are unable to conserve or place objects in order systematically. Responses are scored on 5-point scales, ranging from low to high levels of ability to predict and represent concepts of sequential order as well as concepts of horizontality and verticality.

The Concept of Sequential Order

The aim of the first task is to determine whether a respondent has acquired the ability to predict and represent a sequence. The task presents a series of line drawings of an ice cream soda and six empty glasses and asks the respondent to draw lines in the empty glasses to show how the soda would appear if gradually consumed through a straw. It is based on the premise that a respondent who draws a descending series of horizontal lines in the glasses, without corrections, has acquired the ability to order a sequence systematically (scored 5 points). Erasures and other corrections suggest that the concept has been achieved through trial and error rather than systematically, reflecting a lower level of ability. A drawing that does not represent a sequence of lines suggests that the respondent has not acquired the concept of sequential order.

The other two tasks of the Predictive Drawing subtest are designed to assess concepts of horizontality and verticality and are based on observations by Piaget and Inhelder (1967, pp. 375–385).

The Concept of Horizontality

Zeki (1999) noted that lines of particular orientation are genetically determined, as discussed earlier, and Piaget and Inhelder (1967) have observed that the most stable framework of everyday experience involves horizontals and verticals. They point out that we are so used to thinking in terms of horizontals and verticals that they may seem self-evident; but when asked to draw water in bottles, children aged 4 or 5, tend to scribble round shapes. As they grow older, they draw lines parallel to the base even when the bottle is tilted; then they begin to draw oblique lines, which become less oblique and more horizontal until, around the age of 9, they tend to draw horizontal lines immediately.

To determine whether respondents have acquired the ability to represent horizontality in spite of changes in appearance, the task presents outline drawings of an upright and a tilted bottle and asks respondents to draw lines in the bottles to show how the bottles appear when half-filled with water. The task is based on the premise that a individual who draws a horizontal line in the tilted bottle has learned that the surface of water remains horizontal regardless of the tilt of its container, scoring 5 points. Lower levels of ability are also inferred and scored.

The Concept of Verticality

When Piaget and Inhelder (1967) asked 5-year-olds to draw trees or houses on the outline of a mountain, they drew these inside the mountain. As children matured, they drew trees and houses perpendicular to the slope; and as they reached the age of 8 or 9, began to draw them upright.

To determine whether respondents have acquired the concept of verticality, the third task, Predictive Drawing, presents the drawing of a house on top of a steep mountain and asks respondents to draw the way the house would appear if moved to a spot marked X on the slope. The task is based on the premise that a respondent who draws a vertical house that is cantilevered or supported by posts has acquired the concept of verticality (5 points), and that lower levels of development can be inferred and scored.

The Drawing from Observation Subtest

Drawing from Observation was basic in teaching art when I considered how to teach Charlie and his classmates. Developing this ability was the keystone of art education when I was an art student and for generations of art students before mine. At New York City's famous Cooper Union Art School, my mother started out by drawing plaster casts of Greek sculptures and then progressed to drawing live human models, still limited to the medium of charcoal. Throughout my four years in college, previously in Parson's School of Design and subsequently at the Art Student's League, I drew live human models from observation using charcoal at first, progressing to oil paints, and concluding with modeling clay.

When discussing the neurophysiology of the visual cortex and the significance of straight lines in the brain's search for essentials, Zeki (1999) cited the straight lines in paintings by Mondrian, perhaps unaware of the role of visible and imagined straight lines in the accuracy of any attempt to draw from observation. There is sound reason behind the cartoon cliché of an artist in smock and beret, squinting at the brush he holds vertically at the end of his outstretched, horizontal arm. Art students are taught to do just that because it is the time-honored way to measure horizontality and verticality and to compare the lengths and breadths of objects they are trying to represent, as well as angles and other spatial relationship between objects.

As Zeki observes, many cells in the visual cortex are selective for lines of particular orientation, which are genetically determined and need only to be visually nourished to become permanent fixtures of the visual brain. People who have suffered lesions in distinct areas of the visual brain may lose this capacity (p. 96).

The findings of Piaget and Inhelder (1967) can serve to amplify Zeki's observations. In tracing the development of spatial concepts, they noted that young children tend to regard objects in isolation, their various features perceived in turn. Gradually, children begin to regard objects in relation to nearby objects, linking them into a single system by coordinating different points of view. At the same time, they begin to develop the idea of straight lines, parallels, and angles. This ability to coordinate assumes the conservation of distance—applying relationships of sequential order to three directions simultaneously. Eventually, children arrive at a system embracing objects in three dimensions: left–right (horizontal relationships), above–below (vertical relationships), and front–back (relationships in depth).

The aim of the SDT Drawing from Observation task is to find out whether a respondent has acquired the ability to represent height, width, and depth, as well as assess the level of ability at the time the task is presented. It presents four simple objects arranged in a predetermined way on a straight-sided sheet of paper below eye level so that the surface of the paper is viewed as a flat plane rather than a line. The objects include three cylinders differing in height and width and a small stone. Respondents are asked to draw what they see. Scoring their responses is based on the ability to represent spatial relationships in height, width, and depth, as discussed in detail in chapter 2.

Why the SDT Was Developed and How It Evolved

While teaching the art classes discussed in the introduction, I became increasingly aware of low expectations for children who are deaf, contrary to my own experiences. For example, a journal article had reported that children with severe hearing impairment were unimaginative and their artwork inferior to the artwork of hearing children, in both subject matter and technique (Lampard, 1960). These findings were at odds with my experience and the scores of my students on the Torrance Test of Creative Thinking. It seemed to me that studio art had latent potentials for developing the cognitive and creative skills of children with deafness (Silver, 1962, 1963, 2000a). I enrolled in a doctoral program and began to read the authors cited earlier in this chapter.

Doctoral Project

The principal aim of my doctoral project was to find out whether studio art experiences could be used to stimulate the intelligence and emotional well-being of children who had language deficiencies as well as hearing impairments (Silver, 1966, 1978, 2000b). In addition, I hoped to challenge the claim that the artwork of children who are deaf is inferior to the artwork of hearing children, in both subject matter and technique. With this in mind, I asked two panels of judges to evaluate the artwork produced by my students in four schools for deaf children (Silver, 1966, 1978, 2000b).

One panel included 20 psychologists; psychiatrists; teachers of special education; and educators of children who were deaf, aphasic, and hearing. The judges attended an exhibition of drawings and paintings by my students and responded to a questionnaire, which asked whether they found evidence that art experiences provided opportunities for various kinds of cognition and evidence that would be useful in assessing various characteristics and needs. Of their 337 answers, 315 (93%) were positive, 8 (2%) were negative, and 14 (5%) were qualified.

Judging the same paintings and drawings, the second panel of 20 art educators was asked if they found evidence of spontaneity, planning, story telling, sensitivity, and skill. Of their 260 answers, 243 (93%) were positive, 1 was negative, and 16 were qualified.

The project's findings seemed to support five concluding observations—among them, that drawing and painting could serve as instruments for expressing thoughts and feelings that cannot be verbalized and as instruments for assessing abilities, knowledge, interests, attitudes, and needs. The findings also suggested that art symbols could serve as instruments for organizing thoughts and experiences and developing ability to recall, generalize, evaluate, and imagine.

Subsequently, I received a grant from the U.S. Office of Education to conduct a demonstration project in art education for adults, as well as children, with hearing impairment.

A Demonstration Project for Children and Adults with Hearing Impairment

The aims of this project were to identify effective methods of teaching and to assess aptitudes, interests, and vocational opportunities in the visual arts for children and adults with hearing impairments (Silver, 1967). This project was supported by a grant from the U. S. Office of Education.

A total of 54 children and adults with hearing impairment attended one or two semesters of an experimental art program. They were not selected but were accepted in the order in which they applied, following a public announcement that the classes were available.

After several months of weekly art classes, 12 children and 1 adult volunteered to take the Figural Form of the Torrance Test of Creative Thinking, a test of creativity in general, not of artistic ability. Their average scores were in the the 99th percentile in both originality and elaboration; in the 97th percentile in Fluency, and the 88th percentile in flexibility. Charlie, whose performance was discussed in the introduction, was one of the children who scored in the 99th percentile.

As in the doctoral project, panels of judges evaluated the artwork produced. In one of five assessments, three art educators judged paintings by 22 hearing students and 22 students with hearing impairments, based on originality, expressiveness, and sensitivity. The 44 paintings were identified only by number and the age of the painter. Mean scores of the children and adults with hearing impairment were slightly higher than mean scores of hearing children and adults, whereas the mean score of adolescents with hearing impairments was slightly lower. The other assessments found that the scores of students with hearing impairments were equal or superior to scores of their hearing counterparts.

The findings suggested that further study, comparing the cognitive skills of hearing-impaired students with the cognitive skills of their hearing counterparts, would be worthwhile.

First Pilot Study

The pilot study was an attempt to use art experiences to encourage children with auditory or language impairments to sustain thoughts they could not verbalize and to acquire the three fundamental concepts cited by Piaget (1970) and others.

Rationale

Children who cannot learn language in the usual way are often deficient in cognitive functioning. It generally is assumed that the cause of their deficiency is language retardation, but this may be misleading. Language obviously is related to thinking, but whether it is essential seemed open to question.

Unimpaired children use language to pin down perceptions, organize experiences, and exercise control over their environments. By labeling perceptions with words, they make them usable again and again. In addition, they use language to acquire vicarious experiences. When they cannot obtain a desired result, they can substitute words and, by symbolizing, obtain it in imagination.

In the thinking of children with language impairment, art symbols can take over some of the functions of language symbols. Even though their capacity for acquiring language may be impaired, their capacity for visual–spatial thinking may be intact.

Procedures

The art procedures used in this pilot study were designed to invite exploratory learning, expand the range of communication, and provide self-rewarding tasks. They included Drawing from Imagination and Observation, painting, modeling clay, and manipulating objects such as plumb lines. The procedures are described in detail elsewhere (Silver, et al., 1980; Silver, 2000a, 2001).

Before and after the art program, two classroom teachers responded to a questionnaire about the cognitive and emotional behavior of their students (Silver, 1971). The questionnaire asked whether their students showed aggressive and other behaviors and whether they found it difficult to recall, focus attention, grasp hypothetical situations, and integrate information. The teachers had not been advised that they would be asked to respond again to the same questionnaire after the 11-week art program.

Six of the eight students showed gains in each item of the questionnaire, and seven of the eight showed less difficulty in the four cognitive areas. The single student who did not improve was the only one who did not represent people, animals, or objects, but had experimented with nonrepresentational techniques.

Because the study did not indicate whether the events were causally related—that is, whether the art program might have *caused* the gains in cognition and behavior—a second study was undertaken. This study also attempted to minimize subjective evaluations by providing a control group.

Second Pilot Study

This project was an attempt to find answers to the question of whether art experiences can establish patterns that language might follow—that is, whether drawing representational pictures would enable a child to bypass auditory or language disorders and develop the ability to conserve and classify through art experiences (Silver, 1973, pp. 2–3).

Nine children attended experimental art classes, and nine served as controls. The experimental group included half the number of children in three regular classes in a school for children with these impairments. Chosen at random, the children participated in a weekly art program, meeting for 40 minutes once a week for 15 weeks. Piaget's (1967) task of drawing a container half-filled with water was used as a pretest and posttest. The control group included the children who did not attend the art program, but remained with their classroom teachers doing other schoolwork.

To develop ability to conserve, the children modeled clay. In the pretest, only one of the experimental children and none of the control children demonstrated ability to conserve. In the posttest, five of the eight experimental children who initially demonstrated lack of ability subsequently demonstrated ability to conserve, whereas none of the control children showed this ability.

In the pretest of ability to classify, two of the experimental children and one of the control children demonstrated ability to group on the basis of class or function. In the posttest, six of the seven experimental children who initially demonstrated lack of ability subsequently grouped on the basis of class or function, whereas only one of the eight control children who initially demonstrated lack of ability demonstrated ability.

Eight months later, the tests were administered again to the experimental children by another examiner. Five were still conservers, and five still grouped on the basis of class or function.

State Urban Education Project

Encouraged by the pilot studies and hoping to continue with additional students who had auditory and language impairments, I applied for a grant to conduct a state urban education project (SUEP) in New York (Silver, 1973). Approval of the project arrived late, after the 1972 school year had started in September. Because my project proposal called for pretests in October and a project evaluator had not yet been assigned, I was obliged to improvise the pretest myself. I asked for help from a specialist at a nearby university, who guided me in designing a 30-item criterion-referenced test in exchange for one of my paintings. The pre–posttest included rating scales for assessing ability to sequence, predict, conserve, select, combine, and represent spatial concepts, as well as thoughts and feelings.

The experimental group included 34 children, ages 8 to 15, a randomly selected 50% sample of 12 classes in the school, who attended weekly 40-minute classes for 11 weeks in the fall and 9 weeks in the spring. The other 34 children remained with their classroom teachers and served as the control group. Drawing tasks were developed, some administered as pre–posttests and subsequently used in the SDT. The tasks were also administered once to 68 unimpaired children in a suburban public school.

When pre- and posttest scores of experimental and control groups were compared, significant gains were found in skills related to cognition (the process of knowing), as well as in art skills. The developmental and assessment procedures, statistical findings, and responses by individual students are among the outcome studies reviewed in chapter 5.

National Institute of Education Project

Following the SUEP project, students in the art therapy program at the College of New Rochelle began to use the assessment and developmental procedures, and because I had presented these at conferences and in publications, art therapists elsewhere began to use them and share findings with me.

In addition, students in the art therapy program had participated in a successful study, which asked whether the procedures would be useful with children who had an opposite constellation of skills—verbal strengths and visual–spatial weaknesses—and whether the procedures could be used by art therapists other than the person who developed them (Silver & Lavin, 1977). In the study, 11 graduate students worked under supervision with 11 children. After 10 weekly art periods, the children again showed significant gains.

In another study, a different group of graduate students worked under supervision with 11 children in a suburban school. These children also showed significant gains. Thus, the results of the previous studies were verified again.

In 1979, I received a grant from the National Institute of Education (Silver et al., 1980). The project's principal objective was to develop greater precision in assessing the intelligence of children with disabilities. It proposed that students who have difficulty putting thoughts into words or understanding what is said might nevertheless have intellectual abilities that escape detection on traditional tests, but that may emerge in assessments that are independent of language skills. It hypothesized that art can be a language of cognition paralleling spoken language. Concepts that can be expressed through words can also be expressed through art. Similarly, cognitive skills that can be developed and assessed through language-oriented activities also can be developed and assessed through art activities.

Another objective was to evaluate the procedures developed in the SUEP and to verify the approach to teaching in which art activities take the place of language in receiving and expressing the concepts cited by Piaget (1970) and others as fundamental in reading and mathematics. The project also developed norms and examined the reliability and validity of the procedures. Coauthors of the project report were my former students in art therapy and a colleague who performed the statistical analyses. The project's findings can also be found among the outcome studies reviewed in chapter 5.

The SDT was first published in 1983 by Special Child Publications of Seattle, Washington, and revised editions were published in 1990 and 1996.

This chapter has reviewed the history of the SDT, why it was undertaken, and how it evolved.

The remaining chapters in section I present the procedures for administering and scoring the SDT; summarize studies of the assessment's reliability and validity; and present normative data, outcome studies, and studies of age and gender differences in attitudes and cognitive skills found in responses to the drawing tasks.

Chapter 2

Administering and Scoring the SDT

◇   ◇   ◇

This chapter includes guidelines for administering the SDT and scoring responses to the three drawing tasks. It also presents examples of scored responses. The testing materials and Form B, a second set of stimulus drawings for use other than testing, are reproduced in appendix A. Subsequent chapters in section I present studies of reliability, validity, and normative data, as well as studies of individuals and groups.

The SDT has been administered and scored without prior training by teachers, as well as by mental health professionals, in America, Australia, Brazil, Russia, and Thailand, as discussed in chapter 15. The recommended age range is from 5 years to adult. Individual administration is suggested for children younger than 7 and clinical subjects.

The SDT is not timed, but usually takes about 15 minutes. Although each of the three tasks can be considered separately and is scored separately, they are interconnected and begin with the simplest task—Predictive Drawing. It asks the respondent to predict changes in the appearance of objects by adding lines to outline drawings. The second task, Drawing from Observation, asks the respondent to draw an arrangement of three cylinders and a large pebble to assess ability to represent spatial relationships in height, width, and depth. Both tasks usually are completed in about 5 minutes.

The third task, Drawing from Imagination, aims to stimulate reflection and usually takes about 10 minutes. It is important to prevent interruptions or distractions, particularly because some individuals become deeply absorbed in modifying and elaborating their drawings (or stories). For this reason, I recommend pencils with erasers rather than pens, markers, or crayons. If a respondent prefers a pen, however, do not insist otherwise.

It is important to establish an atmosphere that is encouraging and supportive. As an introduction, say:

> I believe you will have fun with this kind of drawing. You will be asked to draw things you can see, things you cannot see, and things only you can imagine. It doesn't matter whether or not you have talent in drawing.
>
> What matters is using your imagination and expressing your own ideas.

As much as possible, avoid the stress usually associated with testing.

Accommodate reasonable requests and encourage questions before drawing begins. Afterward, however, you should prevent interruptions and postpone discussions as much as possible until all respondents have finished.

Provide a test booklet for yourself, as well as for each respondent.

The Predictive Drawing Task

The Predictive Drawing task is shown in figure 2.1. If a respondent has difficulty reading directions, use pantomime or manual language. For example, hold up your own booklet, point to the first glass on the left and say, "Here is an ice cream soda. Suppose you drank a few sips." Then draw a horizontal line near the top of your second glass and say, "Can you draw lines in the glasses to show how the soda would look if you took a few sips, then a few more, and more, until you gradually drank it all?"

You also might pantomime with a drinking straw, taking care not to make a sequence of gestures or indicate where the lines should be drawn. If you use manual language, modify the directions as needed.

Guidelines for scoring responses are shown in table 2.1 and examples of scored responses in figures 2.2 to 2.8.

Figure 2.1. The SDT Predictive Drawing Task

Suppose you took a few sips of a soda, then a few more, and more, until your glass was empty. Can you draw lines in the glasses to show how the soda would look if you gradually drank it all?

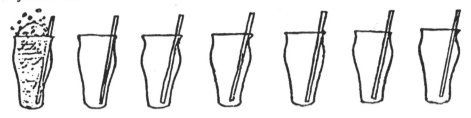

Suppose you tilted a bottle half filled with water. Can you draw lines in the bottles to show how the water would look?

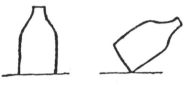

Suppose you put the house on the spot marked x. Can you draw the way it would look?

© 1990, 1996 Rawley Silver

Table 2.1

Guidelines for Scoring the Predictive Drawing Subtest of the SDT

Predicting a Sequence

0 points: No sequence representing the soda inside the glass or glasses.
1 point: Incomplete sequence.
2 points: Two or more sequences.
3 points: Descending series of lines with corrections (trial and error).
4 points: A sequence with unevenly spaced increments but no corrections.
5 points: A sequence with evenly spaced increments and no corrections (systematic). The sequence does not have to continue to the bottom of the glass.

Predicting Horizontality*

0 points: No line representing water surface is inside the tilted bottle.
1 point: Line parallels bottom or sides of tilted bottle (suggesting that the frame of reference is inside the bottle).
2 points: Line almost parallels bottom or side of tilted bottle
3 points: Line is oblique (suggesting that the frame of reference is external but not related to the table surface).
4 points: Line seems related to the table surface but is not parallel.
5 points: Line is parallel to table surface within 5 degrees.

Predicting Verticality*

0 points: No representation of the house or, if examinee is younger than 5, the house is inside the mountain.
1 point: House is approximately perpendicular to the slope.
2 points: House is neither perpendicular nor vertical but on a slant or upside down.
3 points: House is vertical but has no support (may be entirely inside the mountain if examinee is older than 5 years).
4 points: House is vertical but has inadequate support, such as partly inside the mountain.
5 points: House is vertical, supported by posts, columns, platforms, or other structures.

---

*The tasks for predicting horizontality and verticality are adapted from experiments by Piaget and Inhelder (1967). © 1995 Rawley Silver

Example of Scored Responses

Figure 2.2. Predicting a Sequence

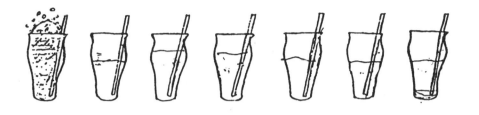

0 points: No sequence representing the soda in the glasses.

1 point: Incomplete sequence.

2. points: Two or more sequences.

3. points: Descending series of lines with corrections (trial and error)

Figure 2.2. continued

3 points: Descending series of lines with corrections.

4 points:Sequence with unevenly spaced increments but no corrections.

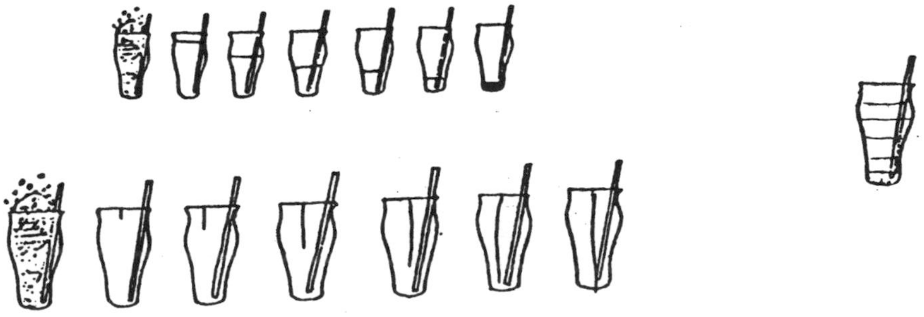

5. Sequence with evenly spaced increments and no corrections (systematic).

Figure 2.3. Predicting Horizontality

1 point: Line parallels bottom or side of tilted bottle.

2 points: Line almost parallels bottom or sides.

3 points: Line is oblique.

4 points: Line relates to the table surface but is not quite parallel.

5 points: Line is parallel to the table surface within 5 degrees.

Figure 2.4. Predicting Verticality

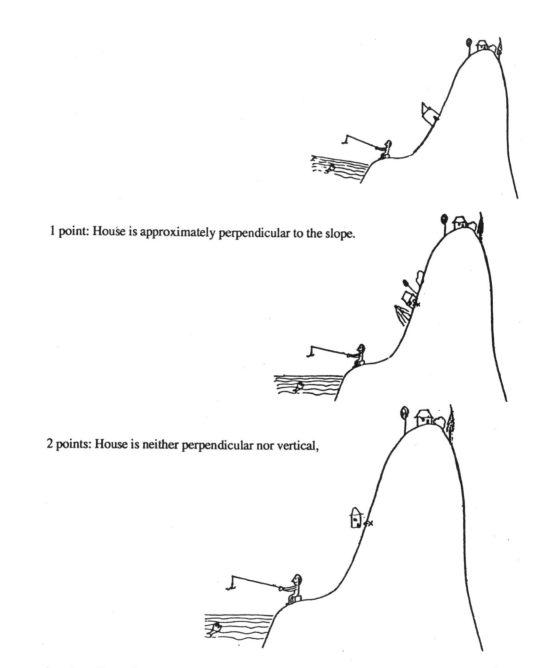

1 point: House is approximately perpendicular to the slope.

2 points: House is neither perpendicular nor vertical,

3. points: House is approximately vertical but has no support.

Figure 2.4. continued

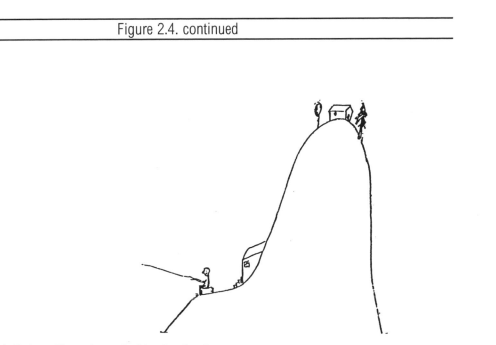

4. Points: House is vertical but has inadequate support.

Figure 2.5. Predictive Drawing by Tania, age 9

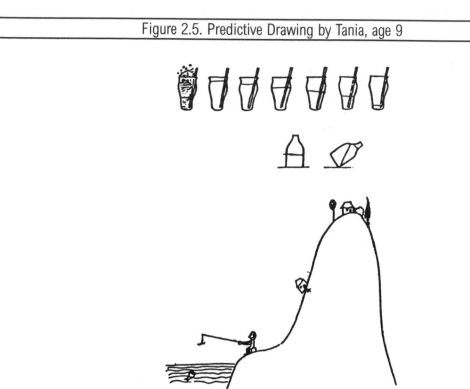

Figure 2.6. Predictive Drawing by an adult in a university audience

Figure 2.7. Predictive Drawing by George, expressive and receptive language impairments

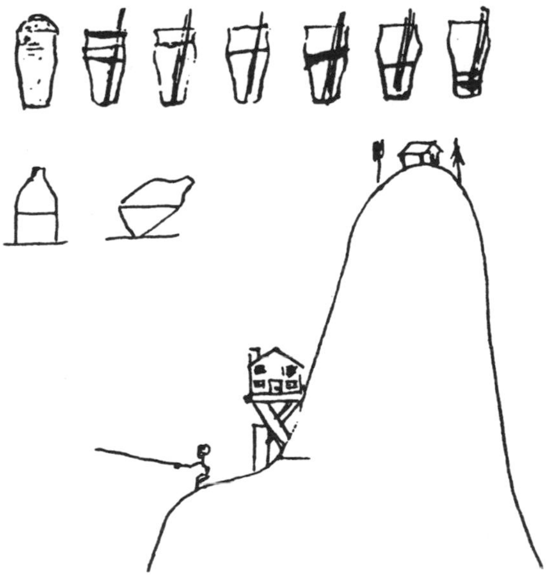

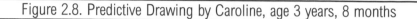

Figure 2.8. Predictive Drawing by Caroline, age 3 years, 8 months

The Drawing from Observation Task

Prepare the arrangement in advance, placing the layout sheet on a table below eye level so that it will appear as a plane rather than as a line (if placed above eye level, it will appear as a line, preventing perception of depth); then place the cylinders and a large pebble or stone on their outlines on the layout sheet. The arrangement should appear as sketched in the guidelines for scoring (table 2.2.); that is, the widest cylinder appears on the left, the tallest on the right, and the smallest to the left of the stone between them.

If the task is to be administered to groups, long, narrow cafeteria tables are useful. An arrangement can be placed at both ends, with chairs along both sides of the table. Check the viewpoint from the farthest seats so that no one sits too far to the left or right of the arrangement.

If a respondent has difficulty reading directions, hold up your booklet at the drawing page shown in figure 2.10, pantomime sketching the arrangement (no more than 5 seconds), then read aloud the directions:

> Have you ever tried to draw something just the way it looks? Here are some things to draw. Look at them carefully, then draw what you see in the space below.

Table 2.2

Guidelines for Scoring the SDT Drawing from Observation Subtest

Sketches of the arrangement are shown below. The front view can serve as the criterion for drawings scored 5 points.

When scoring, note that cylinder #1 (on the left) should be the widest and #4 (on the right) should be is the tallest; cylinder #2 should be in the foreground; and the stone #3, is behind and between # 2 and #4. To examinees seated toward the left, #2 will appear farther from #1 and closer to #3. To examinees seated toward the right, #2 will appear farther from #3 and closer to #1.

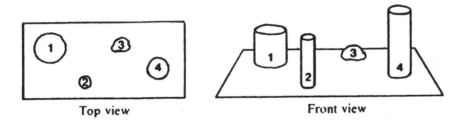

Top view   Front view

Horizontal (left–right) Relationships

0 points: Horizontal relationships are confused. No objects are in the correct left-right order.

1 point: Only one object is in the correct left-right order.

2 points: Two objects are in the correct left right order.

3 points: Three adjacent or two pairs of objects, are in the correct left–right order.

4 points: All four objects are approximately correct in order but not carefully observed or represented.

5 points: All objects are in the correct left-right order.

Three Art Assessments

Vertical (above-below) Relationships (Height)

0 points: All objects are flat; no representation of height.

1 point: All objects are about the same height.

2 points: Two objects (not necessarily adjacent) are approximately correct in height.

3 points: Three objects (not necessarily adjacent) are approximately correct in height.

4 points: All four objects are approximately correct in height but are not carefully observed and represented.

5 points: All vertical relationships are represented accurately.

Front–Back Relationships in (Depth)

0 points: All objects are in a horizontal row even though arrangement was presented below eye level, or else no adjacent objects are correctly related in depth.

1 point: One object is above or below a base line (drawn or implied), or else front-back relationships are incorrect.

2 points: Two objects (not necessarily adjacent) are approximately correct in front–back relationships.

3 points: Three adjacent objects, or two pairs, are approximately correct in front-back relationships.

4 points: All four objects are approximately correct in front-back relationships but not well observed and represented.

5 points: All front-back relationships are represented accurately and the layout sheet is included in the drawing.

Correct,

Examples of Scored Responses

Figure 2.9. The SDT Drawing from Observation Task

Have you ever tried to draw something just the way it looks? Here are some things to draw. Look at them carefully, then draw what you see in the space below.

Figure 2.10. Example of Drawing from Observation

Horizontal relationships: 4 points. (All four objects are approximately correct in left-right order but not carefully observed and represented).

Vertical relationships: 4 points. (All four objects are approximately correct in height but not carefully observed and represented).

Relationships in depth: 1 point. (One object is above the base line).

Horizontal relationships: 5 points.(The horizontal relationships are accurate).

Vertical relationships: 5 points (The vertical relationships are accurate).

Relationships in depth: 5 points (The relationships in depth are accurate and the layout sheet is included in the drawing).

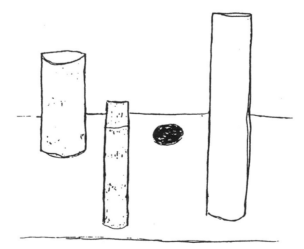

Figure 2.11. Example of Drawing from Observation

Horizontal relationships: 0 points. (No objects are in the correct left-right order).
Vertical relationships: 4 points (All four objects are approximately correct in height).
Relationships in depth: 0 points. (All objects are in a horizontal row).

Horizontal relationships: 2 points (Two objects are approximately correct in left-right order)
Vertical relationships: 3 points (Three objects are approximately correct in height).
Relationships in depth: 1 point: (Relationships in depth are incorrect).

Figure 2.12. Example of Drawing from Observation

Horizontal relationships: 0 points (No objects are in the correct left-right order).
Vertical relationships: 0 points (All objects are flat; there is no representation of height).
Relationships in depth: 1 points (Relationships in depth are incorrect).

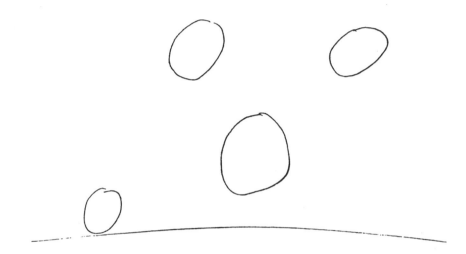

Horizontal relationships: 3 points (Two pairs of objects are approximately correct in left-
      right order).
Vertical relationships: 0 points: (There is no representation of height).
Relationships in depth: 2 points. (Two objects are approximately correct in front-back
      relationships).

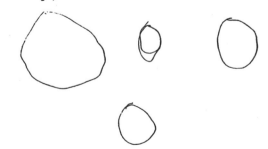

Figure 2.13. Drawing from Observation by an art teacher

Left-right	5
Above-below	5
Front-back	5
Subtest Total	15

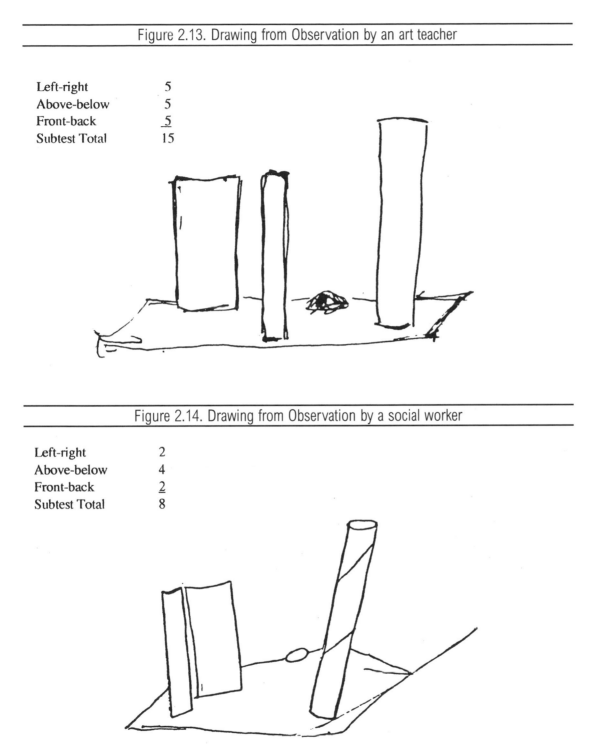

Figure 2.14. Drawing from Observation by a social worker

Left-right	2
Above-below	4
Front-back	2
Subtest Total	8

The Drawing from Imagination Task

If you feel respondents may have difficulty reading directions, point to the Form A set of stimulus drawings (figure 2.15) and the drawing page (figure 2.16), then say:

> Choose two picture ideas and imagine a story, something happening between the pictures you choose. When you are ready, draw a picture of what you imagine. Show what is happening in your drawing.
>
> Don't just copy these pictures. You can make changes and draw other things, too.
>
> When you finish drawing, write a title or story. Tell what is happening and what may happen later on.

If a respondent chooses to draw different subjects or simply copies the stimulus drawings, do not intervene unless you feel the instructions were misunderstood.

After drawings are finished, ask for the information requested below the drawing. With respondents who have difficulty writing, offer to write their stories using the same words.

Whenever possible, discuss the drawings individually so that meanings can be clarified. It is important to make respondents feel it is safe to express thoughts and feelings, "watched only by friends." If they used symbols or metaphors, use them, too. For example, if the principal subject is a cat, you might ask, "Can you tell me how the cat feels or what it is thinking? What has happened and what may happen later on?" Be alert for verbal clues, such as personal pronouns and the subjects of sentences. Metaphoric dialogues often provide opportunities to introduce healthier adaptations or alternative solutions.

Guidelines for scoring the cognitive content of drawings from imagination range from low to high levels of ability, scored 1 to 5 points, as presented in table 2.3. Guidelines for scoring emotional content and self-image range from strongly negative to strongly positive, also scored 1 to 5 points, as shown in tables 2.4 and table 2.5.

It is important to identify principal subjects whenever possible and to consider what the choice of stimulus drawings suggests about those who chose them. Do the drawings reflect anger, fear, conflict, desires, or social isolation? Are other subjects hostile or friendly?

The Form A set of stimulus drawings should be used only for pretesting and posttesting. The second set, Form B, is provided for any other purpose, such as developing cognitive skills or obtaining additional responses so that patterns may emerge. The Form B stimulus drawings may be found in the appendix .

Drawing What You Imagine

Figure 2.15a. Form A, Stimulus Drawings

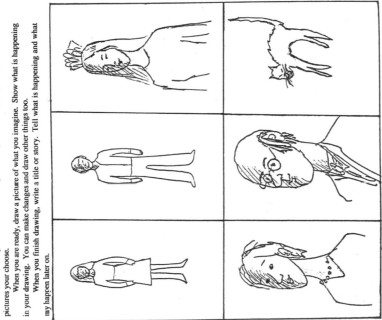

Choose two picture ideas and imagine a story - something happening between the pictures your choose.

When you are ready, draw a picture of what you imagine. Show what is happening in your drawing. You can make changes and draw other things too.

When you finish drawing, write a title or story. Tell what is happening and what my happen later on.

Figure 2.15b. Form B, Stimulus Drawings

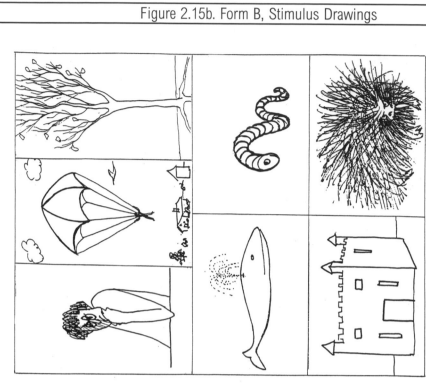

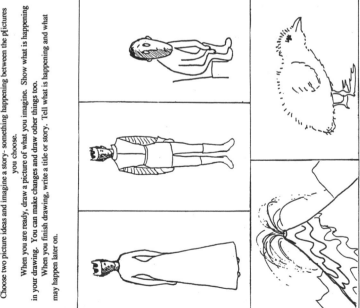

Choose two picture ideas and imagine a story- something happening between the pictures you choose.

When you are ready, draw a picture of what you imagine. Show what is happening in your drawing. You can make changes and draw other things too.

When you finish drawing, write a title or story. Tell what is happening and what may happen later on.

Figure 2.16. Drawing from Imagination Page

Drawing

Story:_____

_____

_____

_____

_____

<u>Please fill in the blanks below:</u>

First name _____ Sex_____ Age _____ Location (state): _____Date:_____

Just now I'm feeling _____very happy _____O.K. _____angry _____frightened _____sad

---

Table 2.3

Guidelines for Scoring the Drawing from Imagination Subtest of the SDT

Ability to Select (the content or message of a drawing and/or story)

0 points:	No evidence of selecting.
1 point:	*Perceptual level*: single subject; or subjects are unrelated in size or placement.
2 points:	Subjects may be related in size or placement, but there is no interaction.
3 points:	*Functional level*: concrete; shows what subjects do or what is done to them; concrete.
4 points:	descriptive rather than abstract or imaginative.
5 points:	*Conceptual level*: imaginative, well-organized idea, implies more than is visible, or show ability to deal with abstract ideas. Art skills are not important here.

Ability to Combine (the form of a drawing)

0 points:	single subject, no spatial relationships.
1 point:	*Proximity*; subjects float in space, related by proximity rather than a baseline.
2 points:	attempts to show relationships, such as arrows or dotted lines.
3 points:	*Baseline*; subjects are related to one another along a base line (real or implied).
4 points:	Beyond the baseline level, but at least half the drawing area is blank.
5 points:	*Overall coordination*: depicts depth or takes into account the entire drawing area, or includes a series of two or more drawings.

Ability to Represent (creativity in form, content, title, or story)

0 points:	No evidence of representation.
1 point:	*Imitative*; copies stimulus drawings or uses stick figures or stereotypes.
2 points:	Beyond imitation, but drawing or ideas are commonplace.
3 points:	*Restructured*: changes or elaborates on stimulus drawings or stereotypes.
4 points:	Beyond restructuring, moderately original or expressive.
5 points:	*Transformational*: highly original, expressive, playful, suggestive, or uses metaphors, puns, jokes, satire, or double meanings.

©1995–2002 Rawley Silver

Table 2.4

Guidelines for Scoring the Emotional Content of Responses in Drawings from Imagination Test

1 point: *Strongly negative themes*, for example,

Solitary subjects portrayed as sad, isolated, helpless, suicidal, dead, or in mortal danger.

Relationships that are destructive, murderous, or life-threatening.

2 points: *Moderately negative themes*, for example,

Solitary subjects portrayed as frightened, angry, dissatisfied, assaultive, destructive, or unfortunate.

Relationships that are stressful, hostile, or unpleasant

3 points: *Neutral themes*, for example,

Ambivalent, both negative and positive,

Unemotional, neither negative nor positive.

Ambiguous or unclear.

4 points: *Moderately positive themes*, for example,

Solitary subjects portrayed as fortunate but passive, enjoying something, or being rescued.

Relationships that are friendly or pleasant.

5 points: *Strongly positive themes*, for example,

Solitary subjects portrayed as effective, happy, or achieving goals.

Relationships that are caring or loving.

Table 2.5

Guidelines for Scoring Self-Images

1 point: *Morbid fantasy*, respondent seems to identify with a subject portrayed as sad, helpless, isolated, suicidal, dead, or in mortal danger.

2 points: *Unpleasant fantasy*, respondent seems to identify with a subject portrayed as frightened, frustrated, or unfortunate.

3 points: *Ambiguous or ambivalent fantasy*, respondent seems to identify with a subject portrayed as ambivalent or unemotional, or else the self-image is unclear or invisible such as the narrator.

4 points: *Pleasant fantasy*, respondent seems to identify with a subject portrayed as fortunate but passive, such as being rescued.

5 points: *Wish-fulfilling fantasy*, respondent seems to identify with a subject who is powerful, loved, assaultive, or achieving goals.

Examples of Scored Responses to the Drawing from Imagination Task

Figure 2.17. "Muscleboy having a snack after school," by Mack, age 12, no impairments

Mack is a presumably normal sixth-grader in an urban public school. Presented with the Form A set of stimulus drawings, he chose the boy, the soda, and the refrigerator. In his drawing, the boy is transformed into a young athlete endowed with large biceps, broad shoulders, and a tiny waist. He spreads his arms wide, holding the soda, which has been enlarged to hold two scoops of ice cream, side by side, and a striped straw that bends toward the smiling athlete. The refrigerator has also been embellished with the manufacturer's name. A fluorescent light hangs overhead and beyond the window, the sun shines.

In emotional content, the theme of Mack's drawing is strongly positive. School has ended for the day and its solitary subject is portrayed as happy and effective. As for self-image, Mack seems to have created a wish-fulfilling fantasy and identified with his admirable subject.

In ability to select, Mack's response is well organized and implies more than is visible (his subject, an athlete). Further evidence that it reflects performance at the conceptual level is the abstract word in his title, *snack*, signifying a class of tasty food. In ability to combine, it shows depth (the window is behind the boy); and in ability to represent, it is expressive, playful, and suggestive.

Emotional projection	5	Solitary subject seems happy, achieving goals.
Self-image	5	Mack seems to identify (or wish to identify) with Muscleboy.
Ability to select	5	Imaginative, well organized.
Ability to combine	5	Overall coordination.
Ability to represent	5	Expressive, playful.

Figure 2.18. Untitled drawing, by Dan, age 15, language-impaired

---

Dan, age 15, attended a special school for children with language impairments. His diagnosis was "congenital expressive aphasia," and he was unable to read.

Presented with the Form A set of stimulus drawings, he chose the boy, girl, and television. In his drawing, the boy sits on a chair watching TV, his feet resting on a footstool. Using a line to separate indoors from outdoors, the girl seems to be outside, skating on the sidewalk. At her side, but presented from a different point of view, another boy rides a bicycle.

In emotional content, Dan's theme seems moderately positive. The boy indoors is passively watching TV. The children outside are playing, but do not seem engaged in active play. In self-image, Dan may identify with one or both of the boys, but without verbal or written clues, it is unclear.

In ability to select, Dan seems to have chosen his subjects at the functional level, showing what they do. In ability to combine, his use of a line to separate inside from outside suggests ability beyond the proximity level but below the base line level. In ability to represent, Dan imitated the stimulus drawing television but drew it on a table. He also restructured the boy and girl and invented the chair, footstool, sidewalk, and bicycle.

Emotional content	4	moderately positive
Self-image	3	unclear
Ability to select	3	functional, shows what subjects do
Ability to combine	2	vertical line separates inside and outside home
Ability to represent	3	restructures stimulus drawings and adds details

Figure 2.19. "The bride and the mouse," by Jody, age 11

Jody is a presumably normal girl in the fifth grade of an urban elementary school, who chose the stimulus drawing bride and the mouse. In her drawing, the bride is transformed. She is drawn full length and seems much younger than the stimulus drawing bride. Jody also added hands with fingers outstretched, and a gown with many details. The mouse is also transformed, holding a bouquet of flowers and leaning toward the bride with tail held high.

In emotional content, Jody's response seems ambivalent, both negative and positive. The bride's fingers and averted gaze suggest feelings of disgust, whereas the mouse (the groom?) seems pleased. As for self-image, the youthfulness of the bride suggests that Jody identifies her with herself.

In ability to select, this fantasy seems to be a well-organized idea, implying more than is visible, in spite of its noncommunicative title. In ability to combine, the bride seems slightly in the foreground, the mouse at a distance slightly behind her, perhaps suggesting their relative status in Jody's esteem. In ability to represent, the contradictory feelings of both bride and groom are evident.

Emotional projection	3	ambivalent
Self-image	2	Jody seems to identify with the disgusted bride
Ability to select	5	implies more than is visible
Ability to combine	4	beyond the base line level
Ability to represent	5	highly expressive

Figure 2.20. "The dying bride," by Connie, age 14, no impairments

---

Emotional projection 1   solitary subject portrayed as isolated, suicidal, and tearful
Self-image   1   Connie may identify the bride with herself.

Ability to select   5   imaginative, well-organized idea; implies more than is visible
Ability to combine   5   takes into account the entire drawing area
Ability to represent 5   highly expressive and suggestive

Figure 2.21. "Victims of death," by John, age 8, no impairments

Emotional projection	1	life-threatening relationships
Self-image	3	unclear; John could identify himself with his predators, victims, or the narrator
Ability to select	5	imaginative, well-organized idea; uses abstract words
Ability to combine	5	two drawings, different subjects illustrate the title
Ability to represent	5	original, expressive

Figure 2.22. Untitled, by Betty, age 13, severe sensori-neural and receptive language disabilities; hearing loss 78 dB in her better ear

Emotional projection 3   unemotional
Self-image   3   unclear, Betty may identify with the girl

Ability to select   2   girl and dog are related by the leash and placement
Ability to combine   3   girl and dog are related along an implied base line
Ability to represent 3   girl and dog are restructured

Figure 2.23. "N-N-N-Nice Doggie," by Bill, age 14, no impairments

Emotional projection 2   fearful and hostile relationships
Self-image   2   Bill seems to identify with the frightened young man

Ability to select   5   imaginative, well-organized idea
Ability to combine   5   shows depth: boy in front of tree, dog behind rock
Ability to represent   5   highly expressive and suggestive

Figure 2.24. Going to the Malt Shop, by Sara, age 14		
Emotional projection	4	moderately positive theme
Self-image	4	Sara seems to identify with the passive girl
Ability to select	3	functional level
Ability to combine	5	overall coordination
Ability to represent	3	Although Sara elaborated on the stimulus drawings, her response is not very expressive or creative.

Figure 2.25. "The dog is chasing the cat," dictated by Caroline, age 3 years, 8 months

Emotional projection	4	both dog and cat are smiling
Self-image	3	Caroline seems to be the invisible narrator
Ability to select	3	functional
Ability to combine	3	implies base line
Ability to represent	3	restructures stimulus drawings

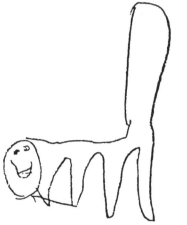

Figure 2.26. "The Great Mouse Murder," by Roy, age 17, no impairments

Emotional projection	1	helpless mouse in mortal danger
Self-Image	5	Roy seems to identify with the unseen murderer
Ability to select	5	Imaginative, well-organized idea, implies more than is visible
Ability to combine	5	takes into account the entire drawing area
Ability to represent	5	original, expressive, suggestive

Figure 2.27. "Mister Man Siting (sic) on a chair," by Teddy, age 9, no impairments

Emotional projection	3	ambiguous and ambivalent
Self–image	3	unclear, Teddy seems to be the invisible narrator
Ability to select	5	implies more than is visible
Ability to combine	5	shows depth
Ability to represent	5	highly expressive and suggestive

	Figure 2.28. "The Great Escape," by Bruce, age 16, no impairments	

Emotional projection	3	the snake is frustrated, the mouse escapes
Self-Image	5	Bruce seems to identify with the successful mouse
Ability to select	5	imaginative, well-organized idea
Ability to combine	5	shows depth
Ability to represent	5	original, expressive, playful, double meaning

◇ ◇ ◇

Figure 2.29. "Jig-a-dig-dig, 2 kids on a pig," by Max, age 13, no impairments

Emotional projection	4	the kids seem fortunate but passive
Self-image	3	Max seems to be the invisible narrator
Ability to select	5	imaginative, well-organized
Ability to combine	5	overall coordination
Ability to represent	5	play on words

Humorous Responses to the Drawing Tasks

Different forms of humor have been observed in responses to the drawing task. Although most responses are not humorous, those that are provide information about the emotional states of individuals and access to coping skills, anxieties, and desires, as well as age and gender differences (Silver, 2001). Guidelines for assessing humor are presented in chapter 14, which also provides normative data on the uses of humor.

This chapter has presented guidelines for administering and scoring responses to the three SDT tasks, illustrated by responses scored as suggested by the rating scales. The following chapter will review the studies undertaken to determine whether the scores are reliable and whether they have validity.

Chapter 3

Reliability and Validity of the SDT

◇   ◇   ◇

This chapter summarizes studies of scorer and retest reliability, as well as the SDT's relationship to traditional tests of intelligence or achievement. To collect data for these and other studies, the SDT was administered to 1,399 children, adolescents, and adults. They included 849 presumably typical or unimpaired respondents and 550 with brain injuries, hearing impairments, emotional disturbances, or learning disabilities. The SDT was administered by 21 art therapists, psychologists, and classroom teachers residing in California, Florida, Idaho, Nebraska, New Jersey, New York, Pennsylvania, Wisconsin, and Canada.

Scorer Reliability

Comparing the Evaluations of Seven Judges

Seven art therapists administered and scored responses to the SDT by children who were participating in the National Institute of Education Project, discussed in chapter 5 (Silver et al., 1980). Four were registered art therapists and three had received master's degrees in art therapy or in education. After several training sessions, the judges scored the responses of six children, selected by school administrators for performing at least 1 year below grade level in reading or mathematics. Separate reliability coefficients were computed for each subtest.

Results

The judges' ratings indicated a high degree of interscorer reliability. The coefficients were .93 in Predictive Drawing, .91 in Drawing from Observation, and .98 in Drawing from Imagination, as shown in table 3.1.

Table 3.1

Interscorer Reliability Coefficients for SDT Subtests by Seven Judges

Subtest	r
Predictive Drawing	.93
Drawing from Observation	.91
Drawing from Imagination	.98

Comparing Evaluations of SDT Subtests by Six Judges

In a second study, six judges scored the SDT responses of 11 children with visual–motor disabilities who participated in a study of children with learning disabilities (Silver & Lavin, 1977).

Results

An analysis of variance (Winder 1962, p. 128) indicated that the six judges had a similar frame of reference and displayed a high degree of agreement in scoring the tests. The reliability coefficient was .852 in ability to select, combine, and represent (Drawing from Imagination) and .944 in spatial orientation (Drawing from Observation, sequencing, and conserving).

Comparing Evaluations of Self-Image and Emotional Content Scores by Five Judges

Five judges evaluated responses to the Drawing from Imagination task in order to determine reliability for the self-image scale and the emotional content scale. Four judges were registered art therapists; the fifth, a graduate student in a university art therapy program.

The judges scored 5 responses selected at random from a group of 15 responses by 7 males, 8 females, 4 children, 5 adolescents, and 6 adults. The judges met for approximately 1 hour to practice scoring the 10 unselected responses, then independently scored the 5 selected responses. The ratings for each of the two scales were analyzed separately.

Using the statistic Intraclass Correlation (ICC), a measure of interrater reliability, the results obtained are shown in table 3.2.

Table 3.2	

Interscorer Reliability for the Self-Image and Emotional Content Scales for Five Judges

	ICC
Emotional Content Scale	0.94
Self-Image Scale	0.74

These data show strong reliability for the emotional content scale and moderate reliability for the self-image scale. Thus, it appears that the scales show interscorer reliability.

Judges with No Special Training

The following studies were undertaken to determine the adequacy of the SDT scoring guidelines for judges who did not participate in training sessions.

Comparing Evaluations of Cognitive Skill by a Registered Art Therapist with No Special Training and the Author

The director of an art therapy program in Pennsylvania scored test booklets administered to 16 tenth-grade students and 20 fourth-grade students. He used the guidelines provided in a preliminary version of the SDT manual. The booklets were subsequently scored by the author (who had not met him).

All correlations were found significant, five at the .01 level and one at the .05 level, as shown in Table 3.3. These data show moderate reliability. They suggest that the scoring guidelines alone are adequate when used by a registered art therapist, and that training sessions for such examiners are unnecessary.

Table 3.3		

Correlations for Subtests Scored by a Registered Art Therapist with No Special Training and the Author

Subtest	r	p
Tenth-Graders ($n = 16$)		
Predictive Drawing	.71	.01
Drawing from Observation	.81	.01
Drawing from Imagination	.79	.01
Fourth-Graders ($n = 20$)		
Predictive Drawing	.86	.01
Drawing from Observation	.45	.05
Drawing from Imagination	.65	.01

Comparing Evaluations of Cognitive Skill by Another Registered Art Therapist with No Special Training and the Author

A registered art therapist in Virginia who learned to score the SDT by reading its manual administered the SDT to nine hospitalized adults with mental handicaps. The test booklets were scored by the art therapist and the author.

The judges displayed a high degree of agreement in scoring the tests, as shown in table 3.4. These data show strong reliability, again suggesting that training sessions for registered art therapists are not necessary.

Table 3.4

Correlations for Subtests Scored by an Art Therapist with No Special Training and the Author ($n = 9$)

Subtest	r	p
Predictive Drawing	.99	.01
Drawing from Observation	.89	.01
Drawing from Imagination	.91	.01
Total	.96	.01

Comparing Evaluations by a Classroom Teacher, a Psychotherapist, and Three Art Therapists

In revising the SDT manual for the second edition, changes were made in the wording of the scoring guidelines in an attempt to make scoring more precise. To determine whether the changes would affect scorer reliability, the test performances of 10 children were scored by 5 scorers using the revised guidelines. Reliability coefficients were computed for their evaluations of the total test scores of 10 third-graders in a public school in Nebraska.

The judges included the children's teacher in Nebraska, who learned to score the SDT by reading its manual; the psychotherapist in Florida; and three art therapists in Pennsylvania. Scorers A and B were registered art therapists who had learned about the SDT by reading its manual, and Scorer C was a graduate student who learned about the test from Scorer A. None of the scorers had met the author.

Significant correlations at the .01 level were found as indicated in table 3.5, suggesting that training sessons also are unnecessary for teachers and psychotherapists.

Table 3.5

Interscorer Reliability Coefficients of Evaluations by Five Judges

Mean = 32.55
SD = 4.5
r = .66
$p < .01$

◇ ◇ ◇

Retest Reliability

To determine the test–retest reliability of the SDT, it was administered on two occasions to groups of children and adolescents. Their responses were scored and reliability coefficients computed.

Comparing Performance Scores of 12 Adolescents with Learning Disabilities After Approximately One Month

Moser (1980) used the SDT in her doctoral project, administering it twice to 12 adolescents with learning disabilities with a time lapse of approximately 1 month, and computed reliability coefficients for each subtest. All correlations were significant at the .05 level. The test–retest reliability scores are strong in Drawing from Observation and "Ability to Represent Spatial Concepts" (Moser's term for Predictive Drawing) but weak in Drawing from Imagination, as shown in table 3.6.

Table 3.6

Test–Retest Reliability Coefficients of Adolescents with Learning Disabilities, Moser Study

Subtest	r	p
Predictive Drawing	.8036	.05
Drawing from Observation	.8401	.05
Drawing from Imagination	.5637	.05

Comparing the Performance Scores of 10 Children After Approximately One Month

The SDT was administered to all children in a third-grade class by their teacher in an urban public school in Nebraska during November 1989. She administered the test again in December 1989 to 10 of the children, whom she described as the "top students across the board." Limiting the retest group to top scorers limits the reliability of the findings.

Responses to the test were scored by five judges. To ensure that the judges would score blindly, the drawings were identified only by first names. The first test performance by each examinee was identified by the child's real name; the second, by a fictitious name beginning with the same letter of the alphabet. For example, Sandra's second booklet was named Susie; Andrew's second booklet, Arthur. Thus, the judges assumed they were scoring one test performance by each of 20 children but were actually scoring two test performances by each of 10 children.

Moderate correlations were found in Drawing from Imagination and in total test scores. Low correlations were found in Drawing from Observation. No significant correlations were found in Predictive Drawing, as shown in table 3.7.

Table 3.7		
Test–Retest Reliability Coefficients of Third-Graders		
Subtest	*r*	*p*
Predictive Drawing	.08	ns
Drawing from Observation	.61	.05
Drawing from Imagination	.70	.02
Total	.72	.02

The inconsistencies in test–retest correlations between Studies 6 and 7 suggest that the Drawing from Imagination subtest may be an unstable construct for adolescents with learning disabilities but not for children, whereas the Predictive Drawing subtest may be unstable for children but not for adolescents.

A review of the children's responses to the Predictive Drawing task found that in the retest, two children failed to draw any lines in the tilted bottle, thus lowering their scores from 4 points in the first test to 0 in the retest. Two other children apparently had learned that water remains horizontal regardless of the tilt of its container, raising their scores from 1 point on the first test to 5 points on the second test.

In addition, one child scored 5 points in the first test, drawing a sequence of descending lines in the soda glasses without corrections. In the retest, however, she erased the lines she drew in the glasses, thus lowering her score to 3 points.

In the Predictive Drawing task, scores are based on observations by Piaget and Inhelder (1967), who found that children use trial and error when they do not know the solutions to problems. When they do know the solutions, however, they proceed systematically without resorting to trial and error. As this child had represented a sequence systematically in the first test, it seems unlikely that her erasures in the second test reflected trial and error. It may be, instead, that the erasures reflected feelings of insecurity or a desire for perfection. At any event, the variations in retest scores suggest that the visuospatial abilities measured by the Predictive Drawing task may be unstable in this age group. This test–retest reliability underestimates the reliability of the test.

Correlations Between the SDT and Traditional Tests

Hayes's Finding of Correlations Between the SDT and SRA Reading Test

Karen Hayes (1978), a classroom teacher in an urban parochial school, had been troubled by her observation that the amount of time given to art education had been diminishing each year and even eliminated altogether by budget cutting or "back-to-basics zealots." She believed it was important for primary teachers and art teachers to become aware of similarities between the mental processes involved in drawing and reading and decided to devote her master's thesis to examining relationships between children's drawings and reading scores.

Procedures

Hayes administered the SDT to 75 children in grades 1 to 3, then compared their SDT scores with their reading scores. She correlated the SDT scores of first-graders with their scores on the SRA Informal Reading Inventory and the scores of second- and third-graders with their scores on the SRA Reading Achievement Test, Form F, Primary II.

Twenty-five children from each of the three grades were randomly selected by their homeroom teachers to participate in the study. The children were then grouped as high, middle-, or low-reading achievers, as determined by the SRA Informal Reading Inventory and the SRA Achievement Series Test. The children had not been exposed to any formal art classes, due to a reduced budget, and any previous art experiences had been provided by classroom teachers. The children lived in predominantly middle-class homes in the Bronx, New York, and spoke English at home. They ranged in age from 6 to 9 years; 38 were girls, 37 were boys.

Hayes administered the SDT to approximately ten children at a time, over a period of two weeks, administering it individually to students who had been absent from their groups. Her study attempted to answer the following questions:

1. Is there a correlation between a children's ability to associate and represent concepts as found in their ability to read and ability to draw from imagination?

2. Do reading scores correlate with ability to perceive and represent spatial relationships when drawing from observation?

3. Do reading scores correlate with ability to order and represent spatial concepts through predictive drawing?

4. Is the relationship between performances, as measured by reading scores and scores on the SDT Drawing from Imagination subtest, stronger for boys than for girls?

Hayes used the Spearman rank-order formula to determine the strength of correlations and compared correlation coefficients for boys and girls to determine whether gender differences emerged.

Results

In all three grades, significant correlations emerged between reading achievement scores and Drawing from Imagination subtest scores. Because all correlation coefficients were statistically significant, the null hypothesis was rejected at the .05 level of significance ($r = .945$, .657, and .668 for grades 1 to 3, respectively). The relationship between reading ability and the SDT was stronger for girls than boys in the second and third grades.

On the other hand, correlations between Drawing from Observation and reading scores were significant for third-graders only, indicating that Drawing from Observation scores did not correlate consistently with reading scores. The finding of one strong correlation suggested that further investigation would be useful.

The correlations between Predictive Drawing and reading achievement were also inconsistent, with weak correlation for the first grade and no significance for the second and third grades. The relationship between reading and artistic performance as measured by Drawing from Imagination was stronger for boys in the first grade and stronger for girls in the second and third grades.

Concluding Observations

Hayes (1978) noted that the Drawing from Imagination subtest provided insight into the child's personality and concepts of reality, in addition to the correlations found between ability to read and represent concepts. She concluded that art instruction should be an integral part of the primary child's school curriculum, because the cognitive skills needed in art do correlate with the cognitive skills needed in reading and other academic subjects. She recommended further investigation of the correlations between reading and Predictive Drawing, as well as Drawing from Observation, to clarify the inconsistencies found in her study and suggested that some other testing device, rather than the SRA Achievement series, be used to assess reading ability.

Anderson's Finding of Correlations Between the SDT and the Gates-MacGinitie Reading Comprehension Test

Victoria Anderson examined relationships between the cognitive skills used in comprehending prose and in composing a Drawing from Imagination, in her master's thesis (2001). She hypothesized that positive correlations would be found between scores on the 1996 edition of the SDT Drawing from Imagination subtest and scores on the Gates-MacGinitie Reading Test (1989). This standardized reading test is used annually in an urban, public, magnet middle school in Pennsylvania to measure the reading comprehension of its students. The test assesses ability to read paragraphs of prose and answer multiple-choice questions.

Both tests were administered (in varying order) to approximately 250 students by the language arts teacher in each grade during the same class period. Twenty-four of these students volunteered to have their scores correlated in order to explore relationships between reading comprehension and Drawing from Imagination. The students, ages 11 to 13, included 14 sixth-graders, 4 seventh-graders, and 6 eighth-graders. Of the 50-minute period, 35 minutes were devoted to the reading test, 15 to the SDT. Reading test scores were based on grade-equivalent norms. Scores on both tests were correlated using Pearson's *r*.

The correlation for the 24 students yielded results significant at the .01 level of probability ($r = .53, p < .01$), showing with 99% certainty that a significant relationship exists between scores on both measures. Anderson's study seems to support the validity of using the SDT to assess the cognitive skills considered fundamental in comprehending written language, as discussed in chapter 1, and provides interesting observations for future investigation, as discussed in chapter 16.

Swanson's Finding of Correlations between the SDT and the SRA Survey of Basic Skills Ability

Joan Swanson, a schoolteacher in Nebraska, volunteered to administer the SDT to 15 of her students (Silver, 1990). The students, ages 13 and 14, comprised one half of her eighth-grade class in a rural public school. Because the class previously had been divided for periods of music and art, she administered the SDT to students attending the art period, then sent the test booklets to me for scoring. In addition, she sent, in a sealed envelope, the students' scores on the SRA Survey of Basic Skills Ability, administered the previous spring to assess ability and progress. I gave the sealed envelope and the SDT scores to a statistician, who analyzed the results.

Results

The statistician found significant correlations between the SRA scores and total SDT scores, as well as between two of the three subtests: Predictive Drawing and Drawing from Imagination, as shown in table 3.8. She did not find significant correlations between the SRA and the Drawing from Observation subtest.

Table 3.8

Correlations Between Scores on the SDT and the SRA Survey of Basic Skills Ability

Subtest	Mean	SD	r	p
Predictive Drawing	11.4	1.8	0.52	0.05
Drawing from Observation	12.2	2.4	0.51	n.s.
Drawing from Imagination	9.8	2.5	0.68	0.01
Total	33.4	5.0	0.76	0.01
SRA	104.7	9.8		

Comparing SDT Scores with Scores on the Metropolitan Achievement Test (Reading and Mathematics)

Madeline Altabe, PhD, used correlational analysis to determine whether the SDT was related to school achievement, as measured by the MAT. She compared the three SDT cognitive subtest scores of 40 children with their reading and mathematics scores on the Metropolitan Achievement Test (MAT, 1931–1993), which had been administered previously by school personnel. The children attended grades 1 to 3 in a suburban public school in a low to middle socioeconomic neighborhood in New York.

Results

The SDT and MAT scales appear to be related, even though the MAT is a language-oriented test of scholastic achievement. The children's scores in Predictive Drawing, Drawing from Observation, and Drawing from Imagination correlated significantly with their MAT Reading and Mathematics scores at the $p < .05$, $p < .01$, and $p < .001$ levels of significance, as shown in table 3.9.

Surprisingly, scores on the SDT self-image scale were also related significantly to the MAT scores.

Table. 3.9

Relationships Between SDT Scales and MAT Scales Among Elementary School Children in Grades 1 to 3 ($N = 40$)

SDT Scales	MAT Reading	MAT Mathematics
Predictive Drawing	.39★	.42★★
Drawing from Observation	.50★★★	.44★★
Drawing from Imagination	.36★	.34★
Emotional Content	n.s	n.s.
Self-Image	.42★★	.40★★

★$p < .05$, ★★$p < .01$, $p < .001$

Horvitz-Darby's Findings of Concurrence with the DATA

Ellen Horovitz-Darby, ART-BC (1991), examined the role of clinical art therapy with deaf children and their families. She based her therapy on four assessments, including the SDT and the Diagnostic Art Therapy Assessment and reported a case study of a 10-year-old boy that found concurrence between these assessments, yielding quantified information.

Correlations Between the SDT and Six Traditional Language-Oriented Tests of Intelligence and Achievement

The 1980 National Institute of Education Project, which provided the study of inter-scorer reliability discussed earlier in this chapter and in chapter 5, also examined relationships between the SDT and the Canadian Cognitive Abilities Test (CCAT), the Metropolitan Achievement Test (MAT), the Otis Lennon School Ability Test, the SRA Math Achievement Test, the Iowa Test of Basic Skills (Composite), and the WISC Performance IQ, which was used in testing children who are deaf.

Although significant relationships were found between the SDT and these traditional tests, the reliability coefficients were low, as shown in table 3.10. The correlations with Drawing from Imagination were modest, while correlations with Drawing from Observation were significant only with the Iowa Composite Test. Thus, the relationships between these tests and the SDT are only moderate.

The traditional tests are heavily weighted with verbal items that do not appear at all on the SDT. On the other hand, the SDT taps cognitive skills that are not included on these tests. All the instruments assess intellectual ability, but they use different assessment techniques and emphasize language and visuospatial cognitive skills to different extents.

Table 3.10

Relationships Between Scores on the SDT and Scores on the CCAT, Otis Lennon, WISC Performance IQ, MAT Reading, and SRA Math

	Predictive Drawing			Drawing from Observation		Drawing from Imagination	
	n	r	p	r	p	r	p
CCAT	25	.33	ns	.05	ns	.50	.01
Otis Lennon	99	.30	.01	.05	ns	.39	.01
WISC Perf.	65	.33	.01	.16	ns	.37	.01
MAT Reading	76	.32	.01	.03	ns	.31	.01
SRA Math	65	.36	.01	−.15	ns	.37	.01
Iowa Comp.	20	.11	ns	.55	.01	.44	.05

What can't be explained by correlations with these traditional tests can be explained by other cognitive strengths not measured by these tests. Joey was not alone in having low scores on a traditional test and high scores on the SDT. In Predictive Drawing, only 18 of 136 children received the highest possible scores, and 8 of the 18 had IQ scores ranging between 50 on the Stanford Binet and 140 on the Draw-a-Man test. Their ages ranged from 10 to 13.

The SDT has been presented to audiences of teachers and other professionals. Without fail, some confuse spatial relationships in Drawing from Observation or draw houses perpendicular to the slope or lines parallel to the sides of the tilted bottle.

How can this finding be explained? The obvious answer: Lack of talent in art seems inadequate, because the drawing tasks call for more than art skills. It may be, instead, that adults who say they cannot draw a straight line have difficulty in processing spatial information. They may have subtle cognitive dysfunctions easily overlooked because our schools emphasize verbal skills, and it does not matter if students cannot draw. By the same token, subtle cognitive strengths may also be escaping detection. It may well be important to identify and evaluate these strengths if they can be used to assist students with language dysfunctions to acquire concepts usually acquired verbally.

The results lend support to the hypothesis that the SDT measures cognitive skills through the use of drawings rather than language. The Predictive Drawing subtest is based on the theory that it measures ability to predict and represent concepts of sequential order, horizontality, and verticality, as stated in chapter 2. The Drawing from Observation subtest is based on the theory that it measures ability to represent spatial relationships in height, width, and depth. The Drawing from Imagination subtest is based on the theory that it measures levels of ability to select, combine, and represent through images instead of words. These cognitive abilities appear relatively independent of language impairment and verbal–analytical thinking, and to some extent independent of age.

The findings support the premise that the SDT can be used to identify cognitive skills in children with known language deficiencies—such as those with deafness, language impairment, learning disabilities, and other disadvantages—as well as adults who cannot communicate well verbally. These results also explain why we have found unexpected cognitive strengths in some children when using the SDT—strengths that do not appear on other tests.

Moser's Finding of Correlations Between the Scores of 70 Adolescents with and without Learning Disabilities on the SDT and the Bender, Draw-a-Man, WAIS Verbal, and WAIS Performance IQ Tests

Joy Moser (1980) administered the SDT to 70 adolescents with and without learning disabilities and compared mean scores as part of the doctrial. The group with learning disabilities received lower scores than the control group to a degree significant at the .001 level of probability on the SDT and on the Goodenough Harris Draw-a-Man test at the .05 level, as shown in table 3.11.

These findings indicate that adolescents with and without learning disabilities, who would be expected to differ in cognition, do differ on the SDT.

Moser also compared the SDT scores of her subjects with learning disabilities with their scores on four other tests. She found significant correlations between SDT total and subtest scores and scores on the Wechsler Adult Intelligence Scales (WAIS) Performance IQ test and the Goodenough-Harris Draw-a-Man test at the .01 and .001 levels. Negative correlations were found between the SDT and the Bender Visual Motor Gestalt and the WAIS Verbal scores, as shown in table 3.12.

Table 3.11

Correlations Between Scores on the SDT and Draw-a-Man Tests by 36 Adolescents with Learning Disabilities and 34 Control Group Adolescents

Variable	Experimental Mean ($n = 36$)	S.D.	Control Mean ($n = 34$)	S.D.	t	p
Predictive Drawing	3.28	1.02	4.65	.63	−6.98	.001
Drawing from Observation	3.93	1.20	4.9	.30	−4.84	.001
Drawing from Imagination	2.48	1.30	3.63	1.14	−4.01	.001
Total	3.20	.95	4.39	.54	−6.65	.001
Draw–a–Man	40.26	10.59	46.95	9.50	−2.45	.05

Table 3.12

Correlation Matrix Between Scores on the SDT and Draw-a-Man, Bender, and WAIS Performance Tests by 36 Learning-Disabled Adolescents

Variable	1	2	3	4	5	6	7	8
1 Drawing from Imagination	1.00							
2 Drawing from Observation	.45**	1.00						
3 Predictive Drawing	.62***	.22	1.00					
4 Silver Test Total	.88***	.71***	.75***	1.00				
5 Draw-a-Man	.75***	.31*	.62***	.72***	1.00			
6 Bender	−.59***	−.17	−.42**	−.50***	−.37**	1.00		
7 WAIS (Verbal)	−.04	.18	−.01	.02	−.12	−.01	1.00	
8 WAIS (Performance)	.59***	.37**	.50***	.60***	.60***	−.45**	.01	1.00

$^*p = .05$
$^{**}p = .01$
$^{***}p = .001$

The lack of correlations with the WAIS Verbal IQ supports the theory that the SDT does not measure verbal ability. Similarly, the lack of correlation with the Bender supports the theory that the SDT measures conceptual skills and creativity. The Bender asks examinees to copy nine abstract designs and, as stated in its title, is a measure of visual–motor skills, whereas the SDT gives copying its lowest score and originality its highest. In presenting the WAIS Verbal Scale, the examiner reads questions aloud and examinees respond orally, thus requiring auditory–verbal input and verbal output. In presenting the SDT, the examiner can bypass language with pantomime, and examinees receive and respond to directions nonverbally through images. Although the Drawing from Imagination task also asks for verbal responses, it can be scored without them.

Conversely, positive correlations between the SDT, the Draw-a-Man, and the WAIS Performance scale suggest that these measures tap similar abilities and assess similar constructs. As no correlations were found between the SDT and the Bender and the WAIS Verbal, they seem to assess different constructs.

This chapter has reviewed 8 studies that seem to support the scorer and retest reliability of the SDT and 10 studies that seem to support its validity, based on significant correlations with traditional, language-oriented tests of intelligence or achievement. The following chapter will review the normative data that has been developed.

Chapter 4

Normative Data

◇　　◇　　◇

This chapter presents new normative data and summarizes the norms in previous editions of the SDT manual. The norms are based on age and gender differences in responses to the SDT by presumably normal children, adolescents, young adults, and senior adults.

Norms make it possible to compare the scores of particular individuals with typical scores. For rough estimates, individual scores can be compared with the mean scores of similar age or gender groups; scores above the mean, indicate above-average performance; and scores below the mean, below-average performance. Percentile ranks provide additional information.

Previous Norms and Case Studies

The norms in the 1996 edition of the SDT were based on the scores of approximately 624 subjects, students ages 6 to 18, and 77 adults. The students attended heterogeneous classes in 13 schools. Five schools were located in New York state: three suburban schools in high, middle, and low socioeconomic suburban neighborhoods (grades 1 to 6); and two urban schools in low to middle socioeconomic neighborhoods (grades 2 to 12). Other schools were located in New Jersey, Pennsylvania, California, and Canada. Although more than 700 students with various disabilities also responded to the tasks, their scores are not included in the normative data.

Three Art Assessments

Approximately 250 adults have responded to the drawing tasks during workshops or lectures in various states. They included art therapists, teachers, social workers, and graduate or undergraduate students. The first 77 were a random sample of adults' responses collected for normative data in table 4.1.

The SDT scores and percentile ranks showed gradual improvement with age. Where reversals occurred amid the prevailing upward trend, they were small and well within chance limits for these sample sizes. Table 4.1 shows mean scores based on ages and grade levels. Tables 4.2 and 4.3 provide percentile ranks for subtest and total scores.

To illustrate how the norms have provided clues to emotional and cognitive difficulties, the responses of a child and an adult are discussed in the following pages.

Table 4.1

Normative Data
Normative Data Based on Mean Scores of Samples of 624 Children and Adults

Grade	Age	n	Mean Score Predictive Drawing	Mean Score Drawing from Observation	Mean Score Drawing from Imagination	Mean Score Total Score
1	6–7	22	4.82	6.27	7.55	18.91
2	7–8	82	7.92	8.05	8.41	24.38
3	8–9	127	8.51	9.02	8.78	26.81
4	9–10	106	8.54	8.36	10.01	26.91
5	10–11	66	9.32	9.42	9.24	27.98
6	11–12	27	8.87	10.27	10.08	29.22
7	12–13	26	9.88	10.04	11.47	31.39
8	13–14	39	11.74	12.32	11.01	35.07
10	15	16	12.06	11.31	10.56	33.93
12	17–18	36	10.97	10.22	10.42	31.61
Adults		77	12.87	14.18	12.29	39.58

Rita

Rita, age 10, was a student in the fourth grade of an urban elementary school. Her classroom teacher described her as normal with average intelligence. Her opinion was supported by Rita's score on the Metropolitan Reading Instructional Test, indicating performance at the fourth grade, 4th month level.

In responding to the Drawing from Imagination task, Rita chose only one stimulus drawing: the girl. In Rita's drawing, however, the girl's eyes are averted and her hands behind her back (figure 4.1). She is a solitary figure near the top of the page; most of the drawing space is filled with Rita's story, entitled, "The Girl who Never Stops Crying." This is what she wrote:

> Once upon a time there was a little girl who lived with her mother and father. And every day the little girl came home from school she was always crying. And every day her ask [sic] why are you crying? She never tells. She will always give her mother a candy and then she would go somewhere. Then day finally that was she came home from school not crying and that was the day she told her mother why she was always crying.

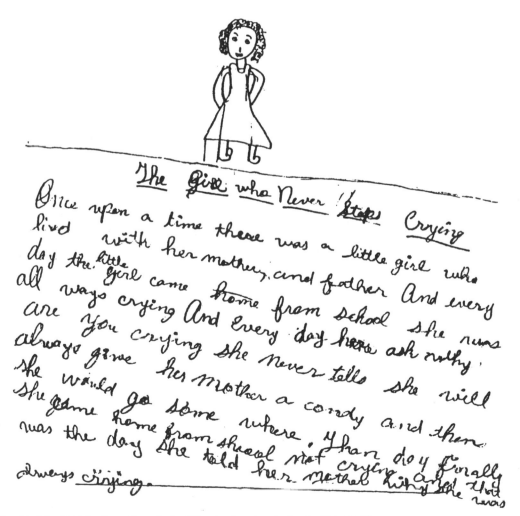

Fig. 4.1. "The Girl Who Never Stops Crying," Drawing from Imagination by Rita, age 10

On the Emotional Projection Scale, Rita's response scores 1 point, since it represents a strongly negative theme. It scores 1 point in ability to select, since Rita did not relate the subject she chose to any other subject or add subjects of her own. In ability to combine, it scores 0 because it does not include spatial relationships. In ability to represent, however, it receives the highest score, 5 points, being highly expressive and suggestive in both form and story-telling content. By drawing the girl with averted eyes and hands behind her back, Rita transformed the stimulus drawing she chose, using graphic symbols to express the secrecy articulated in her story. Her cognitive score in Drawing from Imagination, of 6 points, is below average, the norm of 10.01 points, the mean score of the SDT sample of 106 fourth-graders, as shown in table 4.1. Her Drawing from Imagination scored in the 6th percentile of children in the fourth grade, as shown in table 4.4.

In Predictive Drawing, Rita scored 0 in ability to represent a sequence because she did not draw any lines in the soda glasses. In predicting how water would appear in the tilted bottle, she finally decided to draw an oblique line, after two corrections, scoring 3 points. In predicting how a house would appear on the slope, she again scored 3 points, because she drew a vertical house inside the mountain without support. Her total score of 6 points is below the mean score of 8.54 for children in the fourth grade, as shown in table 4.1; and in the 14th percentile, as shown in table 4.2.

In Drawing from Observation, Rita's drawing scores 0 in ability to represent horizontality, because none of the objects is in the correct left–right order. In verticality, it scores 3 points because three objects are approximately correct in height. In depth, it scores 1 point, because the three cylinders stand in a row and only the stone is above the base line. Her total score of 4 points is again below the mean of 8.36 points for children in the fourth grade, placing her in the 11th percentile, as shown in tables 4.1 and 4.3. Rita's total SDT score, 16 points, is also below average, compared with the mean score of 30.47 points for children in the fourth grade, placing her in the 3rd percentile.

Since Rita usually displays normal intelligence, it may be that she performed poorly on the SDT because she was emotionally distressed when responding to the drawing tasks, as suggested by her strongly negative fantasy. Her failure to respond to some tasks may have been caused by preoccupations that interfered with cognitive functioning, or she may have been aware of cognitive deficiencies that caused emotional distress. At any event, her unusually poor cognitive performances may be associated with the emotional distress expressed in her story, suggesting that follow-up would be appropriate.

Mr. O.

Although Mr. O was not paralyzed, his stroke had left him with expressive and receptive-language impairments. He could not read aloud, confused verb tenses, and had difficulty writing his thoughts. Although his words flowed smoothly, his meanings were unclear. His drawing responses to the SDT seemed to parallel his verbal disabilities. His Drawing from Imagination, entitled "A Lifetime of Growth" (figure 4.2), scored 5 points, far below the adult mean of 12.64 (table 4.1) and even below the 1st percentile (table 4.5). In Predictive Drawing and Drawing from Observation, however, his scores of 14 and 15 points, respectively, were slightly above average for adults. These drawings are shown in figure 4.3.

Figure 4.2. "A Lifetime of Growth," prettest Drawing from Imagination by Mr. O, stroke patient

Figure 4.3. Predictive Drawing and Drawing from Observation by Mr. O

Figure 4.4. "Hedges May Hide Surprises," posttest Drawing from Imagination by Mr. O

After several weeks of speech therapy and art therapy, his posttest Drawing from Imagination, entitled "Hedges May Hide Surprises" (figure 4.4), like his expressive language, improved substantially, reaching slightly below the adult mean (table 4.6). His other responses to the drawing tasks are shown in chapter 12.

Gifted Children

SDT responses by small samples of gifted children were also examined. Eileen McCormick tested a group of eight children in New Jersey previously identified as gifted intellectually. The group produced unusually high scores for its fourth-grade level, and had the highest scores in the Drawing from Imagination subtest of any group tested thus far. Carole McCarthy tested eight children in Connecticut, previously identified as gifted, based on their scores on the Iowa Test of Basic Skills. They included all such children in one fourth-grade class and one combined fifth- and sixth-grade class. Although each scored above the age norm in each subtest, and although their mean scores exceeded the mean scores of their classmates, the number of children previously identified as gifted was too small to qualify for statistical analysis. This preliminary exploration suggests that a study of larger numbers of gifted children would be worthwhile.

Expanded Norms

After the norms in tables 4.1 to 4.5 were calculated, volunteers in various parts of the country administered the SDT to additional adolescents, young adults, and senior adults. The new norms, including scores in emotional projection and self-image, are presented in tables 4.6, 4.7, and 4.8.

The respondents resided in California, Connecticut, Florida, Missouri, Nebraska, New Jersey, New Hampshire, New York, New Mexico, Pennsylvania, Texas, and Canada. The students attended public elementary and secondary schools and one private elementary and high school, including urban schools in Nebraska and New York, suburban schools in New York and Pennsylvania, and rural schools in Nebraska and Ontario, Canada. The schools were in low, middle, and high socioeconomic neighborhoods.

As in the previous norms, the students came from various ethnic backgrounds and were of African American, Hispanic, and Caucasian descent. This information was not recorded, but their educational levels, ages, genders, and disabilities, if any, accompanied their SDT scores.

The younger adults, ages 20 to 50 (average age was 28.7 years) responded to the SDT while participating in workshops or college audiences. They included students, teachers, and mental health professionals in New York, Wisconsin, and Nebraska.

The senior adults had volunteered to respond to the tasks while participating in recreational or other programs provided in Florida and New York. All lived independently in their own homes or retirement communities. Although they had been asked to indicate their ages in increments beginning with 65, 20 of the 57 seniors specified ages, which averaged 80.8 years.

Scores of Adolescents, Young Adults, and Senior Adults

Table 4.6 presents the mean scores and standard deviations (in parentheses) of responses by high school students and adults in Predictive Drawing, Drawing from Observation, and the cognitive content of Drawing from Imagination. The younger adults had higher mean scores than the high school students in each subtest. They also had higher scores than the senior adults in Predictive Drawing, but lower scores in Drawing from Imagination.

Table 4.7 presents mean scores and standard deviations in emotional content and self-image in responses to the Drawing from Imagination task by male and female high school students, younger adults, and senior adults. In most age groups, males tended to have lower scores in emotional content than self-image, indicating that males expressed more negative themes and fantasies than did females. On the other hand, men had higher self-image scores than women, portraying more positive self-images, whereas the sample of high school girls had slightly higher self-image scores than did the sample of high school boys.

Girls in grades 1 to 8 had higher mean scores than boys in the emotional content of responses to the SDT Drawing from Imagination subtest; boys had higher mean scores in self-image, as shown in table 4.8.

Table 4.6

Mean Scores (and Standard Deviations) for SDT Cognitive Content Scales in Responses by High School Students, Young Adults, and Senior Adults

Group	Number	Predictive Drawing	Drawing from Observation	Drawing from Imagination
High School	76	10.93 (2.82)	10.22 (3.68)	10.89 (2.28)
Young Adults	52, 51, 59	12.50 (2.19)	13.88 (1.61)	12.64 (2.11)
Senior Adults	35, 44	11.31 (2.90)	n/a	14.34 (0.83)

Table 4.7

Mean Scores (and Standard Deviations) for SDT Emotional Content and Self-Image Scales in Responses by High School Students, Young Adults, and Senior Adults

Group	Emotional Content	Self-Image
High School Youths Boys (45, 27) Girls (49, 38)	2.56 (1.31) 3.24 (1.22)	3.41 (1.01) 3.42 (0.86)
Younger (av. 28.7 yrs.) Men (18) Women (33)	2.94 (1.41) 3.21 (1.17)	3.61 (1.09) 3.24 (1.09)
Senior (av. 80.8 yrs) Men (17) Women (27)	2.59 (1.28) 3.26 (1.20)	3.71 (0.92) 3.15 (0.91)
Total Scores 219 Males 243 Females	2.70 2.43	3.53 3.25

Table 4.8

Mean Scores (and Standard Deviations) for SDT Emotional Content and Self-Image Scales in Responses by Children in Elementary School, Grades 1 to 8, 112 boys, 96 girls

Grade	Ages	Emotional Content	Self-Image
1st grade	6-7		
Boys (8)		1.63 (0.92)	3.00(0)
Girls (7)		3.71 (1.11)	3.71 (0.95)
2nd grade	7-8		
Boys (9)		3.22 (0.83)	3.22 (0.44)
Girls (8)		3.13 (0.83)	3.00 (0)
3rd grade	8-9		
Boys (9)		2.78 (1.56)	3.67 (1.00)
Girls (7)		2.71 (1.11)	3.29 (0.76)
4th grade	9-10		
Boys (36)		3.03 (0.91)	3.50 (0.77)
Girls (32)		2.94 (1.27)	3.22 (0.79)
5th grade	10-11		
Boys (17)		2.88 (1.17)	3.29 (1.05)
Girls (9)		3.33 (1.12)	3.22 (0.67)
6th grade	11-12		
Boys (8)		2.88 (1.13)	3.50 (0.93)
Girls (12)		3.33 (1.15)	3.50 (1.00)
7-8th grades	12-14		
Boys		2.48 (1.26)	3.52 (0.92)
Girls		3.00 (1.10)	3.29 (0.78)
Mean Score, Boys		2.70	3.39
Mean Score, Girls		3.16	3.32

Frequency of Emotional Content and Self-Image Scores

In addition to mean scores, we examined responses to the SDT for the frequency of each of the five scores. Subjects included children, adolescents, and adults: 163 males and 189 females.

In emotional content, more than three times as many males scored 1 point, indicating that 17% of the males (compared with 5% of the females) portrayed life-threatening relationships or sad or helpless solitary subjects. On the other hand, more females scored 4 and 5 points, indicating that 27% of the females (compared with 15% of the males) portrayed friendly relationships or fortunate or passive subjects; and 13% of the females (vs. 9% of the males) portrayed caring relationships or effective or powerful subjects, as shown in tables 4.9 and 4.10.

The reverse appeared in self-image. Although the neutral, 3-point score predominated, more males than females scored 4 and 5 points: 18% of the males, compared with 12% of the females, seemed to identify with subjects portrayed as powerful, loved, assaultive, destructive, or achieving goals; 18% of the males, compared with 13% of the females, seemed to identify with subjects portrayed as fortunate but passive, as shown in tables 4.11 and 4.12.

Table 4.9						
Frequencies of Female Scores in the Emotional Content of Responses to the SDT Drawing from Imagination Subtest						
n	Age			Score		
		1	2	3	4	5
44 Adults	20–50	0	12	14	18	0
38 Adols.	16–19	2	9	4	14	9
32 Adols.	13–15	2	10	11	5	4
21 Girls	10–12	0	5	9	2	5
32 Girls	9–10	5	7	9	7	4
7 Girls	8–9	0	4	2	0	1
8 Girls	7–8	0	2	3	3	0
7 Girls	6–7	0	1	2	2	2
189		9 (5%)	50 (26%)	54 (29%)	51 (27%)	25 (13%)

Table 4.10

Frequencies of Male Scores in the Emotional Content of Responses to the SDT Drawing from Imagination Subtest

n	Age	Score				
		1	2	3	4	5
18 Adults	20–50	2	6	5	1	4
26 Adols.	16–19	5	7	10	0	4
34 Adols.	13–15	7	15	7	2	3
25 Boys	10–12	5	2	12	4	2
36 Boys	9–10	1	10	13	11	1
9 Boys	8–9	3	1	1	3	1
7 Boys	7–8	0	2	1	4	0
8 Boys	6–7	5	1	2	0	0
163		28 (17%)	44 (27%)	51 (31%)	25 (15%)	15 (9%)

				Table 4.11		

Frequencies of Female Scores in the Self-Images of Responses to the SDT Drawing from Imagination Subtest

n	Age	Score				
		1	2	3	4	5
44 Adults	20–50	0	1	43	0	0
38 Adols.	16–19	0	5	14	10	9
32 Adols.	13–15	0	2	18	9	3
21 Girls	10–12	0	0	16	1	4
32 Girls	9–10	1	1	22	4	4
7 Girls	8-9	0	0	6	0	1
8 Girls	7–8	0	0	8	0	0
7 Girls	6–7	0	0	4	1	2
189		1 (.5%)	9 (5%)	131 (69%)	25 (13%)	23 (12%)

Table 4.12

Frequencies of Male Scores in the Self-Images of Responses to the SDT Drawing from Imagination Subtest

n	Age	Score				
		1	2	3	4	5
18 Adults	20–50	0	4	6	1	7
26 Adols.	16–19	0	1	21	1	3
34 Adols.	13–15	1	0	13	13	7
25 Boys	10–12	1	1	16	3	4
36 Boys	9–10	0	1	21	9	5
9 Boys	8–9	0	0	6	0	3
7 Boys	7–8	0	0	5	2	0
8 Boys	6–7	0	0	8	0	0
163		2 (1.2%)	7 (4.2%)	96 (59%)	29 (18%)	29 (18%)

Table 4.2

Percentile Rank and *t*-Score Conversions for Predictive Drawing

Grade	1		2		3		4		5	
Age	6–7		7–8		8–9		9–10		10–11	
Score	t	%	t	%	t	%	t	%	t	%
1	36.26	4	24.67	1	22.10	1−				
2	36.91	10	28.67	2	25.86	1	24.00	1−		
3	41.55	15	32.67	4	29.63	2	27.86	1		
4	46.20	35	36.67	9	33.40	5	31.72	3	24.90	1
5	50.84	53	40.67	18	37.16	10	35.58	7	29.46	2
6	55.49	71	44.67	30	40.93	18	39.44	14	34.02	5
7	60.14	84	48.67	45	44.70	30	43.30	25	38.57	13
8	64.78	93	52.68	61	48.46	44	47.16	39	43.13	25
9	69.43	97	56.68	75	52.23	59	51.02	54	47.69	41
10	74.08	99+	60.69	86	56.00	73	54.88	69	52.24	59
11			64.69	93	59.76	84	58.74	81	56.80	75
12			68.69	97	63.53	91	62.60	90	61.36	87
13			72.69	99+	67.30	96	66.46	95	65.91	94
14					71.06	98	70.32	98	70.47	98
15					74.83	99+	74.18	99+	75.03	99+

Grade	6		7		8		10		adult	
Age	11–12		12–13		13–14		15–16			
1										
2										
3	21.19	1−					22.18	1−		
4	26.09	1	20.38	1−			25.47	1		
5	30.98	3	25.41	1			28.77	2		
6	35.87	8	30.44	2	23.76	1−	32.07	4	23.82	1−
7	40.76	18	35.48	7	28.52	2	35.37	7	27.82	1
8	45.65	33	40.51	17	33.27	5	38.66	13	31.82	3
9	50.54	52	45.55	33	38.02	12	41.96	21	35.81	8
10	55.43	71	50.58	52	42.76	24	45.26	32	39.81	15
11	60.33	85	55.61	71	47.53	40	48.56	44	43.81	27
12	65.22	94	60.65	86	52.28	59	51.85	58	47.80	41
13	70.10	98	70.72	98	57.03	76	55.15	70	51.80	57
14	75.00	99+	75.75	99+	61.79	88	58.45	80	55.80	72
15					66.54	95	61.75	88	59.80	84

Table 4.3

Percentile Rank and t-Score Conversions for Drawing from Observation

Grade	1		2		3		4		5	
Age	6–7		7–8		8–9		9–10		10–11	
Score	t	%	t	%	t	%	t	%	t	%
1	28.84	2	29.83	2	22.32	1–	28.51	2		
2	32.85	4	32.88	4	25.78	1	31.60	3		
3	36.86	10	35.94	8	29.24	2	34.69	6	23.76	1–
4	40.87	18	38.99	14	32.70	4	37.78	11	27.88	1
5	44.89	30	42.05	21	36.16	8	40.87	18	32.00	4
6	48.91	46	45.11	31	39.62	15	43.96	27	36.12	8
7	52.92	61	51.22	55	43.08	25	47.05	38	40.24	16
8	56.93	75	54.27	67	46.54	36	50.15	51	44.36	29
9	60.95	86	57.33	77	50.00	50	53.24	63	48.48	44
10	64.96	93	60.38	85	53.46	64	56.33	74	52.60	60
11	68.97	97	63.44	91	56.92	75	59.42	83	56.72	75
12	72.99	99+	66.49	95	60.38	85	62.51	89	60.84	86
13			69.55	98	63.84	92	65.60	94	64.96	93
14			72.60	99+	67.30	96	68.69	97	69.08	97
15					70.76	98	71.78	99+	73.20	99+
Grade	6		7		8		10		adult	
Score	t	%	t	%	t	%	t	%	t	%
1	24.53	1–					34.57	6		
2	27.52	1					36.51	9		
3	30.51	3	23.68	1–			38.46	13		
4	33.50	5	27.47	1			40.40	17		
5	36.49	9	31.25	3			42.35	22		
6	39.48	15	35.03	7			44.29	28		
7	42.47	23	38.81	13	23.32	1–	46.23	35		
8	45.46	33	42.59	23	28.41	2	48.18	43		
9	48.45	44	46.37	36	33.50	5	50.12	50		
10	51.44	56	50.15	51	38.59	13	52.07	58		
11	54.43	67	53.93	65	43.69	26	54.01	66	17.79	1–
12	57.42	77	57.71	78	48.78	45	55.95	73	27.40	1
13	60.41	85	61.49	87	53.87	65	57.95	79	37.02	10
14	63.40	91	65.27	94	58.96	82	59.84	84	46.63	37
15	66.39	95	69.05	97	64.05	92	61.79	88	56.25	74

Table 4.4

Percentile Rank and t-Score Conversions for Drawing from Imagination

| Grade | 1 | | 2 | | 3 | | 4 | | 5 | |
| Age | 6–7 | | 7–8 | | 8–9 | | 9–10 | | 10–11 | |
Score	t	%	t	%	t	%	t	%	t	%
1										
2	24.79	1	23.36	1–						
3	29.30	2	27.38	1	24.20	1	22.35	1–	22.23	1–
4	33.81	5	31.40	3	28.79	2	26.39	1	26.66	1
5	38.32	12	35.41	7	33.38	5	30.43	2	31.08	3
6	42.83	24	39.43	14	37.97	12	34.48	6	35.50	7
7	47.34	39	43.45	25	42.56	23	38.52	13	39.93	16
8	51.84	57	47.46	40	47.15	39	42.56	23	44.35	28
9	56.35	74	51.48	56	51.74	57	46.61	37	48.77	45
10	60.86	86	55.50	71	56.33	74	50.65	53	53.20	63
11	65.37	94	59.52	83	60.92	86	54.69	68	57.62	78
12	69.88	98	63.53	91	65.51	94	58.74	81	62.05	89
13	74.38	99+	67.55	96	70.10	98	62.78	90	66.47	95
14			71.57	98	74.69	99+	66.82	95	70.89	98
15			75.59	99+			70.86	98	75.32	99+
Grade:	6		7		8		10		adult	
Age										
1										
2										
3										
4			21.75	1–			24.36	1–		
5	23.84	1–	25.54	1	21.80	1–	27.66	1		
6	29.00	2	29.33	2	26.29	1	30.97	3		
7	34.15	6	33.11	5	30.78	3	34.28	6	23.03	1–
8	39.31	14	36.90	10	35.27	7	37.59	11	27.93	1
9	44.46	29	40.68	18	39.76	15	40.90	18	32.84	4
10	49.62	48	44.47	29	44.25	28	44.21	28	37.74	11
11	54.77	68	48.25	43	48.74	44	47.52	40	42.64	23
12	59.93	84	52.04	58	53.23	63	50.83	53	47.55	40
13	65.08	93	55.82	72	57.72	78	54.14	66	52.45	60
14	70.23	98	59.61	83	62.21	89	57.45	77	57.36	77
15	75.39	99+	63.39	91	66.70	95	60.75	86	62.26	89

Table 4.5

Percentile Rank and *t*-Score Conversions for SDT Total Scores

Grade	1		2		3		4		5	
Age	6–7		7–8		8–9		9–10		10–11	
Score	t	%	t	%	t	%	t	%	t	%
8	22.69	1–	22.80	1–						
9	25.24	1	24.55	1						
10	27.80	1	26.30	1						
11	30.36	3	28.05	1						
12	32.92	4	29.80	2			23.05	1–		
13	35.47	7	31.54	3	22.81	1–	24.90	1		
14	38.03	12	33.29	5	24.90	1	26.76	1		
15	40.59	17	35.04	7	26.99	1	28.62	2	22.82	1–
16	43.15	25	36.79	9	29.07	2	30.47	3	24.88	1
17	45.70	33	38.54	13	31.16	3	32.33	4	26.95	1
18	48.26	43	40.29	17	33.25	5	34.18	6	29.02	2
19	50.82	53	42.04	21	35.33	7	36.04	9	31.08	3
20	55.38	71	43.79	27	37.42	10	37.90	12	33.15	5
21	55.93	72	45.53	33	39.51	15	39.75	15	35.22	7
22	58.49	80	47.28	39	41.59	20	41.61	20	37.28	10
23	61.05	87	49.03	46	43.68	26	43.47	26	39.35	14
24	63.61	91	50.78	53	45.77	34	45.32	32	41.42	19
25	66.16	95	52.53	60	47.85	41	47.18	39	43.48	26
26	68.72	97	54.28	67	49.94	50	49.04	46	45.55	33
27	71.28	98	56.03	73	52.03	58	50.89	54	47.62	41
28	73.84	99	57.78	78	54.11	66	52.75	61	49.68	49
29	76.39	99+	59.52	83	56.20	73	54.61	68	51.75	57
30			61.57	87	58.29	80	56.46	74	53.82	65
31			63.02	90	60.37	85	58.32	80	55.88	72
32			64.77	93	62.46	89	60.18	85	57.95	79
33			66.52	95	64.54	93	62.03	88	60.02	84
34			68.27	97	66.63	95	63.89	91	62.08	89
35			70.02	98	68.72	97	65.75	94	64.15	92
36			71.77	99	70.80	98	67.60	96	66.22	95
37			73.51	99	72.89	99	69.46	97	68.28	97
38			75.26	99	74.98	99	71.31	98	70.35	98
39			77.01	99+	77.06	99+	73.17	99	72.42	99
40							75.03	99	74.48	99
41							76.88	99+	76.55	99+
42										
43										
44										
45										

Note: The *t*-scores are based on the unbiased estimate standard deviation. Percentile ranks are calculated from the table of cumulative normal probabilities, *Biometrika Tables for Statistics*, vol. 1, edited by E. S. Pearson and H. O. Hartley, and assume the scores are normally distributed. These procedures were used to avoid underestimating variability, because, for several grades, the population is small. —Beatrice J. Krauss, PhD.

				Table 4.5 continued						

Grade	6		7		8		10		adult	
Score	t	%	t	%	t	%	t	%	t	%
Age	11–12		12–13		13–14		15–16			
8										
9										
10										
11										
12										
13										
14										
15							26.49	1		
16							27.86	1		
17							29.23	2		
18	24.94	1					30.61	3		
19	27.33	1	26.96	1			31.98	4		
20	29.72	2	28.83	2			31.35	5		
21	32.11	4	30.71	3			34.73	6		
22	34.50	6	32.58	4			36.10	8		
23	36.89	10	34.45	6	24.96	1	37.47	11		
24	39.28	14	36.32	9	27.04	1	38.84	13		
25	41.68	20	38.19	12	29.12	2	40.22	16		
26	44.07	28	40.07	16	31.20	3	41.59	20		
27	46.46	36	41.94	21	33.28	5	42.96	24		
28	48.85	45	43.81	27	35.36	7	44.34	28		
29	51.24	55	45.68	33	37.44	10	45.71	33		
30	53.63	64	47.55	40	39.52	15	47.08	39		
31	56.02	73	49.42	48	41.60	20	48.46	44	27.50	1
32	58.41	80	51.30	55	43.68	26	49.83	50	30.18	2
33	60.80	86	53.17	63	45.76	34	51.20	55	32.86	4
34	63.20	91	55.04	69	47.84	41	52.57	60	35.54	7
35	65.59	94	56.91	75	49.92	50	53.95	66	38.21	12
36	67.98	96	58.78	81	52.00	58	55.32	70	40.89	18
37	70.37	98	60.65	86	54.08	66	56.69	75	43.57	26
38	72.76	99	62.53	89	56.16	73	58.07	79	46.25	35
39	75.15	99+	64.40	93	58.24	79	59.44	83	48.93	46
40			66.27	95	60.31	85	60.81	86	51.61	56
41			68.14	96	62.39	89	62.19	89	54.29	67
42			70.01	98	64.47	93	63.56	91	56.96	76
43			71.89	99	66.55	95	64.93	93	59.64	83
44			73.76	99	68.63	97	66.30	95	62.32	84
45			75.63	99+	70.71	98+	67.68	96+	65.00	93+

This chapter has presented normative data so that responses to the SDT by a particular individual can be compared with the average scores of others who are the same age or gender, in the United States. Chapter 15 provides information about the responses of children and adults in other countries.

Chapter 5

Outcome Studies:
Using the SDT as a Pre–Posttest to Assess Programs

◇   ◇   ◇

This chapter reviews five outcome studies, which used the SDT before and after developmental and therapeutic programs to assess changes, if any, and determine whether the programs were effective.

State Urban Education Project for Children with Auditory–Language Disorders

The first project, supported by a grant from the New York State Department of Education, had three objectives: to help an experimental group of children with impairments acquire concepts basic in reading and mathematics, to devise procedures for developing the concepts through art experiences, and to devise tasks for assessing the procedures (Silver, 1973, 1975b).

The project was conducted in a school for children with language and hearing impairments. It included experimental and control groups selected at random and compared these children with children who had no known impairments. Some educators had claimed that children who are deaf lack aptitude for art. The project also was concerned with reconciling different views. Some art therapists believed that structuring art experience inhibits spontaneity, and some art educators believed that using art for therapeutic purposes interferes with aesthetic development. The project hoped to demonstrate that therapeutic and aesthetic goals need not conflict, that art experiences can be structured without sacrificing spontaneity, and that we can pursue therapeutic and cognitive goals without neglecting aesthetic goals.

The children with language impairments had receptive and expressive language disorders. Receptive disorders cause difficulty in comprehending language. Expressive disorders cause difficulty in producing language. Some children had both, and most had peripheral hearing loss as well.

The experimental group of 34 children included a randomly selected 50% sample of 12 classes in the school. They attended weekly 40-minute art classes for 11 weeks in the fall and 9 weeks in the spring. The remaining 34 children, who did not participate in an art program, served as the control group. Their ages ranged from 8 to 15 years.

Drawing tasks were developed and administered as a pre–posttest for the fall program in September and January; and for the spring program in January and June. The tasks also were administered (once) to 68 unimpaired children in a suburban public school in order to compare groups that had and did not have impairments.

The developmental procedures emphasized exploratory learning to encourage reflection and elicit spontaneous responses. They were designed to establish an atmosphere in which independence and initiative would be self-rewarding. The procedures consisted of drawing and painting tasks meant to be open-ended; when they couldn't be open-ended, corrections were brief and promptly followed by free-choice art activities. The drawing tasks focused on sequencing and grouping, relating subjects to one another. The grouping tasks were designed to help students detect similarities and combine subjects based on form or content, usually both. For example, the children were shown two arrays of stimulus drawings—people and animals on one table, passive animals and things on a table nearby—then asked to select subjects from both tables to use in some way in their own story-telling drawings. I structured the first two classes this way to encourage the children to select, combine, and represent. Thereafter, most selected their subject matter spontaneously, without stimulus drawings.

The sequencing tasks were meant to develop concepts of space through observation and manipulation. In one task, objects on a sheet of paper served as points of reference, with the paper's edges as frames of reference. For example, I placed a cylinder and two building blocks on a sheet of paper and traced their outlines with a pencil, then asked students to select the same objects, arrange them the same way, and trace their outlines. When the drawings were superimposed and held up to a light, the children examined the outlines, noting overlaps and distances.

To develop sequencing abilities, I presented a series of cards in one color but in progressively paler tints. Asked if the colors were the same or different, the children considered similarities and differences. Then they were asked to scramble the cards and finally to place them in order from light to dark tints.

Each student received a paper palette, palette knife, and poster paints in muffin trays. After a demonstration in which paint was mixed into a series of tints, students were asked to place a dab of white in one corner and additional colors in two other corners, then to find out how many colors they could create between them. Finally, they added black in the fourth corner and completed the circle with shades as well as tints. In the remaining time, they were free to paint as they chose. Some children painted abstract designs, whereas others turned to figurative painting.

A third task, locating a doll on a model landscape, was adapted from experiments by Piaget and Inhelder (1967, p. 421). Two identical landscapes were constructed on cafeteria trays—mountains, rivers, paths, trees, houses, and dolls made from plaster, cardboard, matchsticks, and clay. To play the game, children had to place their dolls in the same position as other people's dolls in the other landscape. After a few trials, one landscape was turned 180 degrees, making it necessary to relate the dolls to positions in the landscape, rather than to one's own position. The model landscapes had 17 marked positions.

To develop concepts of space, the children drew from observation. For example, several objects were placed on a table in front of the room—cylinders made from rolls of construction paper and bugs made from pebbles by adding legs and eyes. The arrangement was presented on a drawing board, with another board, supported by the wall, serving as backdrop. After demonstrating with a quick sketch of the arrangement, I asked the children to sketch it, then moved the arrangement to the center of the room (without the backdrop), surrounded by the children's desks. The children were asked to sketch the arrangement from at least three points of view. From one desk, the bug appeared to the left of a blue cylinder and from the opposite desk, to the right.

The project also included in-service workshops for classroom teachers. We met weekly for 1 hour to discuss objectives and methods, and when the first term ended, the teachers scored the posttests and second term pre- and posttests, which included 14 items adapted from tasks in the art program.

In addition, classroom teachers of children in the experimental group responded to a questionnaire indicating the abilities, disabilities, and behaviors of individual children. They responded in October before the art program began, again after the program ended in January, and once again the following June. Although questionnaire evaluations are subjective, they can serve to complement statistical analyses, as suggested in the following pages.

Results

Questionnaire Evaluation by the Classroom Teacher of Burt, Age 13

Burt had receptive and expressive language impairments, as well as severe hearing loss, with a level of 75dB in his better ear. The Stanford Binet test had been administered when he was 9 years old, suggesting an IQ of 43 and a mental age of 3 years, 8 months.

Burt attended 9 of the 11 weekly, 40-minute sessions of the art program. Before it began, his teacher completed the questionnaire, using a 5-point rating scale that ranged from 1 point (Almost Never) to 5 points (Very Often), as shown in table 5.1. After the art program, her questionnaire response indicated that Burt had improved in each of the cognitive categories she had scored 1 point in October. Some behaviors also improved (working independently without asking for help or directions and controlling emotions), others did not change (joining in group activities and cooperating with other children), and some declined (tolerating frustration, interest in learning, playfulness, and self-esteem). These findings may be associated with Burt's art experience but do not indicate cause and effect—that is, whether art experiences may have caused the changes.

Table 5.1

A Classroom Teacher's Evaluation of Burt[a]

	October	January	June
Is (s)he able to:			
1. Select named objects	1	4	4
2. Comprehend words and phrases	4	4	4
3. Follow instructions	4	4	4
4. Find the right word	4	1	2
5. Use nouns, synonyms, antonyms	2	1	3
6. Combine words into sentences	1	1	3
7. Use connective words, pronouns, adjectives, adverbs	3	1	2
8. Sequence events, tell stories	4	3	3
9. Explain his/her thoughts or ideas	4	2	3
10. Discuss hypothetical questions	2	2	1
In nonverbal activities, does (s)he:			
11. Detect similarities between objects	3	3	3
12. Group objects on the basis of invisible attributes, such as class or function	1	2	2
13. Put objects in sequence, such as size or weight	3	3	3
14. Recognize that appearances may be deceiving (knows that spreading out a row of pebbles does not increase the number, for example)	1	3	2
15. Associate new information with what (s)he knows, incorporate and make use of it	1	4	3
16. Concentrate for more than five minutes	3	3	4
17. Retain information and carry a task through to completion	3	1	2
18. Solve problems	1	1	2
19. Engage in imaginary play	5	4	2
20. Originate ideas or forms	1	2	2
Does (s)he tend to:			
21. Work independently without asking for help or direction	1	1	3
22. Control emotions (does not cry easily or hit, shove, fight)	2	1	4
23. Tolerate frustration	4	2	3
24. Join readily in group activities	4	5	4
25. Cooperate with adults			4
26. Cooperate with other children	3	3	3
27. Be interested in learning language	4	2	3
28. Be interested in learning generally	4	2	3
29. Be playful, humorous (Oct.)[b]	5	2	2
30. Have self-confidence, self-esteem	3	2	3

---

[a] Rated on the basis of 1 to 5 points: 1 = almost never, 2 = on rare occasions, 3 = sometimes, 4 = fairly often, 5 = very often.
[b] Wording of item 29 was changed in the January and June rating scale to "have a sense of humor."

Changes in Pretest–Posttest Scores

Burt's scores on the pre–posttest also improved, as shown in table 5.2. His pretest mean score was 2.57, scoring 1 point or 0 in ability to sequence, conserve, select, combine, and represent. His posttest mean score was 4.71, scoring 4 or 5 points in each test item. Burt's drawings and behavior in the art program are described in the project report and chapter 12 (Silver, 1973, 2000).

Table 5.2

Pretest and Posttest Performances by Burt

Cognitive skills	Pretest October	Posttest January	Changes
1. Conserving liquid	0	5	+5
2. Conserving solids	0	5	+5
3. Conserving numbers	5	5	0
4. Ordering a series	5	5	0
5. Ordering a matrix	3	5	+2
6. Ordering colors	1	5	+4
7. Placing objects in given positions	3	5	+2
8. Horizontal orientation	3	5	+2
9. Vertical orientation	5	5	0
10. Grouping three objects	3	3	0
11. Grouping from an array	5	3	−2
12. Selecting	1	5	+4
13. Combining	1	5	+4
14. Representing	1	5	+4
mean	2.57	4.71	2.17

When pre- and posttest scores of experimental and control groups in the fall program were compared, significant differences in favor of the experimental group were found. John Kleinhans, PhD, performed the statistical analyses using distribution-free (nonparametric) descriptive and inferential methods. He used a median test generating a chi-square statistic to evaluate the significance of any difference between control and experimental groups.

The median score for experimental and control groups combined was 9.37. The median of the experimental group was 11.75; of the control group, 8.5. Of the 18 experimental students, 14 had scores exceeding the combined median and 4 fell below. Of the 18 control students, 3 were above and 15 below the combined median. The chi-square value derived from the resulting 2 × 2 contingency table was 11.15. With one degree of freedom, the observed chi square exceeded the criterion value of 10.83 required for the rejection of the null hypothesis of no difference between the groups at the .001 level of confidence. Thus, the observed difference between groups in favor of the experimental group was shown to be highly significant.

Ability to Form Groups and to Represent

In a comparison of pre–post mean test scores of the impaired experimental group ($n =$ 34, fall and spring programs combined), significant improvement was found after the art programs. Pretest mean − 8.0, posttest mean = 11.47, t = 3.62, significant at the .01 level with 33 df (two-tailed test). For the control group ($n = 16$) no significant difference was found (pretest mean = 8.18, posttest mean = 8.44).

In a comparison of groups with and without impairments, no significant difference was found on the pretest, but on the posttest, significant difference was found at the .05 level in favor of the experimental group with impairments. These responses are shown in tables 5.3 and 5.4.

Table 5.3

Comparing Pretest and Posttest Scores of Children with Language or Hearing Impairments, Control and Unimpaired Children

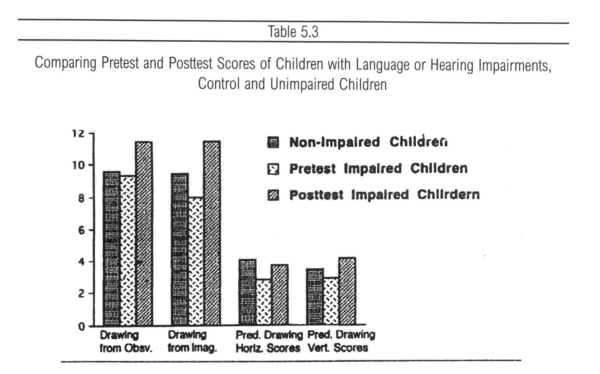

Table 5.4

Comparing Pretest and Posttest Scores of Groups with Language or Hearing Impairments with Experimental and Control Groups

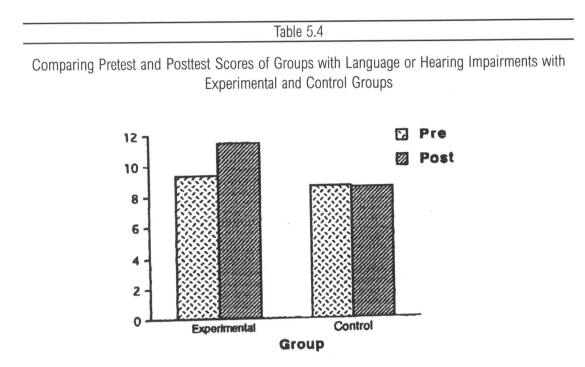

Concepts of Space

In comparison of pre–post mean scores of the impaired experimental group in the spring program (n = 16; teaching and testing procedures were developed during the fall program), significant improvement was found after the art program (pretest mean = 9.37, posttest mean = 11.43, t = 3.03 significant at the .05 level with 15 df [two-tailed test]). For the control group (n = 16), no significant difference was found (pretest mean = 8.56, posttest mean = 8.50).

In a comparison of groups with and without impairments, no significant difference was found.

Horizontal and Vertical Orientation

In a comparison of pre–post mean scores of the experimental groups with impairments (fall and spring programs combined, n = 34), significant improvement was found after the art programs (pretest mean in horizontal orientation = 2.88, posttest mean = 3.76, t = 5.50, significant at the .01 level with 67 df); in vertical orientation, pretest mean = 2.91, posttest mean = 4.11, t = 8.57 significant at the .01 level.

Comparing the 68 Unimpaired Children with Both Groups of Children with Impairments (68)

Significant differences were found on the pretest in favor of the unimpaired group. On the posttest, no significant difference was found in vertical orientation, but significant difference was found in horizontal orientation at the .05 level of probability in favor of the experimental group with impairments.

Changes in Creativity and Art Skills

To test the theory that emphasizing cognition need not interfere with aesthetic and creative growth, two judges—a university professor of art and a registered art therapist/painter—were asked to evaluate three drawings or paintings produced by each child in the fall program experimental group ($n = 18$): the child's first work, the last work, and a work produced at midterm. The 54 drawings and paintings were identified only by number and shown in random order to conceal the sequence in which they had been produced.

The judges, working independently, rated each work on a scale of 1 to 5 points for sensitivity and skill, as well as for ability to represent objects or events. The scale ranged from the low level (imitative, learned, impersonal scored 1 point), to a moderate level (going beyond description to elaborate or edit an experience, 3 points), to the high level (beyond restructuring, highly personal, imaginative, inventive, 5 points).

Both judges found improvements that were significant at the .01 level. As rated by the art therapist/painter, the mean score for artwork produced in the first class was 4.44; the mean score for work produced in the last class was 7.27; $t = 3.13$, significant at the $p < 0.01$ level. As rated by the university professor of art, the mean score of the work produced in the first class was 3.66; the last class, 6.33; $t = 3.29$, significant at the $p < 0.01$ level.

In skill and expressiveness combined, the university professor of art gave four children the lowest score on their first works and the highest score on their last works. The art therapist/painter found the same improvements in six children (Silver, 1973; 1978; 1986; 1989b, p. 225).

Thus, the findings of this study support the theory that emphasizing cognitive development need not interfere with aesthetic and creative development. The study found evidence of pretest–posttest gains in both cognitive and creative skills before and after the 11-week art therapy program, evidence that cognitive, aesthetic, and therapeutic goals can be pursued concurrently.

The study also found evidence of initial cognitive differences between children with language/hearing impairments and children with no known impairments, as well as evidence that art therapy interventions seem to bring about change, enabling the group with impairments to catch up and even excel. Before the art program, the children in the experimental group lagged behind in Drawing from Imagination and Predictive Drawing. After the art program, they equaled or surpassed the unimpaired children.

Subsequently, between 1974 and 1982, the SDT rating scales and developmental tasks were refined and amended in working with additional clinical and nonclinical populations.

Children with Visual–Motor Disorders

In a second study, we asked whether the teaching and testing procedures would be useful with children who had an opposite constellation of skills—verbal strengths and visual–motor weaknesses—and whether the procedures could be used effectively by therapists other than the one who developed them (Silver & Lavin, 1977).

Those who participated were 11 graduate students who had registered for an elective course in art therapy, working individually, under supervision, with 11 unselected children with learning disabilities. The art program consisted of 10 weekly 1-hour sessions. This study used the procedures used previously in the SUEP project to determine whether the developmental and assessments procedures were effective. This study did not have a control group.

The children who participated were not selected. Announcements were sent to newspapers and to the Westchester Association for Children with Learning Disabilities, stating that art classes were being offered to these children at the College of New Rochelle. The first 15 children who applied were enrolled. One child had been diagnosed as hyperkinetic. Another was severely disturbed and attended a day school in a psychiatric hospital. The others attended private schools or special classes in public schools. All but two had disabilities of a visual–spatial motor nature, and these two were eliminated from the statistical analysis. Also eliminated were children who withdrew or whose art therapist became ill, leaving 11 children in the study. The classes were held on Saturday mornings, all participants working in a large studio under my supervision.

The art program provided frequent opportunities to associate and reflect; draw from observation and from different points of view, model clay, mix poster paints into sequences of color; and select and combine colors, shapes, and subject matter while drawing or painting from imagination. Emphasis was on content rather than on form, on meaningful pictures rather than on abstract designs, on exploratory learning rather than on directive teaching, and on eliciting responses rather than on instructing. Other procedures did not involve drawing, such as placing cylinders in order on a matrix. The children's first and last Drawings from Imagination were assessed for ability to select, combine, and represent.

Results

Claire Lavin, PhD, analyzed the results using an analysis of variance to determine interscorer reliability. She found coefficients of .852 in ability to select and combine, and .944 in spatial orientation, as reported in chapter 7. She evaluated the effectiveness of the training program by using a t test ($n = 11$) for correlated means to determine the significance of differences in mean pre- and posttest scores and performed separate analyses for scores on the tests of ability to form groups (select and combine), spatial orientation, and ability to order a matrix. All the obtained t values were statistically significant. Improvement in ability to form groups ($t = 4.79$) and in ordering a matrix ($t = 6.54$) were significant at the .01 level. Improvement in spatial orientation was significant at the .05 level ($t = 2.42$). Thus, the children with learning disabilities who participated in the therapeutic program improved significantly in the three areas of cognitive development that were the focus of the study.

The success of this training program seems to indicate that cognitively oriented art experiences can be used to help children with learning disabilities express concepts nonverbally, through visual–motor channels, in spite of impaired functioning in this area.

Three years after the project ended, four of the graduate students had become registered art therapists who were coauthors of the study that follows.

National Institute of Education Project for Children Performing Below Grade Level

This project, supported by a grant from the National Institute of Education, attempted to verify previous results with a wider variety of settings and more diverse populations (Silver et al., 1980). It also examined relationships between the SDT and traditional, language-oriented measures of intelligence or achievement, as discussed in chapter 3.

The 84 children who participated had been nominated by school administrators, based on performing at least 1 year below grade level in reading or mathematics. They ranged from ages 7 to 11 and attended five schools: a private school for children with learning disabilities, and four public schools that provided classes for children with special needs.

As originally planned, children in the experimental group were to include only those who scored at least 3 points in Drawing from Imagination. As it happened, however, we had to include children with lower scores in order to have 20 children in each school: 10 in the experimental group participating in the art program and 10 in the control group receiving no special treatment. The selected children were randomly assigned to experimental and control groups. During the art program several children were lost for various reasons, and additional children were randomly removed to equate the number in each group for statistical analysis.

In each school, an art therapist worked with two groups of 5 children for approximately 40 minutes a week for 12 weeks. During the first 6 weeks, all art therapists used the same art procedures. During the second 6 weeks, they adapted the procedures to meet the needs of individual children and devised procedures of their own.

Before and after the art program, the children in both experimental and control groups were given the SDT, the Otis Lennon Ability Test, and the Metropolitan Reading and Arithmetic Test. Because some were too severely impaired to take the Otis Lennon and Metropolitan Tests, their school records were used instead. In addition, art therapists and teachers elsewhere had volunteered to give the SDT to other children and send us the test booklets to score, as well as send the children's scores on traditional tests of intelligence and achievement. These scores were correlated and analyzed to determine the relationship of the SDT to these measures. The findings are included among studies of reliability and validity in chapter 7.

The developmental procedures included drawing, painting, modeling clay, and playing manipulative "games" designed to develop conceptual, sequential, and spatial skills, as well as to stimulate reasoning and abstract thinking. The procedures were discussed earlier in this chapter and are presented in detail elsewhere (Silver, 1996a, 2000b, 2001).

To determine the effectiveness of the programs, Claire Lavin, PhD, examined the significance of differences between the pre- and posttest scores of experimental and control subjects, using an analysis of variance for repeated measures. The experimental group improved significantly in total scores between pre- and posttest. The gains made by the experimental group were higher than those made by the control group, but not significantly higher, as illustrated in table 5.5.

Table 5.5

Comparing Pretest and Posttest Mean Scores of Children with Learning Disabilities and Normal Children Performing 1 Year Below Grade Level

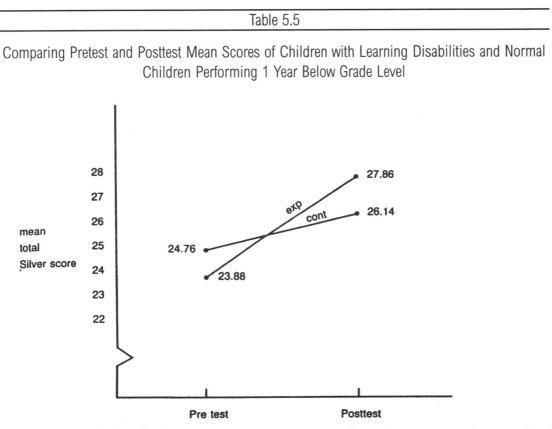

Both posttest scores differed significantly from pretest scores ($p < .05$). In addition, the experimental group's posttest scores differed significantly from the combination of the other three groups of scores. Analysis and table 5.5 prepared by John Kleinhans, PhD.

A similar procedure was performed with respect to gains in general intelligence, as measured by the Otis Lennon test. The experimental group failed to demonstrate significantly higher posttest scores than control subjects.

Another objective was to determine whether improvement in concept formation would transfer to achievement in reading, mathematics, or IQ scores. In an analysis of variance for repeated measures, the *F* ratio for differences between pre- and posttest scores failed to reach significance. The experimental subjects failed to score significantly higher in the math, reading, and IQ posttests, as compared to control subjects.

The final objective of the developmental program was to determine whether children in a specific setting made significantly greater gains than children in different settings. A school-by-school analysis was conducted for each variable, using a series of tests.

In general, the SDT scores of experimental subjects tended to be higher than those of control group subjects. In only three instances, however, were these differences statistically significant. In one school (the school for children with learning disabilities) both the total SDT score and the Drawing from Imagination score were significantly higher for experimental subjects. In another school, the experimental children scored significantly higher in Drawing from Observation.

The project report also included a case study by each art therapist to provide the kind of information that eludes quantification. Although the gains made by some children were not evident in their posttest scores, gains became evident in classroom behavior.

Discussion

In the two previous studies, we found significant improvements in cognitive development within a similar time period. In the National Institute of Education project, the experimental group again improved significantly. Although their gains were higher than control group gains, these were not significantly higher. It may be that the procedures must be extended beyond 12 sessions if a differential impact is to be observed. Another factor that may have affected the findings is that the children in this study were a more heterogeneous group than those studied previously. Many of the children nominated by school administrators were slow learners, not language-impaired. It may be that these children have a generalized low functioning and do not benefit from art experiences as a substitute for language. It had been our intention to select children with high scores on the SDT. The limited number of children with this pattern required us to select children who were not as strong as initially planned.

It is not clear why the school for children with learning disabilities was the only school with significant differences between posttest scores of experimental and control groups, nor why the gains in the previous studies failed to materialize. The finding may reflect the constellations of strengths and weaknesses among children with learning disabilities, superior skills of one art therapist, or too much flexibility in the art program. By specifying what procedures to use in only 6 of the 12 sessions, we may have introduced too many variables.

The results of the testing program reported in chapter 3 indicate that there is a relationship between the SDT and other tests of intelligence and achievement. Although moderate, it nevertheless indicates that the SDT is measuring cognitive skills. As such, the SDT can serve as an instrument for identifying children who have cognitive skills that escape detection on traditional tests. The skills involved in Drawing from Imagination and Predictive Drawing are similar to the skills required in reading, math, and traditional tests. That also explains why some children do well on the SDT, although they do not do well on traditional measures; we are using a different medium to tap these cognitive skills. The SDT was published by Special Child Publications in 1983. Revised editions were published in 1990 and 1996.

Marshall's Study of Children with Learning Disabilities

Marshall (1988) used the SDT to assess the effectiveness of a developmental program designed to enhance the cognitive skills of two groups of children with learning disabilities in the Special Education Program of a school in Maine. Group A consisted of five children, ages 7 to 10, who attended 14 sessions. Group B consisted of four children, ages 13 and 14, who attended 9 sessions. The program included the use of stimulus drawings, painting, Drawing from Observation, modeling clay, and playing "imagination games." The SDT and a second measure of 10 conservation tasks were administered before and after the art program to determine its effectiveness.

After the program, Marshall found that the SDT mean scores of children in Group A had increased in each subtest, their total mean scores increasing from 16.24 to 21.09. The most marked and consistent gain was in Drawing from Imagination. The adolescents in Group B showed little gain, their mean scores increasing from 25.50 to 26.0.

Dhanachitsiriphong's Study of Incarcerated Adolescents in Thailand

The purpose of this experimental research was to study the effects of art therapy and rational emotive therapy on the cognitive and emotional development of incarcerated male adolescents in Thailand. The SDT served as a pretest–posttest to determine whether the interventions were effective. The study was the thesis of Pornchit Dhanachitsiriphong (1999), who was studying for a degree in counseling psychology at Burapha University. She selected her subjects from a group of 100 adolescents, based on their SDT scores, choosing the brightest and most depressed, as measured by their scores on the SDT. Her sample included those whose cognitive scores were higher than the percentile rank of 75 and those whose emotional content scores were lower than the percentile rank of 25. She divided the sample into experimental and control groups, with 6 adolescents in each group, and provided a therapeutic program.

The experimental group participated in art therapy and rational emotive therapy for 12 sessions during a period of 3 months, while the control group continued regular activities. The statistics used to analyze the data included a between-subjects variable, a within-subjects variable, the test for simple effects in the Howell procedure, and the test for difference in pairs in the Newman-Keuls procedure.

Results indicated that after the experiment, the cognitive and emotional scores of the experimental group were significantly higher than the scores of the control group at the .01 level of probability in the eight categories under consideration. The categories included scores obtained after the experiment in cognitive development, during a follow-up period in cognitive development, after the experiment in emotional development, after the follow-up period in emotional development, and other scores.

Dhanachitsiriphong observed that the SDT was useful for access to the unconscious, and she translated the assessment into the Thai language for use in teaching and helping clients in nonprofit programs. This study is discussed in greater detail in chapter 15, along with other cross-cultural studies.

Henn's Study of Adolescents with Multiple Handicaps

Henn (1990) examined the question of whether an integrated approach to teaching can have a significant effect on the understanding of horizontal, vertical, and depth relationships by students with multiple handicaps.

Subjects included 24 racially mixed students who were retarded, ages 16 to 21, from rural, suburban, and urban areas in three New York counties. Some students were nonverbal. The Drawing from Observation subtest served as a pre–post measure. Six lesson plans were designed by Henn to develop spatial awareness and elicit spatial thinking. Each lesson contained a movement activity accompanied by music, an art activity, and a closing activity. Although Henn designed the curriculum, the teaching was implemented by Henn and a movement specialist. Scoring was done blindly by Henn and another certified art teacher. Responses to the drawing task were coded, so that the judges did not know which student produced what drawing, or whether a drawing was a pretest or posttest.

To determine interscorer reliability, a Pearson correlation coefficient was computed. Correlations were .95 for horizontal relationships, .86 for vertical relationships, and .84 for relationships in depth. In addition, a correlation of .92 was found for combined gains on the three variables.

The posttest scores for all three criteria were significantly higher than the pretest scores. The combined pretest mean was 7.88, the combined posttest mean was 14.12. This difference yielded a t-test value of -2.96, which has a probability of .0058. These findings seem to indicate that the teaching approach enhanced understanding of the three spatial concepts to a highly significant degree, and that the SDT was effective as a pre–post measure.

This chapter has reviewed studies of age and gender differences observed in response to the SDT subtests by children and adults in the United States. Age and gender differences in responses to the other assessments will be discussed in sections II and III. Section II presents the second stimulus drawing assessment, Draw a Story: Screening for Depression and Emotional Needs.

Assessing Age and Gender Differences and Similarities in Attitudes and Cognition

◇　◇　◇

This chapter reviews previous studies that found differences between genders in various age groups, as measured by responses to the SDT. It also presents studies in which similarities, as well as differences, emerged in responses by unimpaired children and children with dyslexia, hearing impairments, or learning disabilities. Since the reviews are brief, the reader is referred to the original publications for additional information.

Attitudes Toward Food or Eating

Of the 15 stimulus drawings in Form A of the SDT, only 2 represent food or eating, the ice cream soda and refrigerator, and both seem to trigger associations with feeling deprived. For example, a male adolescent selected the soda and drew "Not having." It shows two young men standing side by side. One scowls, the other smiles. The scowling man is empty-handed; the smiling man holds an ice cream soda, blackened for emphasis. An elderly woman chose two stimulus drawings, the refrigerator and the bride. In her drawing, the bride kneels before the refrigerator, its open door revealing only two items of food. Title: "Food for thought. Does marriage fill a void?"

Other responses seem ambivalent rather than negative. A woman who chose the soda and the girl, drew figure 6.1, titled "I tell her not to eat sugar, then I do." A young girl, age 9, chose the same stimulus drawings, then drew "A Sneaky Snacker" (figure 6.2). The girl's expression and posture suggest guilty desire. Another 9-year-old girl chose the soda and mouse, drawing the soda too tall for the mouse to reach, as shown in figure 6.3. In her written story, however, fate intervenes, and the deprived mouse gets the soda after all:

> The mouse really wanted the drink, but of course he was too small. So the mouse did everything he could to get the drink, but still he couldn't get it. Then suddenly a big hand came down and took the drink away. The mouse was just about to leave sadly when the big hand appered (sic) with the drink. When the big hand was just letting go the drink spilled! The mouse drank his fill (and) after a long hard days work went to bed.

Figure 6.1. "I tell her not to eat sugar, then I do," by a young woman

Figure 6.2. "A Sneaky Snacker," by Charlotte, age 9

Drawing

Story: The mouse really wanted the drink, but of coure he was to small for the mouse did everything he could to ge the drink, but still he couldn't get it then suddenly a b hand came down and took the drink away. The mouse wa just about to leave sadly when the bro had coveered with t drink when the big hand was just betting go when the dri spilled! The mouse dranks his fill after a long, days work ter bed.

Figure 6.3. "The mouse really wated the drink," by Charlene, age 9

Since these and other drawings suggested that choosing the soda or refrigerator might serve to identify respondents with eating disorders, the responses of 293 children, adolescents, and adults were reexamined (Silver, 1998b).

The children, ages 9 to 10, attended fourth grade in three elementary schools in New Jersey, Pennsylvania, and New York. The younger adolescents, ages 12 to 15, attended grades 7 to 10 in five public schools in Nebraska, New York, and Pennsylvania. The older adolescents, ages 16 to 18, included high school seniors in two public high schools in New York. The adults, ages 19 to 70, included a class of college students in Nebraska; adults in college audiences in Idaho, New York, and Wisconsin; and older adults in Florida.

Almost one third of the 293 respondents (29%) and more than twice as many females (59 females, 26 males) drew fantasies about food or eating, proportionally more females than males in each of the four age groups. Among females, these drawings included almost half of the older adolescents, ages 16 to 18 (46.9%) and about one third of the younger girls (34.4%), and among women, 27.9%. Among males, the largest proportions again appeared in the sample of younger adolescents ages 13 to 15 (29.4%), and boys, ages 9 to 10 (25%); followed by adolescents ages, 16 to 18 (22.2%); and ending with the sample of men (10%).

Another notable gender difference was found in responses that were ambivalent, ambiguous, or unclear: 45% of the women and girls, compared with 23% of the men and boys, scored 3 points.

Because adolescent girls tend to be particularly vulnerable to eating disorders, and the sample of older adolescent girls in this study drew proportionally more fantasies about eating than other age or gender groups, further investigation might determine whether the SDT can be useful in identifying those whose preoccupations might be undetected or masked.

Attitudes Toward the Opposite Sex

Previous studies found that respondents tend to draw positive fantasies about subjects the same gender as themselves, but negative fantasies about the opposite sex (Silver, 1992, 1993b). A subsequent study asked whether drawings about the opposite sex expressed negative attitudes to a significant degree (Silver, 1997, 2001).

Reviewing responses to the Drawing from Imagination task by 480 children, adolescents, and adults, the study found that approximately 1 of 4 respondents (116) drew principal subjects of the opposite sex (21% male, 27% female). The responses were divided into age and gender groups, and mean scores analyzed.

The study included 222 males and 258 females: children, adolescents, and adults. The children, ages 8 to 11, attended six elementary schools in New Jersey and New York. The adolescents, ages 12 to 19, who were in grades 7 through 12, as well as freshmen in college, resided in Nebraska, New York, Pennsylvania, and Ohio. The younger adults, ages 20 to 50, included older college students and residents of Nebraska, New York, and Wisconsin. The senior adults, age 65 and older, lived independently in New York and Florida.

Several age and gender trends emerged, showing an age difference of borderline significance. Opposite-sex drawings increased with age, from 29% of the children, to 44% of the adolescents, and 77% of the adults. The remaining subjects chose animal subjects or subjects the same gender as themselves. There was no interaction.

The children and adolescents were more negative toward subjects of the opposite sex than were the adults (F [1,112] = 2.77, p < .10). For example, a girl, age 7, chose the stimulus drawing of the bride and the bed, then drew a sad-looking bride with what appears to be a dark bruise on one cheek, holding a dinner tray presumably intended for the groom lying in bed (figure 6.4). Although the title is noncommittal, the drawing suggests domestic abuse.

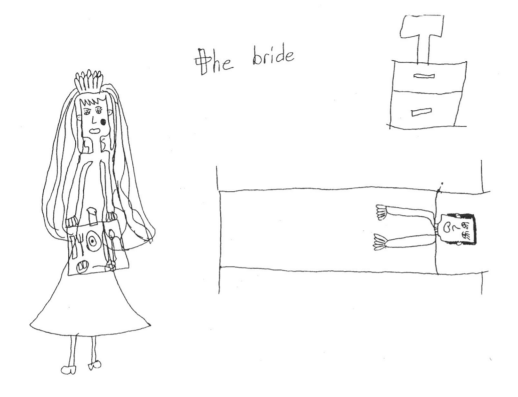

Figure 6.4. "The Bride," by a girl, age 7

Figure 6.5. "The Lady Getting Married to a Dog Who Wants to Kill Him," by a boy, age 8

Figure 6.6. "Woman sees mouse," by a man

Figure 6.7. "Fat couch potato," by a woman

Table 6.4

Portrayals of the Opposite Sex Ranging from Negative to Positive

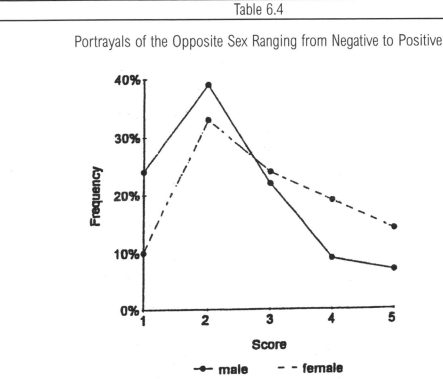

"The Lady Getting Married to a Dog Who Wants to Kill Him" was a negative response by a boy, age 8, who chose the bride, knife, and dog (figure 6.5). With snakes in her veil, the bride holds the knife in one hand, a bouquet in the other.

As shown in table 6.4, more males than females drew fantasies about the opposite sex. Both genders expressed more negative than positive feelings toward their subjects of the opposite sex, peaking at moderately negative (2 points), most portraying them as ridiculous, such as figure 6.6, "Woman sees mouse," by a man; and figure 6.7, "Fat couch potato," by a woman.

Although an analysis of variance found that males expressed significantly more negative feelings toward females than females did toward males at the .01 level of significance (F [1,112] = 6.92, $p < .01$), they were not necessarily expressing misogyny. If it is typical to project self-images through drawings, then drawings about opposite-sex subjects are likely to symbolize the other, not the self. It would seem to follow that feelings of superiority or disgust could be expected in drawings about others, just as drawings about the self tend to elicit positive associations, as the studies have found.

It is important to remember that only 21% of the males and 27% of the females in this study drew subjects of the opposite sex. It may be that unhappy experiences were triggered by the stimulus drawings they chose and associated with their fantasies. The findings suggest that drawings about opposite-sex subjects could provide access to conflicts or troubling relationships and, thereby, opportunities for clinical discussion.

Gender Differences in Self-images, Autonomous Subjects, and Relationships

This study was undertaken because Gilligan, Ward, and Taylor (1998) reported that gender has a profound effect on the ways we organize thoughts and feelings. The masculine way is based on concepts of self-sufficiency; the feminine way, on care and responsibility to others. These investigators based their observations on verbal responses.

The purpose of the study was to find out whether responses to the drawing tasks supported these observations (Silver, 1992). It asked whether males tend to draw autonomous subjects; females, interactions between subjects. It also asked whether respondents tend to draw fantasies about subjects who were the same gender as themselves.

Responses by 145 boys and 116 girls, ages 7 to 10, were examined. The sample included second-, third-, and fourth-graders in suburban and urban public schools in Nebraska, New Jersey, New York, Pennsylvania, and Canada.

Most boys drew pictures about male subjects; most girls, about female subjects. Based on a chi-square test, highly significant gender differences emerged at the .001 level of probability.

No other findings were significant. In drawings about autonomous subjects, boys outnumbered girls, and in drawings about relationships, girls outnumbered boys, but the differences did not reach significance. However, twice as many boys (28%) as girls (14%) drew pictures about autonomous subjects enjoying themselves, and even larger proportions of boys than girls drew pictures about assaultive relationships (19% vs. 05%). In drawings about caring relationships, virtually no gender differences emerged.

Age and Gender Differences in Attitudes Toward Self and Others

A subsequent study asked if there were age as well as gender differences in choosing same-gender subjects and in expressing attitudes (Silver, 1993b). In this study, the subjects included 531 respondents in five age groups: children, ages 7 to 10; younger adolescents, ages 13 to 16; older adolescents, ages 17 to 19; younger adults, ages 20 to 50; and older adults, age 65 and older.

As in the previous study, proportionally more females than males drew pictures about relationships (61% females, 56% males), and more males than females drew pictures about solitary subjects (44% males, 39% females), but these differences did not reach statistical significance. When attitudes toward self and others were examined, however, significant differences were found.

Males expressed positive attitudes toward solitary subjects and negative attitudes toward relationship. These differences were significant at the .001 level of probability ($A^2 = 46.971, p < .001$). Females expressed positive attitudes toward solitary subjects and both positive and negative attitudes toward relationships. These findings, too, were significant at the .001 level of probability ($A^2 = 25.32, p < .001$).

Males showed a significantly higher frequency than did females in drawings about assaultive relationships ($A^2 [1] = 9.38, p < .01$). However, age and gender differences interacted (A^2 [4] = 13.07, p < .05), resulting in a significant age variability in assaultiveness for females but not for males. The proportion of older females who drew assaultive fantasies exceeded the proportion of older men who did so, as well as exceeded the proportion of all other female age groups.

The converse age and gender interaction was found for caring relationships (A^2 [4] = 12.52, p < .05). Whereas females showed significantly higher frequency of caring relationships across age groups, males showed significant age variability. The proportion of younger men who drew pictures about caring relationships exceeded the proportion of younger women who did so, as well as exceeded the proportion of all other male age groups.

Respondents who drew human subjects chose subjects the same gender as themselves to a degree significant at the .001 level of probability. This tendency peaked in childhood and reached its lowest level among adults. The decline continued among older women (19%), but reversed among older men (54%), a proportion almost equal to that found in the samples of boys. Genders were clearly indicated in responses by children and adolescents, but were sometimes unclear in responses by adults, particularly in the drawings of older women.

Attitudes of Older Adults

A subsequent study expanded the previous study by examining more closely the responses of 59 adults over the age of 65, 28 men and 31 women living independently in their communities (Silver, 1993c). Although the sample was too small for statistical analysis, more older women than any other age or gender group drew sad or helpless solitary subjects (1 point). On the other hand, more older women than any other age or gender group drew pictures about active solitary pleasures (5 points).

In drawings about relationships, more older men than older women or any other age or gender group drew fantasies about stressful relationships (2 points). Older men expressed attitudes toward relationships that were proportionally more negative than those of any other male age group. Older women expressed more negative attitudes toward solitary subjects than those of any other age or gender group. Although negative attitudes predominated among older adults, they also used humor more often than did any other age group. Humor was used more often in responses by older men (39%) than in responses by older women (16%). The humor of adolescents tended to be aggressive, making fun of others, whereas the humor of older adults tended to be self-disparaging, directed toward themselves, perhaps reflecting resilience in spite of low self-esteem and the ability (or wish) to survive in spite of adversity.

Attitudes and Spatial Skills of Aging and Young Adults

Although much is known about aging adults in nursing homes, little is known about the attitudes and cognitive skills of those who are psychologically, physically, and financially independent. This study compared attitudes toward self and others, as well as the SDT scores, of 57 aging and 51 young men and women (Silver, 1999, 2000a). The young adults attended colleges or participated in college audiences. The seniors, ages 64 to 95, lived independently in separate households and two retirement residences. Residence A provided many amenities, was relatively expensive, and provided lifetime care. Residence B provided fewer amenities and charged minimal fees. Three procedures were used to assess age and gender differences: individual responses, statistical analyses of mean scores, and top and bottom range scores.

No significant age differences were found, but gender differences emerged to significant degrees. Men had higher scores in sequential order, horizontality, and self-image (portraying powerful or effective principal subjects more often). Both age groups followed similar patterns in emotional content, both peaking at the intermediate 3-point level (ambiguous, ambivalent, or unemotional).

Drawings about unfortunate subjects or stressful relationships predominated in both age groups (32% seniors, 33% young adults), and less than 10% of either group drew sad individuals or life-threatening relationships (1 point).

Top and bottom range scores yielded information not found in the statistical analysis. A larger proportion of seniors than young adults received top scores in ability to represent (55% and 41%, respectively). This trend was reversed for verticality in response to the Predictive Drawing task. More seniors drew vertical houses on the slope without providing adequate support (4 points), perhaps a metaphor for feeling unsteady on one's feet, and reflecting an age-related change in the perception of verticality. Figure 6.8 is an example.

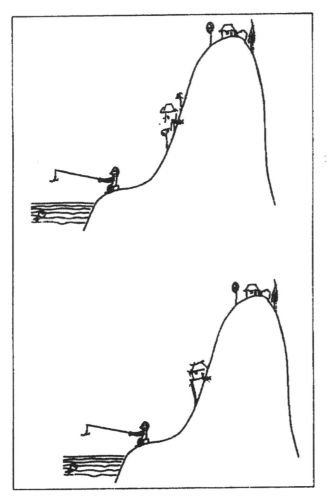

Figure 6.8. Responses to the Verticality Task by Senior Adults

The unexpected finding of gender differences, not age differences, prompted a closer look at the performances of senior women. The 13 women in Community A had higher mean scores than did the 13 women in Community B, suggesting that dread of becoming incapacitated and forced into nursing homes may have affected the cognitive functioning of these residents. The findings suggested that being able to remain physically and financially independent could be a critical factor in successful aging.

To further analyze for potential age and gender differences in Predictive Drawing, the sample was expanded to include four age groups: 53 children, 66 adolescents, 36 seniors, and 51 young adults. Several age trends emerged.

- For horizontality, there was a significant effect of age group (F [1,196] = 18.61, p < .0001). Children (3.15) scored less than adolescents did (4.17). Adolescents scored less than did young adults (4.61), but did not differ from seniors (4.49). The young adults and senior adults did not differ.
- For verticality, a main effect for age group emerged (F [1,197] =

12.30, $p < .001$). Children (1.98) scored less than adolescents did (2.64) who in turn scored less than adults (3.53) and seniors did (3.32). The adult groups did not differ.

- For ability to sequence, there was a borderline significant effect (F [1,147] = 2.68, $p < .10$). Adolescents scored significantly higher than seniors did (4.52 vs. 3.95). Young adults scored in the middle (4.15) and did not differ from either group. Gender differences also were observed, but are not detailed here.

In general, it appears that there are few age-related changes in SDT performances. There may be a slight trend toward a decline in horizontality scores, but more study is needed to test this hypothesis.

Comparing Spatial Skills of Male and Female Adolescents

It seems to be generally agreed that males are superior to females in spatial ability. According to McGee (1979), psychological testing for more than 50 years has concluded that males consistently excel in spatial ability. To test the assumption, this study examined responses to the Predictive Drawing and Drawing from Observation subtests by 33 girls and 33 boys, ages 12 to 15 attending public schools in Nebraska, Pennsylvania, and New York (Silver, 1996b).

Based on a computation of t-test scores, no significant gender differences were found. Although female mean scores (3.70) were higher than male mean scores (3.03) in representing depth, the probability was less than 0.10 and did not reach significance. The girls received higher mean scores on four of the six tasks (horizontality, verticality, height, and depth), whereas the boys received higher mean scores in sequencing and horizontality (left–right relationships), but the differences did not reach significance. The boys' scores, like the girls' scores, tended to be consistent and did not show variability. These findings suggested that further investigation of gender differences would be worthwhile.

Comparing Spatial Skills of Adults, as Well as Adolescents

A subsequent study asked if different scoring systems could explain why other investigators had found males superior to females in performing tasks designed to measure concepts of horizontality and verticality. With this in mind, we re-scored the Predictive Drawing responses previously scored on the 5-point cognitive scale, in terms of success or failure (Silver, 1998a). Only those respondents who drew horizontal lines in the tilted bottle (5 points) or vertical houses on the hill (5 points) were deemed successful. In addition, the numbers of subjects were expanded, including samples of adults.

The subjects included 88 male and 88 female adolescents and adults. The adolescents (mean age 26) included a class of college freshmen in Nebraska, a college audience in New York, and residents of a detention facility in Missouri. The adults included 26 men and 26 women, ages 18 to 50, who had participated in the previous study.

Once again, no significant gender differences were found, either in success–failure scores or in cognitive level scores. Chi-square analyses indicated that both males and females had lower scores in verticality than horizontality; males had lower verticality scores than females. The findings supported the previous study and suggested that perhaps some investigators had been assessing knowledge of physical phenomena rather than natural reference systems based on Euclidean concepts of space. The findings called into question the widespread assumption of male superiority in spatial intelligence and suggested that expressing spatial concepts nonverbally, through drawing, offers unique opportunities for assessing concepts of space. It also may be that self-confidence plays a critical role. Women tend to be less confident about the value of their ideas, and men tend to be more competitive.

Comparing SDT Scores of Hearing Girls and Boys and Those Who Are Deaf

It is often assumed that children who are deaf lag behind children with normal hearing in cognitive abilities, and that females lag behind males in spatial abilities. It has even been claimed that male superiority in spatial thinking has been confirmed and is not in dispute (Moir & Jessel, 1992).

The SDT was designed initially to tap the cognitive abilities of children like Charlie, discussed in chapter 1. It was theorized that children with language and hearing impairments would equal unimpaired children in spatial skills but would fall behind in sequential and verbal skills.

To test these theories, responses to the SDT by 27 children who are deaf and 28 hearing children, ages 9 to 11, were examined and their test performances compared.

Procedures

The subjects with hearing impairments included 13 girls and 14 boys in an urban nonresidential school for children who are deaf in New York. They included all the children in the fourth grade who had responded to the SDT as part of the National Institute of Education project discussed earlier. Their scores on the WISC Performance Scale ranged from 72 to 130. One girl and one boy were severely impaired with multiple handicaps; another boy was "language disordered."

The hearing subjects included 14 girls and 14 boys attending two public elementary schools. They were matched in age and selected at random from responses to the SDT administered by a classroom teacher in New Jersey and an art therapist in Pennsylvania, and scored by teachers or art therapists.

Results

Predictive Drawing

No significant differences were found between children who were deaf and hearing children, or between girls and boys, in horizontal orientation or in ability to sequence. The children who were deaf received significantly higher scores than did the hearing children in vertical orientation (F [1,51] = 14.34, p < .001). Mean scores were 3.13 and 2.00, respectively, as shown in table 6.1.

Drawing from Observation
No significant differences were found between children who were deaf and hearing children, or between genders, in representing left–right, above–below, or front–back relationships.

Drawing from Imagination
The girls received higher scores than did the boys in ability to select (3.54 vs. 3.04), to a degree significant at the .05 level (F [1,51] = 5.49, p < .05). No other gender differences were found. This finding is shown in table 6.2.

The hearing children received higher scores than the children who were deaf in ability to select (F [1,51] = 12.85, p < .001), ability to combine (F(1,51) = 57.66, p < .000001), and ability to represent (F [1,51] = 30.99, p < .000001). The means were 3.68 versus 2.90 for selecting, 3.93 versus 1.98 for combining, and 3.89 versus 2.27 for representing. This finding is shown in table 6.3.

Observations

It was surprising to find the children who were deaf superior in vertical orientation. Only 4 of the 55 children drew vertical houses, and 3 of the 4 were deaf. This suggests they had somehow discovered that houses remain vertical when cantilevered or supported by posts, a discovery that seems to call for visuospatial thinking.

No significant differences were found in the four remaining spatial abilities. This finding supports the theory that children with hearing impairments can be expected to equal hearing children in visuospatial abilities, as measured by the SDT. The results also have support in a study by Craig and Gordon (1989), who found the cognitive task performance of high school students who were deaf above average for the visual and spatial skills measured by the Cognitive Laterality Battery (Gordon, 1986), but below average for sequential skills. In the present study, however, the deaf children equalled the hearing children in ability to sequence, as measured by the Predictive Drawing subtest.

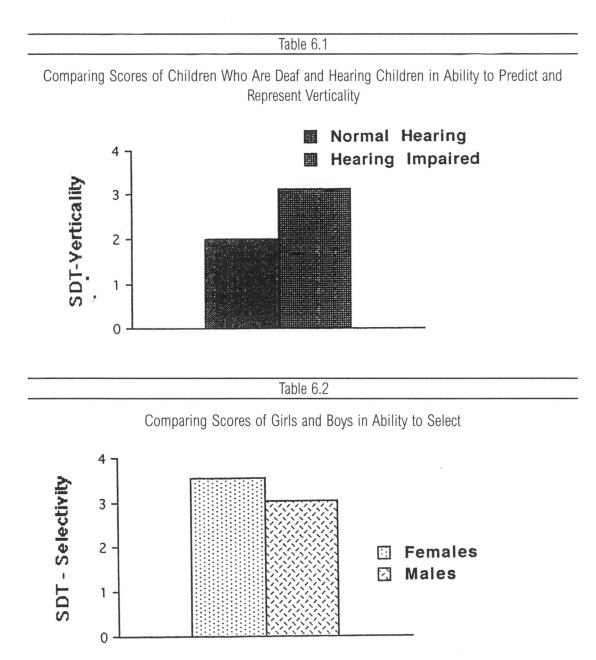

Table 6.1

Comparing Scores of Children Who Are Deaf and Hearing Children in Ability to Predict and Represent Verticality

Table 6.2

Comparing Scores of Girls and Boys in Ability to Select

The significantly lower scores of children who were deaf in Drawing from Imagination suggest that selecting images and combining them into drawings do not parallel the mental operations of selecting words and combining them into sentences. It may be that these mental operations cannot be separated from language skills. On the other hand, it may be that the children who were deaf lagged behind because they had less experience in selecting, combining, and representing because of language deficiences. If so, additional experiences in Drawing from Imagination may lead to improvements that transfer to language skills.

Pollio and Pollio (1991) suggested that assessment should be tied to intervention. Educators of children who are deaf may find useful the intervention techniques for developing cognitive skills listed in chapter 7. Other developmental techniques have been described by Williams and Wood (1977) and by Anderson (1992, 1993).

It was also surprising to find no significant gender differences in spatial abilities because of many reports of male superiority in the Piagetian task of liquid horizontality. In addition, the girls received significantly higher scores than did the boys in ability to select.

The findings of this study support the theory that the SDT can be effective in assessing gender differences and similarities as well as cognitive strengths and weaknesses of children with hearing impairments.

Table 6.3

Comparing Scores of Children Who Are Deaf and Hearing Children in Ability to Combine, and Ability to Represent

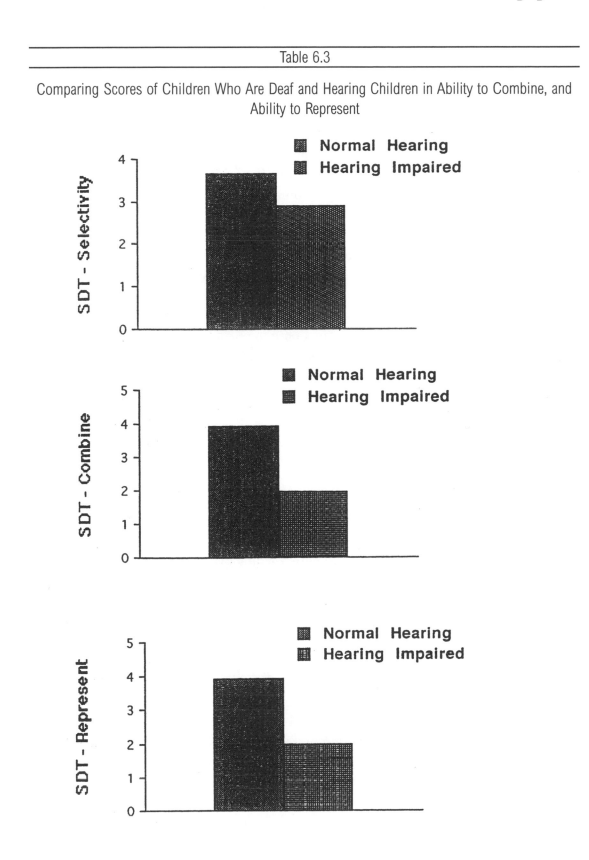

Comparing SDT Scores of Girls and Boys with Learning Disabilities, Deafness, and No Known Impairments

This study extended the previous study by adding a sample of 28 children with learning disabilities. The data were analyzed using ANOVA and LSD tests to determine which groups differed on which measures.

The children who were deaf scored higher in vertical orientation than either the children with learning disabilities or the unimpaired children did at the .05 level of probability. No significant differences were found in sequencing or horizontality.

The unimpaired children and children who were deaf scored higher than did children with learning disabilities in representing left–right relationships. In representing above–below relationships, the unimpaired children scored higher than did the children with learning disabilities, and no significant differences were found in representing front–back relationships.

The unimpaired children scored higher than either children with hearing impairments or those with learning disabilities in ability to select, combine, and represent. The girls scored higher than the boys did in selecting and in combining, whereas the boys had no significantly higher scores.

These findings amplify the evidence found in the previous study and support the theory that the SDT can be effective in assessing and comparing the cognitive strengths and weaknesses of girls and boys with hearing impairments and learning disabilities, with unimpaired girls and boys.

The Hiscox Study of Children with Learning Disabilities, Dyslexia, and No Known Disabilities

Hiscox (1990) hypothesized that children with learning disabilities would fall within the normal range on IQ tests that were not based on language. She administered two tests: the SDT and the California Achievement Test (CAT), including Verbal, Quantitative, and Nonverbal Batteries.

Subjects included 14 children with learning disabilities, 14 children with dyslexia, and 14 normal children in the third, fourth, and fifth grades of three public schools and one private school in California. Selection of the dyslexic group was based on poor performances on the Scott Fresman Oral Reading Inventory.

The CAT and SDT data were analyzed by using a one-way analysis of variance design. Results indicated that each group performed differently (CAT Verbal Battery, $F = 40.97$, $df = 2,39$, $p < .0001$), suggesting that the differences found between groups were real and could not have been due to chance. An examination of reliability showed a high level of scorer agreement; ratings varied by only 1 to 3 points.

The results supported the hypothesis that children with learning disabilities would fall within the normal range. On both tests, normal subjects had the highest mean scores

(CAT: 121.1; SDT: 30.88). Subjects with with learning disabilities had higher mean scores (CAT: 104.9; SDT: 30.54) than did the subjects with reading disabilities (CAT: 98.1; SDT: 25.64), who performed within the middle range of both groups. The difference in the mean and standard deviation between groups validated the rejection of the null hypothesis at the .05 level of significance.

This chapter has reviewed studies of age and gender differences in responses to the SDT tasks by children and adults in the United States. Age, gender, and cultural differences (or similarities) observed by investigators in other countries will be reviewed in chapter 15.

The following section presents the second assessment, Draw a Story, which was designed to screen for depression and emotional needs, as well as for age and gender differences in attitudes toward self and others.

Section II

Draw a Story: Screening for Depression (DAS)

◇   ◇   ◇

Chapter 7

Introducing the Draw-a-Story Assessment

◇   ◇   ◇

This chapter presents the DAS assessment and examples of scored responses. The following chapters in section II review studies of its reliability and validity, as well as studies by various art therapists who used DAS with clients who were abused, brain-injured, depressed, incarcerated, or emotionally disturbed, and also with nonclinical children, adolescents, and adults.

When the SDT was presented to classes of schoolchildren in order to develop norms, a question arose, whether responses to the Drawing from Imagination task can provide access to masked depression. Unexpectedly, a few children drew fantasies about suicide or annihilation. Because childhood depression can be masked by fantasies about death or violence, Draw a Story began as an attempt to screen for depression. It is based on the premise that strongly negative or morbid responses to the drawing task, particularly by children, may reflect depressive illness, and that follow-up would be appropriate.

The DAS Instrument

The DAS task, like the SDT Drawing from Imagination subtest, asks respondents to choose two subjects from an array of stimulus drawings, imagine something happening between the subjects they choose, and then show what is happening in drawings of their own. When the drawings are finished, stories are added and discussed whenever possible and responses scored on the 5-point rating scale shown in figure 7.1.

This assessment also includes two arrays of stimulus drawings. Form A (figure 7.2), consists of 14 stimulus drawings selected from the other two assessments because these drawings seemed to elicit negative fantasies. Form B (figure 7.3), was added to offset the negativity of Form A and to reserve Form A for use as a pretest–posttest measure only. Responses to Form B can serve therapeutic and diagnostic functions by confirming, clarifying, or amplifying an individual's first response.

Administering and Scoring the DAS Task

The task can be presented individually or to groups of examinees. Individual administration is recommended for children and adults who may have difficulty understanding directions, children younger than 7 years, and respondents being examined clinically. The age range is from 5 years to adult. There is no time limit. Most respondents complete the task within 10 minutes. Classroom teachers, as well as art therapists, psychologists, and other clinicians, have administered and scored the DAS assessment.

The examiner should give each respondent a copy of the Form A set of stimulus drawings, the DAS drawing page, and a pencil with eraser. With children younger than 10 and others who may have difficulty reading directions, say,

> I believe you will enjoy this kind of drawing. It doesn't matter whether you can draw well. What matters is expressing your ideas. Here are some drawings of people, animals, places, and things. Choose two of these ideas and imagine a story, something happening between the subjects or pictures you choose.

> When you are ready, draw a picture of what you imagine. Make your drawing tell a story. Show what is happening. Feel free to change these drawings and add your own pictures and ideas.

After drawing has started, minimize discussions and avoid interruptions, including your own. As respondents finish drawing, ask them to write titles or stories and fill in the blanks on the lines below. If respondents have difficulty writing, ask if they would rather dictate their stories to you; and if they do, write their exact words on the lines provided.

As with the SDT it is important to be supportive and encouraging. The experience should be pleasurable and an opportunity for quiet reflection. Respondents should feel free to choose and change stimulus drawings, use their own symbols or metaphors, and express their thoughts and feelings. Erasers are provided so that responses can be revised.

Finally, initiate discussion to clarify meanings, both intended and unintended. For example, if the drawing is about a cat and mouse, you might ask how the mouse feels, what the cat is thinking, what happened before, and what may happen later on. Also look for verbal clues, such as the subject of a sentence or a personal pronoun in the title or story.

Figure 7.4 shows the page for drawings, stories, and other responses.

Examples of Scored Responses

Figure 7.1.

Rating Scale for Assessing the Story Content of Responses to DAS Form A

1 point: Strongly negative, for example,

  a. subjects who are sad, isolated, helpless, suicidal, or in mortal danger

  b. relationships that are destructive, murderous, or life-threatening

2 points: Moderately negative, for example

  a. subjects who are frustrated, fearful, fearsome, or unfortunate

  b. relationships that are stressful or hostile

3 points: Intermediate level: for example,

  a. subjects or relationships that are both negative and positive, suggesting
     ambivalence or conflict

  b. subjects or relationships that are ambiguous or unclear

  c. subjects or relationships that are unemotional, neither negative nor positive;
     no feelings expressed toward the subjects or relationships portrayed

4 points: Moderately positive, for example,

  a. subjects who are fortunate but passive

  b. relationships that are friendly

5 points: Strongly positive, for example,

  a. subjects who are happy or achieving goals (taking action)

  b. relationships that are caring or loving

Figure 7.2. Draw a Story, Form A

Choose two of these drawings and imagine a story - something happening between the subjects you choose.

When you are ready, draw a picture of what you imagine. Make your drawing tell the story. Show what is happening. Feel free to change these drawings and to add your own ideas.

When you finish drawing, write the story in the place provided.

Figure 7.2. continued

Figure 7.3. Draw a Story, Form B

Choose two of these drawings and imagine a story - something happening between the subjects you choose.

When you are ready, draw a picture of what you imagine. Make your drawing tell the story. Show what is happening. Feel free to change these drawings and to add your own ideas.

When you finish drawing, write the story in the place provided.

Figure 7.3. continued

Figure 7.4. DAS Drawing Page

Drawing

Story:_____

_____

_____

_____

_____

Please fill in the blanks below:

First name ____ Sex____ Age ____ Location (state): _____ Date:_____

Just now I'm feeling ____very happy ____O.K. ____angry ____frightened ____sad

© 1992–2002 Rawley Silver

Examples of Scored Response Drawings

1 Point

The score of 1 point is used to characterize strongly negative themes or fantasies about the subjects or relationships portrayed; for example,

1a. Subjects who appear sad, isolated, helpless, suicidal, or in mortal danger

"The man jumps out of his plain and falls into a steaming volcano"

Score: 1 point
Subject in mortal danger

Figure 7.5. "The Man Jumps"

"Mr. Henderson was found guilty of murdering his wife, whom he was married to for 4 years, and got sent to Ryker's Island prison where he was to stay for 50 years. After two weeks there, he got beaten, stabbed, and raped by his inmates. Since he couldn't take any more abuse, he decided to take a knife and stab himself to death with it. He enjoyed his last smoke before he died."

Score: 1 point
Suicidal subject

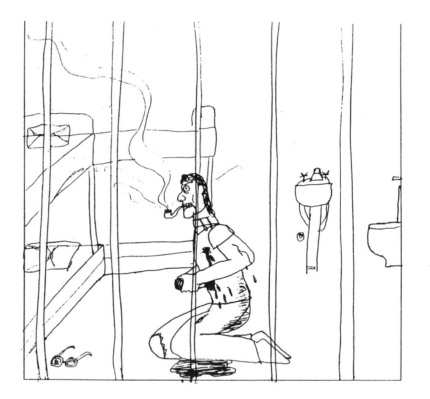

Figure 7.6. "Mr. Henderson"

Score: 1 point
Sad subject

Figure 7.7. "The Sleeping Bride"

Score: 1 point
Isolated helpless subject

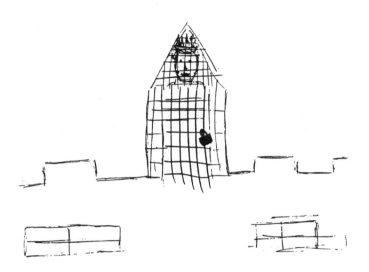

Figure 7.8. "Help!" "No Escape!"

Score: 1 point
Life-threatening relationship

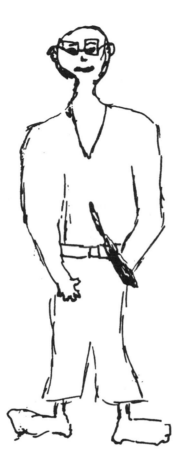

Figure 7.9. "My ex-husband wanting to kill me"

"The Left-out Mouse. One day, a mouse went outside to play with other mice. The mice said that the mouse can't play with us. So the mouse went to bed. The next day a cat came along. The cat said that the mouse could be his friend, but the cat ate up the mouse."
Score: 1 point
Rejecting treacherous and murderous relationships

The Left-out Mouse

Figure 7.10 "The Left-Out Mouse"

2 Points

The score of 2 points is used to characterize moderately negative themes or fantasies about the subjects or relationships portrayed; for example,

2a. subjects who are frustrated, fearful, fearsome, or unfortunate.

Score: 2 points
Frustrated, unfortunate subject

Figure 7.11. "How much she wish the apple"

Score: 2 points
Fearful subjects

Figure 7.12. "One day there was a girl standing by a tree and she was scared because it was moving like a person"

Score: 2 points

"The boy is making fun of the duck and the duck is crying. The boy don't have any feeling for the duck but the duck dose for the boy when he get tisted (teased). The End."

Figure 7.13. "The boy is making fun of the duck."

Three Art Assessments

Score: 2 points
Fearsome subject

Figure 7.14. "The Evil Deprived Young Man"

Score: 2 points
Frustrated, fearful, unfortunate subject

Figure 7.15. "Oops! this isn't the spot they promised me i'd land. a hot seat! pow! zing! zap! yike! hey! i'm outta here!"

3 Points

The score of 3 points, the intermediate score, is used to characterize responses that are both negative and positive, ambivalent, ambiguous, or unemotional, for example

3a. Subjects or relationships that suggest conflict or ambivalence, opposing psychological attitudes, inconsistencies, or complexities

Score: 3a points
Both hostile and caring attitudes and relationships

Figure 7.16. "The cat who tried to save the rat."

Score: 3a points
Suggests conflict. Although volcanos are usually associated with explosive anger, this volcano,
flanked by scowling tornados, suggests a wish to express anger and fear of the consequences.

Figure 7.17. "Why do tornados hate me?"

"This story is about a mice who sits down on a dead branch and stares at the castle with admire feelings with the bright moon and the beautiful stars shining in the night."
Score: 3a points

Suggests low self-esteem and longing for a beautiful, inaccesible world

Figure 7.18. "Mice on a dead branch."

3c. Unemotional; no expression of feeling about the subjects or attitudes portrayed
Score: 3c points
Unemotional

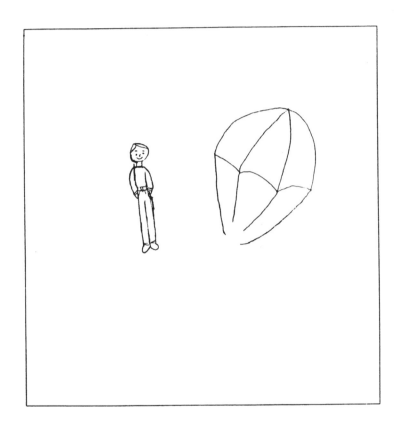

Figure 7.19. "There is no story. He's gonna go take a fly that's all"

Four Points

Score: 4 points
Friendly relationship

Figure 7.20. "Meeting. Hi! Hellow"

"This is a mouse and a baby chick that meet for the very first time. Since the mouse is been around a little longer, he's going to show the baby chick around."

Score: 4 points
Friendly relationship

Figure 7.21. "Mouse and baby chick"

5 Points

The score of 5 points is used to characterize strongly positive themes or fantasies about the subjects or relationships portrayed, for example,
5a. Subjects who are happy or taking action to achieve goals.

Score: 5 points
Successful subject
5b. Relationships that are caring or loving

Figure 7.22. "When birthday balloon took me back in time, I saved my ancestors' castle"

Score: 5 points
Caring relationship

Figure 7.23. "Walking My Dog"

Score: 5 points
Loving relationship

Figure 7.24. "The bride and the prince are getting married"

Chapter 8

Reliability and Validity of the Draw-a-Story Assessment

◇　　◇　　◇

To have reliability and validity, the DAS assessment should provide diagnostic criteria that accords with criteria in the literature. In addition, it should show consistency between scorers and consistency over periods of time, and its premises should be supported by objective evidence. This chapter begins with diagnostic criteria, proceeds to consistency, and concludes with studies of the relationship between clinical depression and strongly negative responses.

Diagnostic Criteria of Depressive Illness

The DAS score of 1 point is used to rate principal subjects who are portrayed as sad, isolated, helpless, suicidal, or in mortal danger, or else relationships between subjects that are destructive, murderous, or life-threatening, as defined and illustrated in chapter 7. This score is based on definitions and observations of depressive illness by clinicians.

As defined by the American Psychiatric Association's Diagnostic Criteria from *DSM-IV*, symptoms of depressive disorder include feelings of sadness, worthlessness, and hopelessness, as well as recurrent thoughts of death and suicidal ideation.

McKnew, Cytryn, and Yahraes (1983) noted the prevalence of violence, annihilation, aggressive behavior, and death in the fantasies of depressed children. Pfeffer (1986) distinguished suicidal from nonsuicidal children by their feelings of hopelessness, worthlessness, and the wish to die. The Beck Depression Inventory (1978) includes feelings of sadness, hopelessness, and thoughts of death or suicide. Shafer and Fisher (1981) studied 100 consecutive people who had committed suicide, most of whom had been diagnosed with depressive illness before their deaths.

Art therapist Linda Gantt (1990) noted that drawings by patients with depression have distinct patterns and seem closer to normal controls than drawings by patients with organic mental disorders or schizophrenia. She found no significant differences between drawings by patients who were depressed and those of the control group patients in problem solving, logic, integration, and realism. They differed from drawings by other psychiatric patients, however, by showing significantly greater use of logic and better problem-solving skills. They differed from drawings by patients with organic mental disorders by showing a significant increase in energy, integration, logic, and ability to solve problems.

Harriet Wadeson (1980) emphasized the formal attributes of drawings, such as the use of color or space. She asked patients with depression to make spontaneous drawings with colored chalks and found that their drawings showed more empty space than did the drawings of nondepressed individuals, showing less color, less effort, and either less affect or more depressive affect, such as harming others.

The DAS assessment emphasizes the emotional content of responses to the drawing task, rather than their formal attributes. Originally published in 1988, a revised edition was published in 1993 and updated in 1998. The questions whether strongly negative emotional content is linked to clinical depression and whether it persists over time were examined in the studies that follow.

Reliability

The DAS task has been administered to 1,028 children, adolescents, and adults by art therapists in various parts of the country who volunteered their assistance. They included 14 art therapists who administered the task to 446 subjects with no known impairments, residing in Florida, Kansas, New Jersey, New York, Ohio, Minnesota, and Missouri. In addition, 34 art therapists administered the task to 449 subjects with emotional disturbances, clinical depression, delinquency, or learning disabilities in Arizona, California, Florida, Georgia, New Jersey, New York, Maine, Montana, Pennsylvania, Minnesota, and Oregon. Most of these responses may be found in the archives of the American Art Therapy Association.

To determine the scorer reliability of the rating scale, three registered art therapists scored (blindly and independently) 20 unidentified responses to DAS Form A. The responses were chosen at random from five clinical and nonclinical groups of children and adolescents. Before scoring, the judges met for about an hour to discuss scoring procedures. The correlations between scores were highly significant, at the .001 level of probability. Between Judges A and B, the correlation coefficient was .806; between Judges A and C, .749; between Judges B and C, .816.

To determine test–retest reliability, 24 third-graders were presented with the Form A task on two occasions. Twelve of these presumably normal children responded with strongly or moderately negative fantasies. When they were retested after an interval of approximately 1 month, 7 received the same scores, 3 had higher scores, and 2 had lower scores (from 2 points to 1 point). When 12 other children were retested after an interval of approximately 2 years, 11 received the same scores they had received previously. The consistency of the responses suggests that the scale is reliable.

Based on these findings, the DAS assessment seems to be reliable. The findings also suggest a link between depressive illness and strongly negative responses. Although strongly negative responses do not necessarily indicate depression and, conversely, positive responses do not exclude depression, they suggest that a child or adolescent scoring 1 point may be at risk for depression.

The findings also indicated that negative feelings persisted over time, suggesting that they reflected characteristic attitudes rather than passing moods.

A third observation was that a comparatively large proportion of subjects with learning disabilities scored 1 point, and that no significant differences emerged between their scores and the scores of patients diagnosed as clinically depressed. These findings suggested that additional studies would be worthwhile.

Additional Studies of Reliability

Subsequently, two studies examined the test–retest reliability or validity of the DAS assessment (Silver, 1993a). In the first, three registered art therapists presented the Form A set of stimulus drawings to children and adults who responded on two occasions. One therapist presented the task twice after a 1-week interval to 8 children with emotional disturbances in a New Jersey public elementary school. The second presented the task without a time interval to 6 adolescents with emotional disturbances, ages 14 to 18, in a summer art therapy program in Florida. The third presented it to 17 men and women in Florida who volunteered to participate anonymously. Significant correlations were found between first and second responses of the 31 subjects (.70262, $p < 0.000$). Correlation for the 8 children was 0.93277, $p < 0.000$; for the adolescents and adults combined, .45095, $p < .05$.

In addition, the retest and scorer reliability of DAS Form B was examined (Silver, 1993). In this study, 33 children, adolescents, and adults responded twice. They included normal subjects, as well as those who had been diagnosed previously as depressed or emotionally disturbed, or else had attention deficit disorders or learning disabilities.

Two judges independently scored the responses, which were identified only by number. They scored first and second drawings on different days. To determine the degree of their agreement in assigning scores, separate interscorer correlations were calculated for the first 33 responses marked A, the 33 second responses marked B, and the combined 66 A/B responses. Interscorer correlations were significant. The correlation for A scores was .83943, $p < 0.000$; for B scores: .74054; for combined A and B scores: .80806, $p < 0.000$.

In addition, 17 students in a graduate art therapy program presented the DAS Form B task on two occasions to 34 children, adolescents, and adults. The interscorer reliability was .59, .63, and .60.

These studies also suggest that DAS Form A is a reliable measure.

Screening Children and Adolescents for Depression

The first study asked whether drawings could be used for the early identification of depressive illness (Silver, 1988a). We had noticed that children and adolescents seemed to be less guarded in expressing themselves through drawings than through talk, and that a few drew about suicide when responding to the SDT Drawing from Imagination task and more than a few drew fantasies about death, dying, or hopeless situations. Were they depressed? In search of answers, we selected 14 stimulus drawings from the Stimulus Drawing Assessment (Silver, 1986) and revised its rating scale.

Subjects included 254 children and adolescents between the ages of 8 and 21. Of these, 111 were presumably normal, 21 had clinical depression, 61 had emotional disturbances with nondepressive psychopathology, 31 had learning disabilities, and 24 were nondepressed children who responded to the Drawing from Imagination task on two occasions. Nineteen art therapists, teachers, and school counselors volunteered to administer the task or score responses. They resided in Arizona, Montana, New Jersey, New York, Oregon, and Pennsylvania. Their names and my appreciation are in the acknowledgments to this book.

Approximately 56% of the subjects with depression responded with strongly negative fantasies, scoring 1 point, compared with 11% of the normal subjects, 21% of the emotionally disturbed, and 32% of the subjects with learning disabilities.

To determine whether the differences were significant, a chi-square analysis found that significantly more subjects with depression than nondepressed subjects scored 1 point (27.63, $p < .001$). The proportion of subjects with depression scoring 1 point was also greater than the proportion of subjects with emotional disturbances scoring 1 point (10.54, $p < .01$), but was not significantly greater than the proportion of subjects with learning disabilities scoring 1 point (3.269, $p < .05$).

Second Study of Depression

Building on these findings, a second study increased the number of subjects to 350 children and adolescents and again asked whether strongly negative responses to the DAS task were associated with clinical depression (Silver, 1988b). Twenty-four art therapists, teachers, and school counselors volunteered their assistance.

The subjects included 35 children or adolescents with depression, 15 adults with depression, 117 presumably normal children and adolescents, 74 children and adolescents with emotional disturbances and nondepressive psychopathology, 64 adolescents with learning disabilities, 18 children and adolescents with hearing impairments, and 27 older adults residing in Pennsylvania, Arizona, Georgia, Montana, Illinois, New Jersey, New York, and Oregon. Their responses were evaluated on a scale ranging from strongly negative to strongly positive themes.

Results and Observations

Approximately 63% of the children and adolescents with depression responded with strongly negative themes, scoring 1 point, whereas approximately 10% of the nondepressed children and adolescents scored 1 point, as shown in figure 8.1 and table 8.1.

To determine whether the differences between subjects with depression and nondepressed subjects were significant, a chi-square analysis was conducted. The proportion of children and adolescents with depression scoring 1 point was significantly greater than the proportion of any other group scoring 1 point: Compared with the presumably normal children and adolescents, the chi square was 43.2, $p < .0005$, compared with that of people who had emotional disturbances, 20.6, $p < .0005$; compared with that of subjects who had learning diasbilities, 11.1, $p < .001$; compared with that of subjects who had hearing impairments, 19.5, $p < .0005$; compared with that of older persons, 20.0, $p < .0005$; and compared with the chi square of adults with depression, 10.4, $p < .005$ (see table 8.2).

These findings suggest that strongly negative responses to the DAS task are associated with adolescent or childhood depression. They also suggest that the DAS instrument could serve as a first step in identifying some, but not all, children and adolescents with depression. Although strongly negative responses did not necessarily indicate depression—and, conversely, positive responses did not exclude depression—the findings seem to indicate that a child or adolescent who responds with a strongly negative fantasy may be at risk, and that further examination by a mental health professional would be justified.

The findings about children and adolescents with depression did not apply to adults with depression. Only 2 of the 11 adults with depression scored 1 point, whereas 9 received the neutral score of 3 points (ambivalent, ambiguous, or unemotional).

Did this indicate that responses by depressed adults tend to be ambivalent, ambiguous, unemotional, or more guarded than responses by children and adolescents with depression? Where the adults being treated more successfully? Would a self-report or evaluation of formal elements, such as the use of space or detail, clarify the responses by adults with depression? A follow-up study was undertaken.

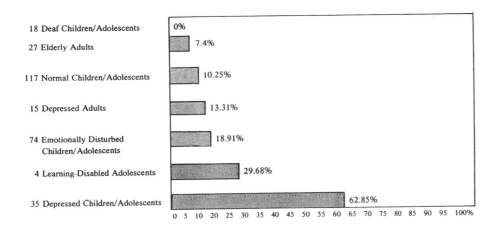

Figure 8.1. DAS Responses by Depressed and Nondepressed Subjects

---

Table 8.1

Comparing Responses to the Draw-a-Story Task by Children, Adolescents, and Adults Who Are Depressed, Normal, Emotionally Disturbed, Learning-Disabled, and Deaf

Ages: Scores*	35 Chil/Adols with Depression 6–17	117 Normal Chil/Adols 5–19	74 Chil/Adols w/Emot. Disturb. 8–21	64 Adults w/Learn. Disabil. 14–20	18 Chil/Adols w/Deafness 9–18	27 Older Adults	15 Adults w/Depression 24–59
1 point	22 (62.9%)	12 (10.3%)	14 (18.9%)	19 (29.7%)	0	2 (7.4%)	2 (13.3%)
2 points	3 (8.56%)	46 (39.3%)	23 (31%)	14 (21.8%)	9 (50%)	2 (7.4%)	2 (13.3%)
3 points	1	12	6	3	0	2	0
4 points	5 (14.3%)	18 (15.3%)	18 (24.3%)	12 (18.8%)	-3 (16.7%)	4 (14.8%)	9 (60%)
5 points	2	7	10	4	3	11	0
6 points	1	18	3	8	2	5	1
7 points	1	4	0	4	1	1	1

---

* 1 point: strongly negative responses
 2 points: moderately negative responses
 3 points: mildly negative responses, self-disparaging humor
 4 points: unemotional, ambivalent, or unclear responses
 5 points: mildly positive responses, survivor humor
 6 points: moderately positive responses, aggressive humor
 7 points: strongly positive responses

Use of Space
1 point: less than one fourth of the area is covered by the drawing
2 points: less than one third of the area
3 points: approximately half of the area
4 points: approximately two thirds of the area
5 points: entire drawing area

Use of Detail
1 point: copying or stick figures, no added detail
2 points: few new details or changes
3 points: moderate amount of details are added
4 points: many details, moderately original or expressive
5 points: many details, highly original and expressive

Self-Report
1 point: sad or very unhappy
2 points: angry, frightened, or unhappy
3 points: response is unclear
4 points: O.K. or happy
5 points: very happy

Figure 8.2. Rating Scales for Assessing the Use of Space, the Use of Detail, and the Self-Report, Later Eliminated

---

Table 8.2

Analysis of Differences in the Proportion of Strongly Negative Responses Among Children, Adolescents, and Adults Who Are Depressed, Normal, Emotionally Disturbed, Learning-Disabled, and Hearing-Impaired

---

	Depressed Children & Adolescents	Normal
1 point	22	12
2 or more points	13	105 $\chi^2 = 43.2$
		$p < .0005$

	Depressed Children & Adolescents	Emotionally Disturbed
1 point	22	14
1 or more points	13	83 $\chi^2 = 20.6$
		$p < .0005$

	Depressed Children & Adolescents	Learning-Disabled
1 point	22	19
2 or more points	13	45 $\chi^2 = 11.1$
		$p < .001$

	Depressed Children & Adolescents	Deaf
1 point	22	0
2 or more points	13	18 $\chi^2 = 19.5$
		$p < .0005$

	Depressed Children & Adolescents	Elderly
1 point	22	2
2 or more points	13	25 $\chi^2 = 20.0$
		$p < .0005$

	Depressed Children & Adolescents	Depressed Adults
1 point	22	2
2 or more points	13	13 $\chi^2 = 10.4$
		$p < .005$

Although most of the findings supported the findings of the first study, there was one significant difference. In the field trial, no significant difference was found between the scores of 31 subjects with learning disabilities and the scores of the group with clinical depression. In the second study, however, with a larger group of 64 subjects with learning disabilities, a significant difference was found between their scores and the scores of the group with depression, at the .001 level.

Third Study of Depression

This study examined age and gender differences in responses to the DAS task by 103 adults and adolescents who had and did not have depression (Silver, 1993a). The sample with depression included 47 patients hospitalized for depression in Georgia (18 girls and women, ages 12 to 69; and 23 boys and men, ages 17 to 53). The nondepressed sample included residents of a nursing home in Pennsylvania and undergraduate university students in Florida (34 women, ages 19 to 72, and 26 men, ages 20 to 77).

In addition to the DAS stimulus drawings and rating scale, the study included experimental scales for assessing the use of space and detail (figure 8.2) and a self-report was added below the drawing and story (as shown in figure 7.4).

Based on an analysis of variance for depression and the use of space and detail, no significant effects emerged for the depression groups, no difference in the use of space and only gender differences in the use of detail (F [1,103] = 4.27, p < .05). Females used significantly less detail (mean = 1.84) than males (mean = 2.31).

Results

The following analyses were conducted to evaluate differences between subjects with depression and nondepressed subjects on various indicators of the DAS (content, use of space, and use of detail).

A depression group (depressed, nondepressed) by gender (male, female) analysis of variance was conducted for depression, use of space, and use of detail. There was a significant gender difference in use of detail (F [1,103] = 4.27, p < .05). Females use significantly less detail (mean = 1.84) than males (mean = 2.31). No significant effects for the depression group were found.

In the 1988 study, the DAS score of 1 point was associated with depression, whereas all other scores were not. In addition, the scores are used to mean different things: 1–2 for negative themes, 3 for neutral themes (ambivalent, ambiguous, or unemotional), and 4–5 for positive themes. Thus, the DAS scores may be looked at as a categorical variable. Chi-square analyses were conducted to look for differences in the proportion of negative, neutral, and positive themes for various groups.

A group with depression (depressed, nondepressed) by drawing affect theme (negative, neutral, positive) 2 × 3 chi-square analysis was conducted. Overall, the two groups with depression did not differ significantly in the proportion of negative, neutral, and positive drawings.

A gender (male, female) by drawing affect theme (negative, neutral, positive) 2 × 3 chi-square analysis was conducted on the group with depression, nondepressed group, and the total group. Chi square was significant for the group with depression only (chi square (1, 2) = 8.61, p < .05). The males with depression tended to have drawings with negative themes, whereas the females with depression tended to have drawings with neutral themes. Nondepressed men and women did not differ significantly.

Comparing subjects with depression and nondepressed subjects within gender, we found no significant effects at the .05 level of significance. However, at the $p < .10$ level, there were differences in the proportion of negative drawings for males with depression and nondepressed males. Men with depression tended to have more negative drawings than nondepressed men (chi square $[1, 2] = 4.96$, $p < .10$). Since this level of statistical significance is considered borderline, further study seems warranted.

Discussion

Findings of the three studies suggest that strongly negative responses to the DAS task are associated with childhood depression and may be associated with depression among adolescents and men. The association with adolescent depression is unclear, because the adolescent samples were combined with other samples in both studies. In the 1988a study, adolescents with depression were combined with children who had depression because the samples were too small for separate statistical analyses. For the same reason, the 1993 study combined the sample of 7 male adolescents with depression with the 15 men who had depression, and the 7 female adolescents with depression with the 18 women who had depression.

Although the men with depression responded with negative themes to a significant degree, the significance of their difference from nondepressed males was borderline.

The studies did not find that strongly negative responses to the DAS task were associated with depression in women. However, the question remains as to whether neutral responses are associated. The 1988a study found that 9 of the 11 adults with depression responded with neutral themes; the 1993 study found that the chi-square analysis was significant for the group with depression and that females with depression tended to produce drawings with neutral themes. This raises the question of whether depression among women is associated with ambivalent or ambiguous themes (comparatively few women drew pictures with unemotional themes).

When the two formal attributes of drawings were evaluated, female drawings showed significantly fewer details than male drawings, but no difference was found between drawings of subjects with depression and those of nondepressed subjects, either in the use of detail or in the use of space. Consequently, the scale for assessing space and detail was eliminated.

Because no significant difference was found between respondents with depression and nondepressed respondents, either in the use of detail or the use of space, scales for assessing space and detail have been eliminated from the DAS assessment. The self-report, however, has been retained for the following reasons.

The Self-Report and Masked Depression

The brief self-report below the written story asks respondents to check the appropriate empty space in following sentence: "Just now I'm feeling ____very happy ___ O.K. ____ angry ____ frightened ___sad."

Surprisingly, most examinees responded by checking "very happy" or "O.K.," even when they were hospitalized for clinical depression and drew pictures about sadness or death. The inconsistency suggested that they were in fact depressed, but that their

It may be that drawings are less guarded than words; less vulnerable to denial than traditional, verbal self-reports; or less vulnerable to conscious deception and the desire to please. In addition, we found that even misleading self-reports were valuable in follow-up discussions. Consequently, the self-report remains in the DAS assessment.

This chapter concludes the review of studies concerned with the reliability and validity of the DAS assessment. The following chapter reviews studies in which 10 art therapists have used DAS in different ways for different purposes in working with clinical and nonclinical children, adolescents, and adults.

Chapter 9

Using DAS with Clinical and Nonclinical Populations

◇   ◇   ◇

This chapter reviews 10 studies by art therapists who used Draw a Story for different purposes. Their subjects included respondents with no known disabilities, as well as children, adolescents, and adults with emotional disturbances, clinical depression, delinquency, brain injuries, learning disabilities, and those who were abused.

Adolescents with and without Emotional Disturbances

This study examined responses to DAS Form A by 95 adolescents, ages 13 to 17, who had been diagnosed previously as having emotional disturbances. Sixty-eight presumably nondisturbed adolescents served as controls. The adolescents included four subgroups: 35 girls with disturbances, 60 boys with disturbances, 42 control girls, and 26 control boys. Thirteen art therapists or teachers administered the task to the disturbed students in special schools, special classes in public schools, or psychiatric facilities in Florida, Georgia, Nebraska, New York, and Oregon. Six art therapists or teachers administered it to the control students in four public schools and one private school in Florida, Minnesota, New York, and Ohio. Chi-square analyses were performed by Madeline Altabe, PhD, to determine the proportions of each group in obtaining certain scores.

Results

Significant differences were found between groups that were disturbed and control groups. As might be expected, fewer adolescents with disturbances than control adolescents responded with positive themes, scored 4 and 5 points, as shown in table 9.1. The chi square for this analysis was significant (chi square [1] = 13.26). The group of normal girls had the most positive scores (43%) followed by the boys with disturbances (26%), normal boys (16%), and girls with disturbances (14%).

In scoring 5 points, twice as many adolescents in the control group drew fantasies about caring relationships or effective solitary subjects (18% controls, 9% disturbed), as shown in figure 9.1. More than six times as many control girls as control boys scored 5 points (26% vs. 4%), while about twice as many boys with disturbances than girls with disturbances scored 5 points (20% vs. 11%).

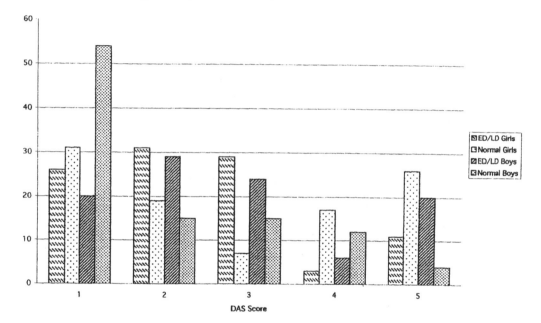

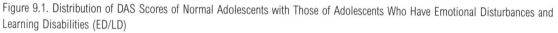

Figure 9.1. Distribution of DAS Scores of Normal Adolescents with Those of Adolescents Who Have Emotional Disturbances and Learning Disabilities (ED/LD)

In scoring 4 points, five times more control than adolescents with disturbances drew pictures about friendly relationships or fortunate but passive solitary subjects (15% of control, 3% of disturbed). Even greater differences emerged between the two groups of girls (3% of girls with disturbances, 17% of controls). This difference also was statistically significant (chi square [1] = 9.8). Although more control boys than boys with disturbances scored 4 points, only twice as many did so (12% vs. 6%), not significant.

In negative responses to the DAS task, boys in the control group had most of the extreme negative scores (1 point). This result also was significant (chi square [1] = 4.88). No significant differences were found between the girls who scored 2 points.

There were no significant patterns within the groups for a score of 2, 3, or 4 points. The pattern of results for a score of 5 points (control girls being more positive than their counterparts with disturbances; control boys received this score less frequently than their counterparts with disturbances) was significant (chi square [1] = 16.72). Thus, it can be said that control boys had more of the most negative scores and less of the most positive scores.

Observations

It was surprising to find the girls with disturbances less inclined to portray friendly relationships or fortunate solitary subjects than were girls in the control group, to significant degrees. It was also surprising that no significant differences emerged between the two groups in portraying stressful relationships or unfortunate solitary subjects. These findings may reflect denial of loneliness or avoidance of painful associations and suggest that the absence of positive themes in their responses may be more meaningful than the presence of negative themes.

The finding that the presumably normal boys drew morbid fantasies about assaultive relationships significantly more often than the boys with disturbances is less surprising because similar findings emerged in a previous study that compared incarcerated male adolescents with a control group (Silver, 1996b). This study is reviewed later in this chapter.

The findings raise the question of whether expanding the age range or increasing the number of respondents will produce similar results. If so, the paucity of positive scores may prove more useful than the prevalence of negative scores, in screening for emotional disturbance or masked depression.

Table 9.1

Comparing DAS Scores of 95 Adolescents with Disturbances, Ages 13 to 16, with 68 Controls

Adolescents	Scores					
	Mean	1pt	2 pts	3 pts	4 pts	5 pts
68 control	2.39	40%	18%	10%	15%	8%
95 disturbed	2.25	36%	31%	21%	3%	9%
42 control girls	2.88	31%	19%	7%	17%	26%
26 control boys	1.89	54%	15%	15%	12%	4%
35 girls with disturbances	2.43	26%	31%	29%	3%	11%
60 boys with disturbances	2.07	20%	29%	24%	6%	20%

Age and Gender Differences in Attitudes Toward Self and Others

Although previous studies had noted gender differences in response to the other two assessments (Silver, 1987a, 1992, 1993a), this pilot study was undertaken, in part, because it was reported that males tend to focus on independence and competition, whereas females focus on relationships and caring for others (Tannen, 1990; Gilligan, Ward, Taylor, & Bardige, 1988). These investigators had relied on verbal communication, raising the question of whether responses to the DAS task provided similar information.

DAS responses by 360 subjects were separated into drawings about solitary subjects and drawings about relationships, assigned to age and gender groups, and scored on the rating scale (Silver, 1993a). The respondents included children, adolescents, and adults who had clinical depression, emotional disturbances, learning disabilities, and those who were presumably unimpaired. Age and gender groups were then compared.

The respondents included 203 females and 157 males in five age groups: children ages 9 to 12; younger adolescents, ages 13 to 16; older adolescents, ages 17 to 19; younger adults, ages 21 to 64; and adults, age 65 or older. The 56 children included 32 girls and 24 boys. Thirty-three had been diagnosed as emotionally disturbed (ED) or learning disabled (LD), 14 were hospitalized as clinically depressed, and 9 were presumably normal. The 147 younger adolescents included 71 girls and 76 boys. Thirteen were hospitalized patients with depression, 78 had been diagnosed as ED or LD and attended special schools, and 56 were unimpaired. The 68 older adolescents included 30 girls and 38 boys: 1 hospitalized for clinical depression, 27 diagnosed as ED or LD, and 40 unimpaired. The 79 adults included 7 hospitalized women with depression and 53 non-depressed women and 19 men. Thirteen art therapists in 10 states volunteered to administer the DAS assessment. They resided in Arizona, Florida, Georgia, Maine, Montana, New Jersey, New York, Ohio, Pennsylvania, and Washington.

Results

In drawings about solitary subjects, no gender differences emerged. Both males and females expressed more negative than positive attitudes toward the subjects they portrayed, as indicated in table 9.4. Across the five female age groups, 41% of the responses portrayed sad or helpless (1 point) or angry or fearful subjects (2 points), compared with 28% who drew fantasies about passive or active pleasures (4 and 5 points). Across male age groups, 49% scored 1 and 2 points, compared with 27% who scored 4 and 5 points. The young boys expressed the most negative attitudes, 75% scoring 1 point, whereas none of the girls scored 1 point. The older women were the most positive: 41% drawing solitary subjects engaged in active pleasures; 12%, in passive pleasures.

In drawings about relationships, however, gender differences emerged. Male responses tended to be more negative—72% portraying assaultive and stressful relationships—compared with 34% of the females, as shown in table 9.5. On the other hand, 9% of the males and 29% of the females portrayed friendly and caring relationships.

The most negative relationships appeared in drawings by boys (80%), younger adolescents (75%), and older adolescents (67%), whereas female relationships tended to be mixed (34% negative, 29% positive, 37% neutral).

More positive relationships appeared in drawings by older women than any other age or gender group, 46% scoring 4 and 5 points. Proportionally more women than men portrayed active solitary pleasures (41% women, 20% men).

Proportionally more adolescent girls than any other female age group drew fantasies about sad, helpless, or isolated solitary subjects, scoring 1 point (35% of girls ages 13 to 16; 43% of those ages 17 to 19), as well as stressful relationships, scoring 2 points (30% of those ages 13 to 16, 38% of those ages 17 to 19).

These findings are inconsistent with the observation that females tend to focus on relationships and responsibility to others and males on independence and detachment. More males than females portrayed relationships, and both genders drew relationships more often than they drew solitary subjects.

Responses to the drawing task suggest that gender differences are reflected in the *emotional content* of the relationships portrayed. Males tended to portray negative relationships; females, positive relationships.

Table 9.4

Age and Gender Differences in Fantasies About Solitary Subjects: Comparing Proportions of Scored Responses to the DAS Task

Score:			1 Sad or Helpless	2 Angry or Fearful	3 Ambiv./ Ambig.	4 Passive	5 Active
Gender Age		No.					
Female							
	9–12	12	0	1 8%	8 67%	1 8%	2 17%
	13–16	34	12 35%	4 12%	10 29%	1 3%	7 21%
	17–19	14	6 43%	2 14%	4 29%	1 7%	1 7%
	21–64	8	2 25%	2 25%	2 25%	0	2 25%
	65+	17	3 18%	3 18%	2 12%	2 12%	7 41%
	Totals	85	23 27%	12 14%	26 29%	5 6%	19 22%
			Negative: 33 41%		Positive: 24 28%		
Male							
	9–12	4	3 75%	0	0	0	1 25%
	13–16	15	1 7%	3 20%	4 27%	2 13%	5 33%
	17–19	11	6 55%	2 18%	3 27%	0	0
	48–65	2	0	0	1 50%	1 50%	0
	65+	5	1 20%	2 40%	1 20%	0	1 20%
	Totals	37	11 30%	7 19%	9 24%	3 8%	7 19%
			Negative: 18 49%		Positive: 10 27%		

			Table 9.5				

Age and Gender Differences in Fantasies About Relationships: Comparing Proportions of Scored Responses to the DAS Task

Score: Gender Female	Age	No.	1 Assaultive	2 Stressful	3 Amb.	4 Friendly	5 Caring
	9–12	20	1 5%	5 25%	7 35%	3 15%	4 20%
	13–16	37	5 14%	11 30%	12 32%	2 5%	7 19%
	17–19	16	2 13%	6 38%	6 38%	0	2 13%
	21–64	17	0	4 24%	10 59%	1 6%	2 12%
	65+	28	4 14%	2 7%	9 32%	7 25%	6 21%
	Totals	118	12 12%	28 24%	44 37%	13 11%	21 18%

Negative: 40 34%   Positive: 34 29%

Male	Age	No.	1 Assaultive	2 Stressful	3 Amb.	4 Friendly	5 Caring
	9–12	20	10 50%	6 30%	3 15%	0	1 5%
	13–16	16	32 52%	14 23%	11 18%	3 5%	1 2%
	17–19	27	13 48%	5 19%	6 22%	3 11%	0
	49–64	3	1 33%	0	2 66%	0	0
	65+	9	2 22%	3 33%	2 22%	2 22%	0
	Totals	120	58 48%	28 24%	24 20%	8 7%	2 2%

Negative: 86 72%   Positive: 10 9%

Ellison and Silver's Study of Adolescents Who Are Delinquents

Joanne Ellison, ATR-BC, investigated the possible benefits of using DAS to provide rapid assessment of its young male offenders in a probation camp, so that more accurate and timely mental health referrals could be made (Silver & Ellison, 1995, part 2). She found very little resistance, in part because of the structured setting, but, for some, she noted, "it was like giving food to the starving." She observed that DAS circumvented stereotyping and written components with symbolic pictures that provide clues to intentions. She illustrated these and other observations with case studies. She also observed that many of her clients were more kinesthetic than verbal, that sad and aggressive stories may indicate depression, and that happy fantasies may indicate denial on the part of youths who are equally depressed, and who may be more resistant to treatment.

Ellison concluded that a structured art assessment, such as DAS Forms A or B, can be useful in the evaluation of juveniles with conduct disorders. Their drawings can help us understand the concerns and occasionally the underlying dynamics of these individuals.

This study also investigated three questions: Can art therapists identify self-images without knowing who drew them? Can they agree when identifying self-images? Can social workers agree when identifying self-images?

Ellison presented DAS Form B to 53 boys, ages 13 to 18, in the residential detention facility in California, then discussed their drawings with them individually and asked them to identify subjects who might represent themselves. Reserving their responses and her own judgments in a sealed envelope, she sent the drawings for blind evaluation to me in New York. After evaluating the drawings blindly, I sent my scores and Ellison's scores in the sealed envelope to Madeline Altabe, PhD, who analyzed the three sets of evaluations. She used the level of agreement between the 39 adolescents, Ellison, and myself, as an index of the validity of the self-image measure.

In addition, three other art therapists and five social workers rated self-images in 10 of the 53 response drawings selected at random. Agreements between the respondents, therapists, and social workers also were analyzed.

Of the 53 adolescents, 39 identified characters in their drawings as themselves. Ellison, who knew their histories and conducted the interviews, accurately matched 77%. Judging blindly, I matched 72%. Interscorer agreement between Ellison and myself was 94.3%. The average agreement among the social workers was 54.0%; among the art therapists, 78.2%; and among the subgroup of three registered art therapists, 93%.

Approximately three out of four respondents agreed with Ellison and me about the self-images in their drawings (74.4%). Ellison agreed with two respondents who disagreed with me, suggesting that the absence of discussion caused me to judge, incorrectly, 2 of the 39 responses.

Although five respondents disagreed with both Ellison and me, we agreed with each other in identifying their self-images. Because our interscorer agreement of 94.3% suggests strong reliability, the five drawings that prompted disagreement were reexamined. For example, one of the five adolescents—Chris, age 16—was enrolled in the special education program. He performed at the eighth-grade level in reading, the seventh-grade level in mathematics, and fourth-grade level in spelling, as measured by tests used in the facility. In responding to the DAS task, he selected two stimulus drawings: the dejected person sitting on a chair and the couple with arms entwined. In discussing his drawing with Ellison, he said the seated man was sad and the couple was happy, because they had scored As on a spelling test while the man had scored an F. Asked how he would feel if he had been included in his drawing, Chris replied, that he "would be part of the group." The art therapists, judging independently, disagreed. Both identified the seated man as his self-image, suggesting that he felt a need to deny feeling sad or unfortunate, as well as a need to gratify a wish-fulfilling fantasy.

The findings suggested that discussion is not required for identifying self-images. Although discussion is preferable—and the more discussion, the more accurate interpretations and assessments are likely to be—the findings seemed to indicate that discussion can be bypassed in order to expedite screening, particularly in urgent situations, such as the need to identify someone who may be depressed or at risk for suicide, when circumstances or time limitations make interviews impossible.

Gender Differences in the Fantasies of Adolescents Who Are Delinquent and Those of Nondelinquent Adolescents

Self-images expressed in response to the DAS task were examined for differences in gender, age, and delinquency (Silver, 1996b). Building on the previous study, the subjects included 64 adolescents in detention in California and 74 normal controls attending schools in Ohio, New York, and Florida; 82 were males (53 were delinquent, 29 were controls) and 56 were females (11 were delinquent, 45 were controls). Their ages ranged from 13 to 17. The responses were divided into four groups: gender, delinquency, drawings about solitary subjects, and drawings about relationship. Mean scores were analyzed and compared.

The first analysis asked whether gender or delinquency was related to self-image scores; that is, to fortunate, unfortunate, or aggressive self-images. No significant differences were found. The male mean score was 2.52; the female mean score was 2.92.

The second analysis asked whether the proportions of drawings about solitary subjects or assaultive relationships differed, depending on delinquency or gender. Significant gender differences emerged in both solitary and assaultive content, and the finding of assaultive content was reversed for solitary content. Overall, males and females differed in both aggressive content (chi square [1] = 11.00, $p < .01$) and solitary content (chi square [1] = 6.33, $p < .05$); 31.7% of the males drew pictures about assaultive relationships, compared with 5.4% of the females.

In solitary content, however, 37.5% of the females drew pictures about solitary subjects, compared with 15.9% of the males. Solitary content also distinguished between delinquent and control groups: 33.8% of the control subjects drew solitary subjects as compared with 14.1% of the subjects who were delinquent.

Table 9.2 shows, the proportional differences in assaultive content found in drawings by delinquent and control, male and female adolescents. These differences reached significance (chi square [1] = 9.11, $p < .01$). The difference between males and females who were delinquent, however, did not reach significance (28.3% of the males drew assaultive relationships; no females who were delinquent drew assaultive relationships). Although males in the control group differed significantly from females in the control group, males who were delinquent did not differ significantly from females who were delinquent.

Table 9.2

Assaultive Content in the Drawings of Delinquent and Control, Male and Female Adolescents

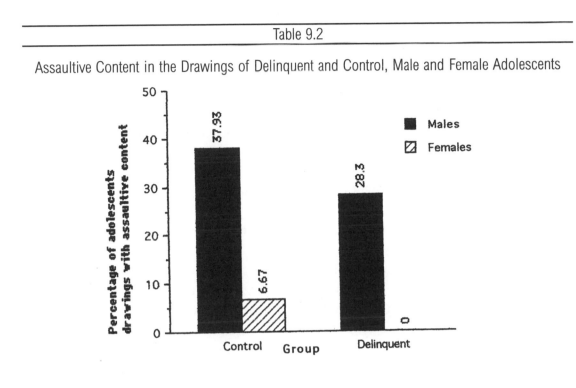

Table 9.3

Solitary Content in the Drawing of Delinquent and Control, Male and Female Subjects

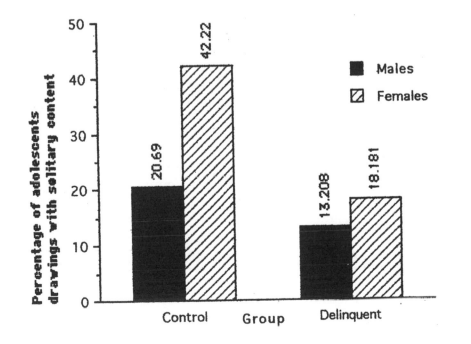

Control group males used aggressive humor in 45.4% of their assaultive drawings, but aggressive humor did not emerge in any other group. A group (delinquent vs. control) by gender (male vs. female) 2 x 2 ANOVA was conducted on the self-image rating. No significant results were found.

In drawings about solitary subjects, gender differences were large in the control group and small in the group that was delinquent, as shown in table 9.3. When negative attitudes toward solitary subjects were examined, gender differences emerged in both delinquent and control groups. Proportionally more females than males drew sad or helpless solitary subjects (females who were delinquent, 18.1%; control females, 17.8%; males who were delinquent, 9.4%; control males, 6.9%). When positive attitudes toward solitary subjects were examined, control groups predominated (control females, 20%; control males, 13.8%; males who were delinquent, 3.7%; females who were delinquent, 0.)

The gender difference was large in the control group but small in the group that was delinquent. Drawings by females who were delinquent were more like the male drawings of both groups. Thus, greater gender differences were found among normal adolescents than among adolescents who were delinquent.

To summarize, no differences in gender or delinquency were found when mean scores were examined, but differences appeared when drawings about assaultive relationships or solitary subjects were examined. Gender made a difference in negative responses scored 1 and 2 points. More than twice as many females as males drew sad or helpless solitary subjects (18% of females and 8% of males). Delinquency also made a difference in positive responses scored 4 and 5 points. Nondelinquent males outnumbered males who were delinquent (14% vs. 4%) in portraying fortunate subjects. No females who were delinquent, but 20% of the nondelinquent females, drew fortunate subjects. The effect was reversed for aggressive content. Females who were delinquent were more like males, regardless of delinquency.

It was surprising to find that proportionally more nondelinquent males than males who were delinquent drew fantasies about assaultive relationships. Perhaps the difference can be explained by the difference between fantasizing about violence and acting violently, or it may be that incarceration inhibits the expression of aggressive fantasies.

The finding that no females who were delinquent expressed positive feelings toward their solitary self-images suggests that they may be more at risk, or that incarceration has dimmed or extinguished their wish-fulfilling fantasies. On the other hand, the sample may have been too small.

Turner's Use of DAS with Adolescents Who Have Experienced Abuse

Christine Turner, ATR-BC (1993), has used the DAS with adolescent clients in a psychiatric hospital as one of a five-assessment series to assess possible history of abuse. She found it useful in assessing the extent of abuse, the meaning attached to abuse, and the effects of abuse on her clients' defenses, coping skills, sense of self, relationships, and worldview. She then made treatment recommendations to assist ward therapists in working with clients, and for after-care, as needed.

Turner asked her clients to respond to five requests: free subject, scribble drawing, kinetic family drawing, self-drawing, and Draw a Story, Form A, placing DAS last because she found that its more cognitive nature provided closure.

The emerging themes often confirmed impressions derived from the preceding four drawings and other sources. Occasionally, however, the adolescent who had produced four guarded, stereotypical images experienced greater freedom in working with the DAS cartoon figures and metaphorical story telling. Conversely, the client who accessed and expressed painful feelings might use the DAS to "regroup" and condense the content of the other four drawings into a safely distanced metaphor.

The client's areas of greatest need may be depicted and described in responses to the DAS. Cognitive schemas relating to the need also may be apparent. Beliefs concerning attribution of causality, locus of control, concerns about self-protective abilities, trust and mistrust, self-value, and community attachments suggested by DAS responses became topics for discussion in the assessment interviews. During the discussion, whether clients remain metaphorical or relate the DAS drawing to events in their own lives, the therapists have the opportunity to begin addressing treatment needs, confirming reality, and laying the groundwork for future therapy.

Wilson's Use of DAS with Patients Who Had Brain Injuries

Mary Wilson, ATR (1993), used DAS Form A to assess the emotional outlook and skills of inpatients and outpatients who had sustained brain injuries in accidents, assaults, strokes, or aneurysms. To assess word-finding difficulty, identification skills, and speaking ability, she presented the stimulus drawings mounted on a cardboard background, asking patients to identify each image. To assess ability to establish relationships and to create and organize images, she noted the patient's ability to combine subjects and show something happening between them. She also examined executive functioning, reasoning, problem-solving abilities, and field-neglect problems, which became evident if the patient drew closer to one side of the page or the other. During the story-writing stage of the task, she observed reading and writing skills.

As a member of the clinical treatment team trying to assess a patient's strengths and weaknesses, Wilson found that DAS served to reinforce the findings of other therapists, and in many instances, contributed information about emotional outlook, depression, and fantasies. She found that patients almost always projected themselves into their drawings and stories, offering material about their emotional inner lives. They revealed issues of low self-esteem, concerns about adjustment to disability, and depression over losses.

Wilson's Use of DAS with Adolescents Who Had Contemplated or Attempted Suicide

Wilson, ATR (1990), also has discussed using the assessment with hospitalized adolescents who are depressed and suicidal. She administered it during the first session of a biweekly treatment program and again months later to gain insight into changes in emotional outlook and how the sense of self and environment were evolving. Of 13 respondents, 12 drew pictures about negative or severely frightening events. Only 1 response was positive. Wilson found the task useful for assessing her patients' emotional states and how they viewed their situations.

Dunn-Snow's Use of DAS with Children and Adolescents Experiencing Emotional Disturbances

Peggy Dunn-Snow, ATR-BC (1994), used DAS Form A to assess the needs of students who were diagnosed with severe emotional disturbances but were able to attend elementary and secondary schools in a large urban school district. She also adapted DAS for use as a therapeutic technique, presenting a case study in which she used the task to determine whether a high school student was depressed. After he responded with self-destructive thoughts, she checked school records and discovered he had history of clinical depression; she then used the task to help him resolve feelings about the death of his father.

Dunn-Snow also used DAS in working with students who became anxious when asked to do relatively free-choice artwork. She found that it provided a second-grader with sufficient structure and support to begin making art, and it broke down resistance among students who previously refused to participate.

In addition, Dunn-Snow adapted DAS for group therapy and to resolve conflicts. In working with fifth-grade boys, she used it to provide structure and set limits, inviting each boy to choose a subject, then collaborate with others in the group by combining their images into a single drawing with a common theme, title, and storyline. She noted that in accomplishing this task, her students followed directions, accepted limits, solved problems, made compromises, and communicated effectively.

Coffey's Use of DAS in a Psychiatric Hospital

C. M. Coffey, in her master's thesis (1995), found that male and female patients in the psychiatric units of two hospitals seemed to have different needs and suggested that gender be considered in planning therapeutic treatment. Males seemed more reticent to reveal themselves to anyone. Females seemed less apt to recognize their rights or self-worth and were fearful that moving toward one goal forecloses other goals. Some patients were very agitated, some abused equipment or themselves, and others displayed a heavy, pervasive sadness. She observed that projective drawing appeared less threaten-ing to evasive or resistant patients than tests like the TAT or Rorschach, and served to establish rapport, uncover areas of patient interests, indicate abilities, and reveal defense mechanisms.

Brandt's Comparison of Adolescents with Depression and Those Who Committed Sex Offenses to Typical Adolescents

Michele Brandt, in her master's thesis (1995), examined the importance of visual arts in assessing and treating adolescents who committed sex offenses, comparing them with typical adolescents and adolescents who are depressed. Participating in her study were 14 males in a residential facility who committed sex offenses, ages 12 to18, averaging 16 years. She compared their mean score on the DAS (1.89) with the mean scores of typ-ical adolescents (2.73) and adolescents with depression (3.14). The findings suggested that those committing sex offenses are likely to be depressed and to perceive themselves and their world in negative ways. The findings also suggested that art expression enables those who work with adolescents committing sex offenses to tap into emotionality and therefore is useful in treatment programs, which tend to emphasize cognition and behavior.

This review of studies by seven art therapists concludes section II. The following section presents the third assessment, Stimulus Drawings and Techniques.

Section III

Stimulus Drawing Techniques in Therapy, Development, and Assessment

Chapter 10

Introducing the Stimulus Drawing Techniques Assessment

◇   ◇   ◇

This chapter presents objectives, procedures, and guidelines for administering and scoring the third SD assessment. It also presents examples of scored responses. The assessment includes 50 stimulus drawings in four categories: people, animals, places, and things. Some are specific to suggest particular feeling states; others are ambiguous to encourage individual recollections and associations. This set of stimulus drawings is presented on 3" x 5" cards, instead of on pages in a test booklet. It can be found in appendix C.

The SD assessment, the first developed, uses 7-point rating scales to evaluate the emotional content of the principal subjects and environments portrayed in responses to the drawing task. Because distinguishing between "mildly" and "moderately" negative or positive themes provided little useful information, the distinction was eliminated in the SDT and DAS rating scales.

Objectives and Procedures of the SD Techniques

Therapeutic Techniques*

Materials: Drawing paper 8 1/2 x 11 inches or larger;
pencils with erasers, colored chalk, or marking pens;
the 50 stimulus drawings in Appendix C cut apart so that they can be handled individually.

Objectives	*Procedures*
1. to provide structure and support for those who may need them as an introduction to art therapy.	Present the SDs spread out in adjacent groups. You might say, "Here are some drawings you may find interesting. Do you think you can draw a picture using two of these picture ideas? Try to think of something happening between the drawings you choose. Then when you are ready, draw a picture of your own. Make your drawing tell a story. Show what is happening. Feel free to change these drawings and to use your own ideas."
2. to stimulate conscious and unconscious associations for insight into emotional needs and opportunities for follow-up.	
3. to provide opportunities to relieve tensions, ventilate anger, express fears indirectly, and fulfill wishes vicariously.	
4. to build self-esteem and a sense of achievement.	Minimize talk while drawing is in progress. Avoid interruptions, including your own.
5. to provide a record of emotional projections available at any time for discussion or review, or for evaluation on the rating scale, (page 191).	After response drawings are finished, ask for titles and initiate discussion.

---

*Caution: Psychotherapy is the province of mental health professionals. If someone without professsional training attempts to use psychotherapy, harm may result. Consequently, techniques of intervention and interpretation are beyond the scope of this book.

Developmental Techniques

Materials: Stimulus drawings in the categories of People, Animals, and Things presented in adjacent groups, the name card of each group surrounded by the appropriate drawings. Reserve the drawings of Places as indicated below.

At first, use paper and pencils with erasers. Later on, painting, pastels, clay, or other art materials.

Objectives	*Procedures*
1. to bypass language deficiencies in developing ability to form concepts, particularly the concept of a class or group of objects. This concept is said to be fundamental in mathematics (Piaget, 1970) and possibly in reading (Bannatyne, 1971).	ask students to look over the array of SDs, select one from each group, and imagine something happening between the subjects selected, then show what is happening in drawings of their own.
Although concepts usually are developed verbally, they also can be perceived and interpreted through visual thinking and drawing.	when response drawings are finished, ask for titles, and initiate discussions about the form and content of the drawings.
The ability to form concepts involves making selections and combining them into a context, such as selecting words and combining them into sentences. The drawing tasks involve selecting images and combining them into narrative pictures.	ask each student to return the SDs to the groups "where they belong."
2. to develop ability to select. Disturbance in this ability is associated with receptive language disorders (Jakobson, 1964).	scramble the SDs and present tasks such as "find the ones that belong together" or "this drawing goes with this one. Can you find another that belongs with them?"
3. to develop ability to combine as well as concepts of space which are also said to be fundamental in reading and mathematics.	add the SDs in the category of Places. In the time reserved for discussion, point out spatial relationships such as foreground and background.
4. to develop creativity and ability to represent.	show appreciation of originality and expressiveness.
5. to reinforce these experiences.	introduce other art materials.

Three Art Assessments

Assessment Techniques

Materials: Stimulus drawings, paper, pencils, and the scales for rating emotional content or cognitive skills.

Objectives	*Procedures*
1. to evaluate response drawings for emotional content: concepts of self, attitudes toward others, or clues to conflicts and concerns that may not be verbalized.	score response drawings as indicated in the scale on page 191.
2. to evaluate response drawings for cognitive and creative skills. These techniques may avoid the stress often associated with testing by using drawings rather than words as the principal instruments for receiving and expressing ideas.	score response drawings as indicated in the scale on page 192.
3. to assess individual progress or the effectiveness of therapeutic or educational programs.	date, number, score, and photocopy first and last response drawings as well as other key drawings. Score and examine for changes.

Table 10.1

Scale for Evaluating the Emotional Content of Principal Subjects and Environments of the Stimulus Drawing Assessment

Principal Subject(s)

1 point: Strongly negative, for example, subjects who are dead, dying, helpless, sad, or in grave danger.

2 points: Moderately negative, for example, subjects who are angry, frustrated, frightened, or suffering.

3 points: Mildly negative, for example, subjects who are dissatisfied or unfortunate.

4 points: Intermediate level, for example, subjects who are ambivalent (both negative and positive) or ambiguous (unclear or neither negative nor positive).

5 points: Mildly positive, for example, subjects who are smiling or enjoying something.

6 points: Moderately positive, for example, subjects who are effective, strong, or fortunate.

7 points: Strongly positive, for example, subjects who are loved, loving, or escaping or overcoming powerful forces.

Environment (including people, objects, and events)

1 point. Strongly negative, for example, life-threatening situations, dripping knives, or smoking guns.

2 points: Moderately negative, for example, dangerous, frustrating, stressful, or unfortunate situations.

3 points: Mildly negative, for example, unpleasant activities or scenes, rain, snow, dark clouds, deserts, storms, sunsets, or bare trees.

4 points: Intermediate level, for example, ambivalent situations (both negative and positive) or ambiguous situations (unclear or neither negative nor positive).

5 points: Mildly positive, for example, pleasant activities or scenes, flowers, fruits, sunrises, or leafy trees

6 points: Moderately positive, for example, tasty, friendly, pleasurable, or fortunate situations or events.

7 points: Strongly positive, for example, loving or deeply gratifying relationships.

Table 10.2

Scale for Evaluating Cognitive and Creative Skills Through Response Drawings*

<u>Content (Ability to Select)</u>
1 point: perceptual level: Subjects are unrelated in size or placement.
3 points: functional level: Concrete associations; what subjects do or what can be done to them.
5 points: goes beyond concrete associations: Abstract, imaginative idea; implies more than is visible.

<u>Form (Ability to Combine)</u>
1 point: subjects float in space, related only by proximity.
3 points: subjects are related along a base line, real or implied.
5 points: drawing shows overall coordination.

<u>Creativity (Ability to Represent)</u>
1 point. imitative, stick figures, or stereotypes.
3 points: changes or elaborates on SDs or stereotypes.
5 points: highly original, expressive, or playful; many details.

*Score 2 or 4 points for intermediate levels.

Score: 1 point, strongly negative

Figure 10.1. Untitled drawing by an 8-year-old boy who chose the stimulus drawing of the interior of a room

Score: 2 points, moderately negative

Figure 10.2. "The Desert Man," by another 8-year-old boy who chose the desert landscape

Score: 3 points, mildly negative

Figure 10.3. Untitled drawing About a Chick

Score: 4 points, neither negative or positive

Figure 10.4. "What goes up must come down," by an older woman

Score: 5 points, mildly positive

Figure 10.5. "Return from outer space," by another older woman

Score: 6 points, moderately positive

Figure 10.6. "Rappin Saurus," by an 18-year-old boy

Score: 7 points, strongly positive

Figure 10.7. "Midnight Break," by a young man

Chapter 11

Reliability and Validity

◇   ◇   ◇

To determine whether judges agree in scoring principal subjects and environments on the 7-point scales, three registered art therapists scored 24 responses to the SD drawing task (Silver, 1982a; 1997b). The responses included four drawings selected at random from each of six populations of normal children and adults.

Before scoring, the judges met for 1 hour to discuss the scale and to score and discuss practice drawings. Then the 24 response drawings were presented individually at random to the judges, who scored without further discussion.

In addition, the relationship between this assessment and the SDT was examined. We asked whether the scale could be used to evaluate responses to both this assessment and the SDT Drawing from Imagination subtest. With this in mind, 12 of the 24 responses in the reliability study were responses to this assessment, and 12 were responses to the subtest.

In the five analyses performed, agreement coefficients ranged from .924 to .549, as measured by Beatrice Krauss, PhD, using Finn's r^* (Whitehurst, 1984). For example, an $r = .80$ denotes 80% agreement beyond chance agreement.

The agreement coefficients were .803 for principal subject ($M = 4.86.$ $SD = 1.90$) and .549 for environment ($M = 4.06$, $SD = 2.10$). Thus the scale seems reliable.

No significant differences emerged in mean ratings of the subjects of this assessment and the SDT subtest ($T [22] = .8$, not significant). The results are shown in tables 11.1 and 11.2.

---

*Whitehurst, G. Interrater agreement for journal manuscript reviews, American Psychologist (1984, 39, 22–28). For example, an r = 80 denotes 00% agreement beyond chance agreement.

Thus, there appears to be consistency of measurement in the scale when it is used to assess responses to the set of stimulus drawings and the SDT Drawing from Imagination subtest.

Table 11.1

Agreement Coefficients for the Emotional Content Scale

Stimuli	Finn's *r*
Stimulus Drawing—Subject	.806
Stimulus Drawing—Environment	.549
SDT Subtest—Subject	.778
SDT Subtest—Environment	.924

Table 11.2

The Means and Standard Deviations of the Ratings for Each Set of Response Drawings

	M	SD
SDT Test—Subject	3.75	1.90
SDT Test—Environment	3.67	2.01
Stimulus Drawing—Subject	4.86	1.90
Stimulus Drawing—Environment	4.06	2.10

To examine retest reliability, 24 children in the third grade of a suburban public elementary school responded to the SD task on two occasions. When 12 children who had responded with negative fantasies were retested approximately 2 years later, 11 received the same scores. In addition, when 12 other children who responded with negative fantasies were asked to respond again 1 month later, 7 received the same scores, 3 were less negative, and 2 were more negative (Silver, 1988a).

The SD task was administered to 559 children and adults by Eileen McCormick Holzman, ATR-BC; Patricia Schachner; and myself during the early 1980s. At the time, statistical analyses were not yet available to me. Consequently, the remainder of this chapter is limited to consistency in responses to the drawing task by 5 individuals after an interval of 3 years. They responded for the first time when they were third-graders in the public school of a middle-class New York suburb and again when they were sixth-graders in the middle school of the same community, the only sixth-graders who had responded previously.

Mike

In the third grade, Mike, age 8, responded twice to the drawing task. For his first drawing, he chose stimulus drawings of the king, queen, and worm, then drew figure 11.1. As he finished drawing, he asked me to write inside the balloons, as he dictated the following dialogue:

Queen to pig: "Why did you bother me?"
Pig: "Oink! Oink! Because the butterfly is teasing me."
Butterfly, "I am not, liar."
Worm to king, "I want you to help me."
King to worm, "Why do you bother me like that? I am busy. I have to do my duty."

Mike's first response suggests that the king and queen represent his parents; the butterfly, his sister; and the worm and pig, himself. It received scores of 2 points in both principal subject and environment.

For his second response, Mike chose the chick, bear, and person hiding behind a tree. As he explained, "The bear was going to eat the little bird and the boy saw and he started to cry." In his drawing (figure 11.2), the person beside the tree is crying as well as watching and, with no arms or hands, seems unable to help the little bird. This drawing also scores 2 points in both principal subject and environment. In both responses to the drawing task, Mike seemed to represent himself as weak and helpless, living in a hostile environment.

Figure 11.1. "Why do you bother me?" by Mike, age 8

Figure 11.2. "The bear was going to eat the little bird," by Mike, age 8

At age 11, now in the sixth grade, Mike responded with five drawings; and for two of these drawings, Mike again chose the stimulus drawing of a person behind the tree. In a drawing entitled "Wach (sic) it. How's ther (sic)?" (figure 11.3a), the person is hiding behind a tree from the prince, who holds on a leash the toothy, open-mouthed dog. In the stimulus drawing, however, the leash hangs from the dog's collar.

In his second drawing, entitled, "The Killer" (11.3b) the person hides from the stimulus drawing of a man shooting an arrow at an unknown target. In Mike's drawing the target is the person behind the tree.

Three of Mike's five responses seem to be about weak or helpless protagonists in dangerous or rejecting worlds. In figure 11.3c, Mike chose the mouse, princess, and interior of a room, then drew the princess on a table; one mouse seems heading for a mousetrap, and, as he explained, the other mouse's tail is in the electrical outlet and the mouse is shocked.

Figure 11.3a. "Wach (sic) it. How's ther (sic)?" by Mike, age 11

Figure 11.3b. "The Killer," by Mike, age 11

Figure 11.3c. "The mouse is schocked (sic)," by Mike, age 11

Figure 11.4. "The man in the gabich (sic) can," by Mike, age 11

Like the fantasies he drew at age 8, Mike's subjects live in dangerous worlds and are rejected by a king, queen, princess, and prince. For his fourth drawing (not shown), Mike chose the lion and the parachutist. In the drawing, the parachutist is about to land near the lion onto the skull and bones of a previous meal.

For Mike's fifth and last drawing, he chose the city street, the scowling person leaning on an elbow, and the girl with a valise. His response, entitled "The man in the gabich can" (sic) is shown in figure 11.4.

Each of Mike's seven responses, at ages 8 and 11, seem to score 2 points, suggesting that anxiety, low self-esteem, and feelings of rejection were personality traits rather than passing moods.

Andy

At ages 8 and 11, Andy responded to the drawing task with fantasies about unidentified aggressors stabbing or shooting victims. For his first response (age 8) he chose the sword, man, and ladder and dictated this story: "The sword was on a ladder. It hit the man's butt and he fell in the pool" (figure 11.5). For his second response, he chose the ladder and amplified his first drawing with many details, as shown in figure 11.6. In both drawings, the sword seems responsible.

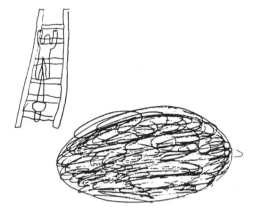

Figure 11.5. "The sword was on a ladder," by Andy, age 8

Figure 11.6. "The sword hit the man's butt," by Andy, age 8

At age 11, Andy chose the boots, gun, and alligator, then drew, "A strange kill" (figure 11.7). As he wrote, "The boots fell on the gun and the gun shot the alligator." Apparently, the gun did it. For his second drawing, Andy again chose the sword, dinosaur, and parachute, then drew "To Kill" (figure 11.8). The sword hangs from the parachute, and seems to be stabbing the dinosaur in the back.

Andy consistently drew fantasies about assailants and victims. He also consistently failed to identify the aggressors, suggesting that he was not ready to take responsibility or feared to express anger or reveal the identity of his aggressor.

Figure 11.7. "A strange kill," by Andy, age 11

Figure 11.8. "To kill," by Andy, age 11

Sam

Sam made only two responses to the drawing tasks: once in the third grade, and once in the sixth grade. At age 8, he chose the prince, dinosaur, old tree, and chick, then drew figure 11.9. As he explained, "The dinosaur was going to eat the bird. The knight shot it and the bird was safe."

At age 11, he chose the prince and dinosaur again, then drew "The Fight," figure 11.10. His prince now faces the dinosaur, instead of shooting it in the back, and draws blood with his sword.

The responses of these three children seem to show consistency in their fantasies, attitudes toward self and others, and the subjects they selected at age 8 and age 11, suggesting that their responses to the drawing task reflect personality traits rather than passing moods.

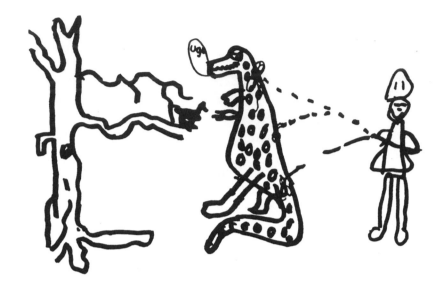

Figure 11.9. "The dinosaur was going to eat the bird," by Sam, age 8`

Figure 11.10. "The fight," by Sam, age 11

Using the Stimulus Drawing Assessment with Clinical and Nonclinical Children, Adolescents, and Adults

◇　　◇　　◇

T his chapter will review the ways art therapists have used the stimulus drawing assess-ment with individuals for development and rehabilitation, as well as for assessment. It also will review its use in assessing age and gender differences between groups of unimpaired children and adults.

Burt: A Child with Auditory and Language Impairments

The original set of approximately 70 stimulus drawings was developed in an attempt to communicate with children who had auditory and language impairments during the 1960s, as discussed in the introduction. Subsequently, the drawings were used in the 1973 state urban education project discussed in chapter 5. Burt, one of the children in the project's experimental group, participated in 9 of the 11 weekly sessions of the first semester program. Table 5.1 shows his classroom teacher's evaluation of his behavior before and after the program; table 5.2, his pretest and posttest performances. This chap-ter will review his behavior in the art program, as well as his responses to the stimulus drawing task presented in 4 of the 9 sessions he attended.

Burt, age 13, had both receptive and expressive language disorders and a hearing loss of 75 dB in his better ear. When tested at age 7, his IQ was estimated at 40 and his men-tal age at 3 years, one month (Stanford-Binet).

At our first meeting, the children were shown an arrangement of four toy animals on a sheet of paper and asked to select the same animals from a pile and arrange them the same way on their sheets of paper.

After this brief task, the stimulus drawing cards were displayed on two tables, people and animals on one, places and things on another. The children were asked to walk around the tables—choose one or two cards from each, then return to their seats and draw or paint from imagination, as described in the procedures suggested in chapter 10. The children were free to return to the tables and exchange their cards for others whenever they wished.

Burt chose the boy and the knife, drew a faceless boy, then stopped. I asked if he would like to give the boy a face. He said no, but asked me how to draw a face. I began to draw on the blackboard, but Burt made it clear that he wanted me to draw his face on a sheet of paper, which I did (figure 12.1).

Burt then drew the boy's face in his drawing, and added the stabbing knife with skull and crossbones on its handle, as shown in figure 12.2. Next, he returned his stimulus drawings to their tables, replacing them with stimulus drawings of a car, airplane, and the city street.

Figure 12.1. Sketch of Burt

Figure 12.2. Burt's Sketch

For our second meeting, I presented the stimulus drawings and art materials again. Burt chose the boy and the knife, changed his mind, replaced them with the plane and seascape, and drew airplanes dropping bombs on ships and buildings (figure 12.3). Although the emotional content of both drawings were strongly negative, there is a difference in the way he represented spatial relationships. In his first drawing, his subjects were related through proximity, the most elementary way, according to Piaget (1970). Except for the boy and knife, he did not relate his subjects appropriately, in size or placement. In his second drawing, however, the planes are related to their targets by scribbled lines suggesting smoke, a conventional symbol.

The third and fourth meetings were devoted to painting and modeling clay, but the fifth returned to the stimulus drawing cards. Burt chose the nurse, a head-and-shoulders sketch, then painted figure 12.4, drawing the nurse with crutches and full length. This painting shows no fragmentation and is well organized, as though the edges of his paper served as a frame of reference. The functional relationship between the nurse and crutches suggests that he had a story in mind.

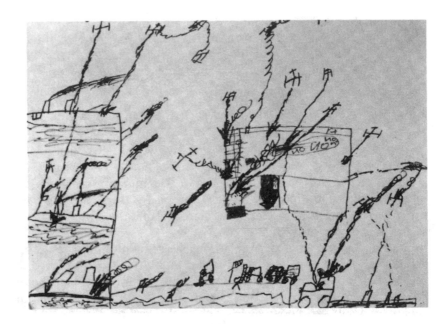

Figure 12.3. "Planes Dropping Bomb"

Figure 12.4. "Nurse on crutches"

Burt's painting of a nurse on crutches was his last response to the stimulus drawing cards. Subsequent meetings involved manipulating objects, Drawing from Observation, and Predictive Drawing. His progress in ability to select, combine, and represent is apparent in figures 12.2, 12.3, and 12.4. His gains in ability to draw from observation are shown in figure 12.5.

Figure 12.5. Burt's Drawings from Observation

Mrs. M

The original group of stimulus drawings has been used for remediation, as well as for development and assessment. To illustrate, Mrs. M's recent stroke had left her paralyzed on her right side and unable to talk. Presented with the SDT, she was able to perform the Drawing from Observation and Predictive Drawing subtests without difficulty; but in Drawing from Imagination, she seemed unable to combine the drawings she chose into meaningful images. This disability seemed to parallel her loss of speech, just as the ease with which she selected subjects seemed to parallel her ability to understand what was said. As noted previously, disturbance in ability to combine words into sentences is associated with expressive language disorders, whereas ability to select remains intact (Jakobson, 1964).

At our second meeting, I presented an array of stimulus drawings. Mrs. M chose a man, a hammer, and a car, then copied them, one above another, the hammer almost as long as her car (figure 12.6).

To suggest how she might relate her subjects, I sketched a man breaking a car window with a hammer, then invited her to choose from a different group of stimulus drawing cards. She chose and drew a man, motorcycle, and tray of food. When I asked if she could show how they might be related, she responded by adding lines, suggesting the man's arms reaching toward the tray (figure 12.7).

Figure 12.6. Mrs. M's First Drawing from Imagination

Figure 12.7. Mrs. M's Second Drawing from Imagination

During subsequent meetings, I continued to present stimulus drawings, and Mrs. M continued to choose the man together with various subjects. When she selected the man and the dog, drawing them side by side, I asked again if she could show how they might be related. When she did not respond, I copied her sketch, adding a leash to connect the man's hand to the dog's collar. She then reinforced the leash with her own pencil, emphasizing the relationship between them. Offered the stimulus drawings again, she chose the banana and drew it in the man's other hand (figure 12.8).

At our last meeting, Mrs. M selected the stimulus drawings of the phone and the interior of a room, placing the man in the foreground; then, without prompting, she added lines suggesting that the man was reaching toward the phone (figure 12.9). This drawing suggests that her ability to select (relating subjects on the basis of function) and ability to combine (appropriate sizes and representing depth) had improved, at least in her drawings. In emotional content, it seems moderately positive, the man is smiling as he reaches toward the phone. (Will he call her? Has she called him?)

Figure 12.8. Mrs. M's Third Drawing from Imagination

Figure 12.9. Mrs. M's Fourth Drawing from Imagination

Mrs. M's responses raise the question of whether gains in ability to select, combine, and represent through drawings will carry over to gains in expressive language, or vice versa. This question remains unexplored.

Mr. O

The stimulus drawings also were used for remediation with Mr. O, whose pretest and posttest responses to the SDT tasks were discussed in chapter 4.

Mr. O had suffered a cerebral hemorrhage. Although he spoke fluently, he tended to confuse verb tenses and had difficulty following directions and expressing concepts.

On the SDT pretest, Mr. O performed well in Predictive Drawing and Drawing from Observation, but in Drawing from Imagination, his performance was comparable to that of children in the second grade. His pretest and posttest responses were shown in figures 4.2 and 4.3.

Mr. O and I met once a week for seven weeks. At each session he chose stimulus drawings, combining and representing the images appropriately, although his titles and stories were, at first, incoherent. He chose stimulus drawings that seemed to be symbols or metaphors for himself and his experiences, such as the stimulus drawing of a whale, water spouting from its head (figure 12.10). At another meeting, he chose the mountain climber, then drew him climbing a steep slope with flowers on the peak, perhaps metaphors for his struggle to overcome aphasia (figure 12.11). His posttest drawing, entitled, "Hedges May Hold Surprises," scored 5 points in Drawing from Imagination and is shown in figure 4.3.

Figure 12.10. "Come home quick there's a whale in sight"

Figure 12.11. "Gathering magic herbs"

Senior Adults in Community Recreational Programs

The stimulus drawing cards have also been used in recreational programs provided in urban and suburban communities for senior adults living independently in the communities in New York and Florida. Previously, the seniors had volunteered to participate in research studies by responding to drawing tasks. Their responses tended to be humorous, and their humor was self-disparaging. Four of the drawings are shown in chapter 14 (figures 14.17 to 14.9).

Joey: A Child with Learning Disabilities

Soon after the 1980 National Institute of Education Project began, a remediation teacher in Canada asked if she might participate informally by working with one of her students, using the same procedures used by art therapists in the project. We arranged that she would work along with us, supervised via telephone and correspondence, seeing Joey once a week for 12 weeks.

Joey, in the second grade of a public school, had difficulty learning to read and "tended to lash out at his peers, sometimes justified but often unjustified." He had been diagnosed as learning disabled and assigned to a behavior modification program. As measured by the Canadian Cognitive Abilities Test (CCAT), his IQ was 91, below average. Only 2 of the 24 children in his class had lower scores. As measured by the SDT, he received the lowest score in his class in Drawing from Observation (14th percentile).

In Drawing from Imagination, however, Joey received the highest score in his class, scoring in the 99th percentile in cognitive skills. His response, entitled "The Killier" (sic), (figure 12.12), seems to represent a doctor operating on a patient who calls for help even though anaesthetized. Upstairs, someone lies in bed snoring. Although his fantasy is strongly negative in emotional content (1 point), it is unclear whether he identifies with the victim, the smiling "killier," the sleeper above, or the narrator of his story.

Figure 12.12. "The Killier (sic)"

To clarify relationships between the SDT and the Canadian tests, scores on both were analyzed. Correlations between the CCAT and the SDT Drawing from Imagination subtest emerged at the .01 level ($r = .50$). No significant correlations emerged between the Drawing from Observation subtest and the CCAT.

The following week, Joey responded to the stimulus drawing cards. He chose the elephant, the old leafless tree, and a leafy tree. In his drawing, entitled "The elephant's journey," birds are nesting and the elephant smiles as it walks between the trees, but clouds are overhead (figure 12.13). With time for another drawing, he chose the whale and the alligator, drew them facing one another, and again clouds. He entitled this drawing, "The Fight Is Going to Begin."

Figure 12.13. "The elephant's journey"

The third week, Joey chose the bear, car, and leafy tree, then drew "The Bear Chased Them Amay (sic)." The bear stands between two trees, and behind one, facing the bear, is a red car with yellow flag, blue roof lamp (police car?), and a dark cloud overhead. Joey's title seems to contradict his drawing. The trees seem to block the bear as they block the sun (figure 12.14).

Figure 12.14. "The Bear Chased Them Amay (sic)"

The following weeks called for painting, modeling clay, self-portraits, and family portraits.

After a series of unfortunate events, Joey's remediation teacher became ill, postponing the art program for 5 weeks, and his classroom teacher canceled two sessions as punishment for his misbehavior.

For Joey's next and final response to the stimulus drawings, he chose the airplane and mountain climber together with his previous choices of the elephant and green tree.

Once again, his drawing seems to contradict his title, "Seeing an Elephant in the Woods" (figure 12.15). The mountain climber, now climbing a tree, could not possibly see the elephant behind him. Furthermore, the climber wears dark glasses and has no ears. In addition, the trees would hide the elephant from the airplane above, even if Joey had given the plane windows. Like his previous drawings, trees block the elephant's progress and, for the first time, the cloud extends across the sky.

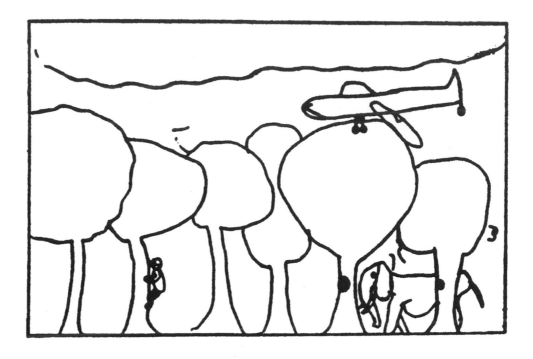

Figure 12.15. "Seeing an Elephant in the Woods"

Joey's responses suggest that he may identify the elephant with himself—frustrated, invisible, and isolated by the trees around him. Joey's responses to the SDT tasks and the developmental procedures are discussed elsewhere (Silver, 2001).

Vilstrup's Study of Adolescents in a Psychiatric Hospital

Kristen Vilstrup, ATR-BC (Sandberg, Silver, & Vilstrup, 1984), used the stimulus drawing assessment with hospitalized adolescents as a projective technique to stimulate symbol formation and for access to their strengths, conflicts, and maladaptive defenses.

She presented the stimulus drawings in four groups, based on category, and asked the patients to choose two or three from different categories, then draw pictures using *ideas* from the cards to illustrate a story. She also asked them not to copy the cards, but to use them as starting points. As the patients finished drawing, Vilstrup asked for stories with beginnings, middles, and ends and finally, for morals or titles.

Vilstrup found that the adolescents used personal symbols and metaphors in selecting stimulus cards and creating narrative drawings, revealing individual experiences and current affect. In conjunction with story telling, she used what she called "corrective" drawing, allowing the respondent or herself to make changes on the original drawing to help alleviate threatening situations, such as containing a dragon by adding a fence. She also found that an individual's own symbols and story provided a vehicle to facilitate conflict resolution.

Sandburg's Study of Adults with Chronic Schizophrenia

Louise Sandburg (1984) used the stimulus drawings with adults in a psychiatric hospital, asking them to choose two or three cards and think of a story that would include the images. The instructions remained the same from week to week to establish consistency. After 1 year, the adults constructed their own story cards, using collage techniques.

Sandburg's patients worked in a closed room at a table seating eight, drawing on 12" X 18" white paper with colored chalks. Finished drawings were displayed on a wall, patients' chairs placed in a semicircle for viewing. She encouraged patients to talk about their work and to interact with others and used questions such as, "Is there anything you would like to know about one of the pictures?"

When patients were too agitated to draw, she encouraged them to choose cards and participate in the verbal exchanges, rejoining the group as full participants the following week. She found that the stimulus drawings helped patients focus on specific ideas and stem the flow of loose associations. The drawings also served for communication, evoking images from past history and developing social skills.

White-Wolff's Study of Twins

White-Wolff (1991) used the cards in working with four sets of twins. She found correlations between the SD assessment and the House, Tree, Person Test (Buck, 1948); *Kinetic Family Drawings* (Burns & Kaufman, 1972); and *Human Figure Drawings* (Koppitz, 1968).

Malchiodi's Use of Stimulus Drawings with a Child Who Had Experienced Sexual Abuse

Cathy Malchiodi, ATR-BC, has used the three assessments for evaluation and as interviewing techniques (1998). She noted that the children's personal narratives, rather than symbols or specific art elements, tend to reveal depressive affect, and that four themes were particularly important in their narratives and portrayed in their drawings: isolation, despair, self-destruction, and destruction, mourning, or bereavement.

In a previous book, *Breaking the Silence* (1997), Malchiodi discusses the importance of drawing about sexual abuse and how the therapist responds. As she observes, many children do not want to discuss sexual abuse for various reasons. Because interviews can create crises due to the nature of the information solicited, art expressions can be a way to determine whether such abuse exists before it can be verbalized. Drawings enable a child to tell a story in the third person. Drawings are less traumatic than verbal communication and can demonstrate the therapist's attentiveness, support, and interest in the child.

As an example, Malchiodi presents the responses of a 13-year-old girl who had been abused for at least 5 years. She chose and drew the stimulus drawing of boots, then told a story about finding warnings in the boots, her fears, jumping out the window, and resting in peace. Malchiodi found the Drawing from Imagination task helpful in obtaining critical information for structuring immediate interventions.

Couch's Use of Stimulus Drawings for Patients with Dementia

Janet Beaujon Couch (1996) noted that patients with dementia are difficult to engage, and that spontaneity is often a problem, but that enlarging the stimulus drawings on a copying machine produced almost immediate reaction and engagement. Her enlarged images seemed to decrease anxiety and stimulate thinking and humor. They also provided access to fantasy and reflected self-images and social attitudes.

Initially, Couch asked groups of patients to chose one enlarged image, then add color with art media. When they finished, she requested titles. She encouraged patients to paint as many images as they wished; then she lined up the artwork in front of the patients and asked them to compose stories. She found that the emotional content of stories and the use of color reflected aspects of each person's past and present concerns and provided information about the stage of the disease. As dementia progressed, the images seem to bring comfort, reducing the anxiety of performing with art media. Some patients did not make use of the art materials, but simply held a chosen image, which then became the stimulus for memory recall and reminiscence.

Images that reflected anger or frustration sometimes appeared to cause strong verbal or behavioral reactions, or both. Couch found that reducing the size of the images appeared to make these feelings easier to tolerate and still provided an outlet for aroused emotions.

She also cut out enlarged or reduced images for use in collage. Each person chose images, which then were placed and pasted on paper. Art media were available to enhance the images and provide the therapist with additional information about emotional content, such as media pressure and color usage.

In addition, Couch found that adapting the stimulus drawings for patients with dementia provided a way for them to express humor and gave her access to wishes, concerns, and memories that often are unavailable.

Age and Gender Differences Among Groups of Unimpaired Children and Adults

The set of 50 stimulus drawings has also been used to assess age and gender differences among typical populations (Silver, 1987a). This study reviewed the responses of 326 subjects. They included males and females in four age groups: third-graders; high school seniors; young adults age 20 to 30; and senior adults, ages 65 and over. Each response was scored for principal subject and environment.

Although both males and females portrayed principal subjects more positively than they portrayed environments, significant gender differences emerged across age groups, exceeding the .05 level of probability, as measured by a 2 x 4 x 2 factorial analysis of variance. The women and girls received nearly identical scores for principal subject and environment. The men and boys consistently received higher scores for principal subject and lower scores for environment. In other words, females consistently portrayed their unfortunate subjects in unpleasant worlds, their fortunate subjects in pleasant worlds. On the other hand, males consistently portrayed more negative surroundings inhabited by more positively seen subjects, as shown in tables 12.1 and 12.2, and figure 12.16.

Age differences approached but did not achieve significance. A Newman-Keuls Multiple Range Test supported these findings (significance of score type by sex interaction).

To the extent that the principal subject of a drawing represents the self–image of the person who draws it, and the environment represents the way that person perceives the world, the findings support the observation that males, from boyhood through old age, have more positive self-images and greater self-confidence than females do.

In subsequent studies of age and gender differences, I used the SDT and DAS assessments.

Table 12.1

Analysis of Variance

Source	df	Sums of Squares	Mean Square	f	p
Sex	1	.10	.10	.03	n.s.
Age Group	3	25.32	8.44	2.57	n.s.
Sex by Age Group	3	21.05	7.01	2.14	n.s.
Subjects within Sex, Age	72	236.50	3.28		
Score Type	1	10.00	10.00	5.75	.05
Score Type by Sex	1	7.22	7.22	4.15	.05
Score Type by Age	3	5.75	1.91	1.10	n.s.
Score Type by Sex by Age	3	5.52	1.84	1.06	n.s.
Score by Subjects within Sex, Age	72	125.50	1.74		

Table 12.2

Table of Means for 80 Randomly Selected Subjects

	Principal Subject		Environment		Total
	Males	Females	Males	Females	
Third-Graders	4.1	2.8	2.9	2.9	3.2
High School Students	4.4	4.7	3.3	4.6	4.3
Adults	3.8	3.3	4.1	3.2	3.6
Senior Citizens	<u>4.4</u>	<u>4.4</u>	<u>2.7</u>	<u>4.2</u>	<u>3.9</u>
Total	4.2	3.8	3.3	3.7	3.7
		3.99		3.49	

Statistical Analyses were prepared by Beatrice Krauss, PhD.

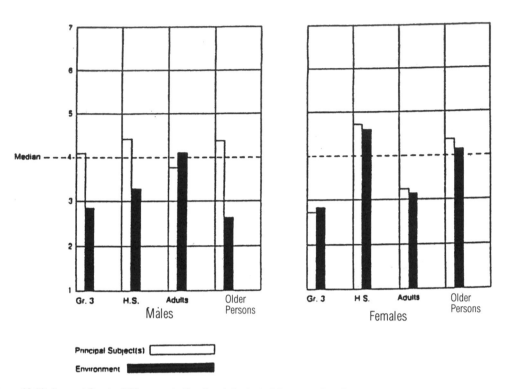

Figure 12.16. Age and Gender Differences in Emotional Content of Response Drawings

Concluding Observations

When the SD assessment was first published, the original group of stimulus drawings was reduced to 50 cards. The present edition has been expanded to a tenth page, to include some of the original cards chosen by stroke patients and others. For example, Mrs. M, who could not talk, chose a stimulus drawing phone, associating it with the man who appears in each of her responses. In figure 12.9, he reaches toward the phone but does not touch it, perhaps representing her frustrated desire to talk with him. Mr. O, who had expressive language impairment, also chose and drew the phone (figure 12.10). Mrs. M chose the car, as did Burt, who added windows that seem to be eyes and black smoke pouring from its roof (figure 12.2). Joey seems to have transformed the car into a police car (figure 12.14). Both Joey and Mr. O chose and transformed the mountain climber (figures 12.15 and 12.11). Mr. O, Joey, and Burt chose and drew the airplane (figures 12.3, 12.10, and 12.15).

This chapter concludes section III. Appendix C includes the stimulus drawings and guidelines for using them. Section IV is concerned with findings about the three assessments: correlations between them, the uses of humor in responding to their tasks, and studies of cultural differences and similarities.

Section IV

Correlations Between the Assessments, the Use of Humor, and Cross-Culture Studies

◇   ◇   ◇

Correlations Between the Silver Drawing Test, Draw a Story, and Stimulus Drawings and Techniques

◇   ◇   ◇

What is the relationship between the three assessments? They use virtually the same Drawing from Imagination task and rating scales, but different stimulus drawings. Is this difference important? If not, the three measures could be interchangeable. Art therapists and others who use the Drawing from Imagination tasks in the SDT could also screen for depression, DAS users could also assess cognitive skills, and SD users could use the 5-point scales in assessing principal subjects and environments.

To determine whether the measures assess the same emotional and cognitive constructs, responses to the three measures were reexamined.

Relationships Between the SDT Drawing from Imagination Subtest and Stimulus Drawings and Techniques

To determine the relationship between these two assessments, the SD reliability study reported in the previous chapter included 12 responses to the SD task and 12 responses to the SDT Drawing from Imagination task. We asked whether the SDT scale could be used to evaluate responses to both tasks.

No significant differences were found in mean ratings of responses to the SD and SDT subtest t (22) = 8, not significant. Thus, there appears to be consistency of measurement in the scale when it is used to rate responses to the SD task, as well as to the SDT subtest, as shown in tables 13.1 and 13.2.

Table 13.1

Agreement Coefficients for the Emotional Content Scale

Stimuli	Finn's r
Stimulus Drawing Subject	.806
Stimulus Drawing Environment	.549
SDT Subject	.778
SDT Environment	.924

Table 13.2

Means and Standard Deviations of Ratings for Each Set of Response Drawings

	Mean	SD
SDT Subject	3.75	1.90
SDT Environment	3.67	2.01
Stimulus Drawing Subject	4.86	1.90
Stimulus Drawing Environment	4.06	2.10

Relationships Between Draw A Story and Stimulus Drawings and Techniques

The second study investigated interscorer relationships between the DAS and SD assessments at two points in time (Silver, 1993a, pp. 52–53). Two art therapists administered the tasks to 30 children, adolescents, and adults. One therapist administered both tasks to 13 adolescents and 4 adults after a 1-week interval. She also administered the DAS task to a child, age 11, who had previously responded to the SD task at the age of 7. The other therapist administered DAS Form A to 12 children, age 10, in a public elementary school. Previously, when these children were 8 years old, she had administered the SD task.

When responses by all 30 subjects to the two measures were evaluated, the intertest correlation was found to be .49784, significant at the $p < .005$ level of probability. When responses by the 26 children and adolescents were evaluated, the intertest correlation found was .44294, significant at the $p < .023$ level of probability.

Relationships Between Draw A Story and the SDT Drawing from Imagination Subtest

In comparing responses to the two measures, this study examined 448 responses in three age groups: younger adolescents, older adolescents, and older adults (Silver, 1993a). Most of those who responded to the DAS task were emotionally disturbed, whereas the SDT respondents had no known disturbances.

When responses to both instruments were examined, similarities and differences emerged, as shown in tables 13.3 and 13.4. Although the number of respondents in each category was too small for statistical analysis, there were notable age and gender differences in fantasies about the solitary subjects and relationships portrayed.

The most notable difference between DAS and SDT assessments appeared in drawings about sad or helpless solitary subjects, scored 1 point (78% of the DAS female adolescents and 62% of the DAS male adolescents compared with *none* of the SDT male adolescents or older female adolescents).

On the other hand, there were several notable differences in both assessments. Proportionally more girls than boys drew sad, isolated, or helpless subjects (DAS: 35% of girls, 7% of boys; SDT: 11% of girls, no boys), as well as stressful relationships (DAS: 30% of girls, 23% of boys; SDT: 53% of girls, 26% of boys). Among adolescents, proportionally more males than females drew assaultive relationships (DAS: 48% of males, 13% of females; SDT: 47% of males; 23% of females), as well as angry, fearful, or fearsome subjects (DAS: 20% of males, 14% of females; SDT: 33% of males, 19% of females). Among older adults, proportionally more men than women drew frustrated or frightened subjects (DAS: 40% of men, 18% of women; SDT: 21% of men, 6% of women), as well as stressful relationships (DAS: 33% of men, 7% of women; SDT: 64% of men, 20% of women). Proportionally more women than men drew active solitary subjects, scored 5 points (DAS: 41% of women, 20% of men; SDT: 31% of women, 21% of men). None of the older men drew caring relationships compared with 21% of the DAS and 13% of the SDT older women.

Table 13.3

Comparing Fantasies About Solitary Subjects Expressed in Response to the Draw a Story and Silver Drawing Test Tasks

Score: Age	Gender	N.	1 Sad or Helpless	2 Angry or Fearful	3 Ambiv/ Ambig.	4 Passive	5 Active
13–16							
	Female						
	DAS	34	12 35%	4 12%	10 29%	1 3%	7 21%
	SDT	9	1 11%	0	0	6 67%	2 22%
	Male						
	DAS	15	1 7%	3 20%	4 27%	2 13%	5 33%
	SDT	15	0	3 20%	3 20%	3 20%	6 40%
17–19							
	Female						
	DAS	14	6 43%	2 14%	4 29%	1 7%	1 7%
	SDT	16	0	3 19%	2 13%	8 50%	3 19%
	Male						
	DAS	11	6 55%	2 18%	3 27%	0	0
	SDT	6	0	2 33%	1 17%	2 33%	1 17%
65+							
	Female						
	DAS	17	3 18%	3 18%	2 12%	2 12%	7 41%
	SDT	16	2 13%	1 6%	6 38%	2 13%	5 31%
	Male						
	DAS	5	1 20%	2 40%	1 20%	0	1 20%
	SDT	14	0	3 21%	5 36%	3 21%	3 21%

Table 13.4

Comparing Fantasies About Relationships Expressed in Response to the Draw a Story and Silver Drawing Test Tasks

Score: Age 13–16	Gender	N.	1 Assaultive	2 Stressful	3 Ambitious	4 Friendly	5 Caring
	Female						
	DAS	37	5 14%	11 30%	12 32%	2 5%	7 19%
	SDT	19	3 16%	10 53%	2 11%	3 16%	1 5%
	Male						
	DAS	61	32 52%	14 23%	11 18%	3 5%	1 2%
	SDT	23	8 35%	6 26%	6 26%	2 9%	1 4%
17–19							
	Female						
	DAS	16	2 13%	6 38%	6 38%	0	2 13%
	SDT	22	5 23%	3 14%	2 9%	6 27%	6 27%
	Male						
	DAS	27	13 48%	5 19%	6 22%	3 11%	0
	SDT	15	7 47%	5 33%	1 7%	0	2 13%
65+							
	Female						
	DAS	28	4 14%	2 7%	9 32%	7 25%	6 21%
	SDT	15	4 27%	3 20%	4 27%	2 13%	2 13%
	Male						
	DAS	9	2 22%	3 33%	2 22%	2 22%	0
	SDT	14	3 21%	9 64%	1 7%	1 7%	0

A subsequent study focused on responses by senior adults to the SDT and Stimulus Drawings assessments (Silver, 1993c). Proportionally more senior women than any other females drew sad, solitary subjects. Proportionally more senior men than any other males drew fantasies about stressful relationships, producing more than twice as many such drawings, three times as many as the senior women.

Because the respondents in this study drew subjects the same gender as themselves to a significant degree, the negativity of the senior adults may reflect the ways they perceive themselves and their worlds. Even though negative attitudes predominated, it is important to note that many negative responses were also characterized by humor. Proportionally more older men (39%) used humor than did older women (16%). Their humor tended to be self-disparaging, such as joking about frustrating experiences, ridiculing themselves rather than others.

Two examples of this self-disparaging humor are shown in chapter 14:

"I am a Pisces, so where is the other fish?" the response of an older woman, (figure 14.7), and "Gid-a-up bronco." "Sez Who?" (figure 14.8).

Comparing the Negativity of Responses to the SDT and DAS Tasks

This study asked whether the DAS task is more likely to trigger negative responses than the SDT, and whether negativity could be attributed to emotional disturbances, regardless of the set of stimulus drawings (Silver, 1996a).

Five art therapists rated four sets of stimulus drawings: Forms A and B of the SDT and Forms A and B of the DAS, using a 5-point scale that ranged from 1 ("not at all likely to trigger negative responses") to 5 ("extremely likely to trigger negative responses"). Using a one-way analysis of variance (stimulus set), Madeline Altabe, PhD, found no significant differences, as shown in table 13.5. The mean ratings were 3.1 and 3.8. Although not significant, differences do exist and may be significant with larger numbers of raters.

Table 13.5

Likelihood of Triggering Negative Responses for SDT and DAS Stimulus Drawings

Drawing Set	Mean Scores	Standard Deviations
SDT Form A	2.8	.84
SDT Form B	3.4	.89
DAS Form A	4.0	1.00
DAS Form B	3.6	1.14

This finding suggested that the similarities between the DAS and SDT were still open to debate. However the studies of respondents with depression reported in chapter 8 indicated that the DAS is able to discriminate between subjects with depression and nondepressed subjects. There seemed no reason to doubt that the SDT also can be used to screen for depression. The following study continued to examine these issues.

Comparing Emotional and Cognitive Constructs

This study asked whether the DAS and SDT Drawing from Imagination tasks measure the same constructs (Silver, 1998b). Both tasks were presented without a time interval to samples of children and adults. Half of each group responded first to the SDT task, then to the DAS task; the other half responded first to the DAS, then to the SDT. After their responses were scored for cognitive and emotional content, Madeline Altabe, PhD, used correlational analyses to determine the relationship between test scores.

The sample of children included 7 boys and 12 girls, ages 7 to 8, in a public elementary school in California. A classroom teacher administered the tasks, supervised by JoAnne Ellison, ATR. The adults included 7 men and 12 women in a retirement residence in Florida who volunteered to participate anonymously. Their ages ranged from "65 plus" to 85 years, with a mean age of 80.89 years.

Correlations Between the Silver Drawing Test, Draw a Story, and Stimulus Drawings and Techniques

Results

In emotional content, scores of both the SDT and DAS were correlated significantly ($r = 0.57$, $p < .0001$). Only one difference emerged—a difference between age groups: more than 25% of the children drew moderately positive fantasies (4 points), compared with 6% and 11%, respectively, of the adults.

Responses for cognitive content also were consistent across test scores ($r = .66$, $p < .0001$). Within test scores (e.g., SDT emotional content vs. cognitive content), no consistency was found (for SDT, $r = .13$, not significant; for DAS, $r = 0.02$, not significant).

One respondent, an older woman (age 83), drew strongly negative fantasies in responding to both assessments. Responding first to the DAS task, she drew a solitary person on a plane without fuel, falling into the sea, adding, "I'm in an airplane without fuel headed downward to the sea. I can't imagine what I'd be thinking so I can't draw it" (see figure 13.1).

Responding to the SDT task, she drew a solitary figure in a sailboat, adding, "I was on a sailboat wrecked in a storm. I was washed overboard. I can only imagine sinking wondering what . . . No way to draw that—because I don't have any image of dark space." (figure 13.2). Her use of the first-person singular suggests that the solitary subject in her drawing represents herself in life-threatening danger, without hints of escape or rescue. Because she had participated in the study anonymously, there was no opportunity to discuss her response.

Figure 13.1. "I'm in an airplane without fuel headed downward to the sea. I can't imagine what I'd be thinking so I can't draw it." DAS response by a woman, age 83

Figure 13.2. "I was on a sailboat wrecked in a storm. I was washed overboard. I can only imagine sinking wondering what . . . No way to draw that because I don't have any image of dark space." Her SDT response.

Another older resident, a man, age 82, drew humorous responses to both tasks. Responding first to the SDT, he drew "The Snake and the Mouse," shown in figure 14.12. Responding to the DAS task, he drew a fantasy in which a pilot, dangling from his parachute caught on a turret, reaches toward a window and the extended hand of a princess. In both drawings, his meanings and the identity of his subjects are ambiguous. Like the mouse, his pilot seems helpless and in life-threatening danger; his bride, like his snake, could be either caring or treacherous.

Discussion

The findings of this study suggest that DAS and the SDT assess the same constructs. Although it is not possible to generalize from small numbers of participants, they lend evidence to the validity of emotional and cognitive scores across test formats. They also suggest consistency of measurement when the scale is used to rate responses to both instruments. They seem to indicate that the SDT Drawing from Imagination subtest, like DAS, can be used to screen for depression, and that DAS, like the SDT, can be used to assess levels of ability to select, combine, and represent.

Based on these findings, the differences between sets of stimulus drawings seem irrelevant. What seems to matter is whether they elicit associations with past experiences, and whether responses provide access to fantasies, emotional needs, and cognitive skills.

Chapter 14

The Uses of Humor

◇   ◇   ◇

This chapter examines the humor expressed in responses to the Drawing from Imagination task in the three assessments. It presents five forms of humor that were observed, proposes a rating scale for evaluating humorous responses, and reports a study of age, gender, and other differences in using humor. The findings suggest that humor can be measured reliably.

Background Literature

In examining the humor of psychiatric in-patients, Christine Mango, ATR, and Joseph Richman, PhD (1990), hypothesized that humorous drawings express emotional states. They divided their sessions into a warm-up period in which they told jokes, a drawing period ("Draw something funny that happened to you"), and a discussion period. They noted that interpersonal interactions were either absent or negative in most drawings, and that patients presented themselves as social misfits compelled to face a dangerous and hurtful world. Although few of the situations depicted were amusing, the assignment brought problems into the foreground, enabled patients to experience empathy, and enabled the art therapists to direct group discussions toward solving problems.

Wende Heath, ATR (2000), diagnosed with cancer herself, discussed the importance of humor in her life and the lives of other patients, as she helped them cope with pain and medical treatments. She drew cartoons about experiences with cancer, "Cancer

Comics," and "The Humor of the Tumor," sending them on the Internet, and receiving grateful e-mails.

Avner Ziv (1984) suggested that humor serves five functions: aggressive, defensive, intellectual, sexual, and social. We use aggressive humor to feel superior, punish others, and conceal aggressive desires by permitting their expression in a socially acceptable way. We use defensive humor to us help face reality, challenge dangers, achieve a sense of mastery, and relieve tension by making dangers ridiculous. We use self-disparaging humor to lessen anxiety and gain sympathy or admiration; intellectual humor, to amuse and create new meanings through absurdity or incongruity. Sexual humor allows us to face problems, deal openly with sex, and derive vicarious pleasure without social censure. Social humor, such as satire, is generally aggressive, but its primary function is to achieve social acceptance.

In responses to the Drawing from Imagination task, both aggressive and defensive humor have appeared frequently, but not sexual or social humor. Instead, the humor expressed seems to take additional forms.

Lethal Humor

Humorous responses about death or annihilation seem to have two forms. One form suggests that respondents take pleasure in fantasizing about causing pain and annihilation and expect their viewers to be amused. For example, "GODZILLA VS MIGHTY MOUSE" (figure 14.1) was the response of a male adolescent in high school who chose the DAS dinosaur and mouse. He seems to identify with Godzilla, who bites off the mouse's tail and, as the mouse prays, "gobbles him up."

Another example is the response of a boy, a third-grader, who chose the stimulus drawing of a chick, then drew an arrow aimed at its tail, causing the chick to cry, "Ouch" (figure 14.2).

"Survival of the Fittest" is a series of drawings by a male adolescent, who chose two stimulus drawings, the snake and the mouse (figure 14.3). The frightened mouse cries "help" and "I'm dead," as the snake chases, then devours it head first. Although innate cruelty may inspire fantasies of inflicting pain, traumatic experiences also can trigger rage and a desire for vengeance.

The second form of lethal humor does not depict pain or suffering, even though it may show predators killing prey. It has appeared rarely and only in responses by adults. For example, in a response drawing entitled "Cat Eats Mouse," by a young woman, all we see of the mouse is its tail.

Although both forms are strongly negative and score 1 point on the Emotional Content scale, the scale for assessing humor distinguishes between the forms, rating the first 1a, and the second, 1b. In either event, both forms seem to disguise strongly hostile intent.

Figure 14.1. "GODZILLA VS MIGHTY MOUSE"

Lethal humor,
scored 1a

Figure 14.2. "Ouch"

Lethal humor,
scored 1a

Figure 14.3. "Survival of the Fittest," by Walter, age 17

Lethal humor,
scored 1a

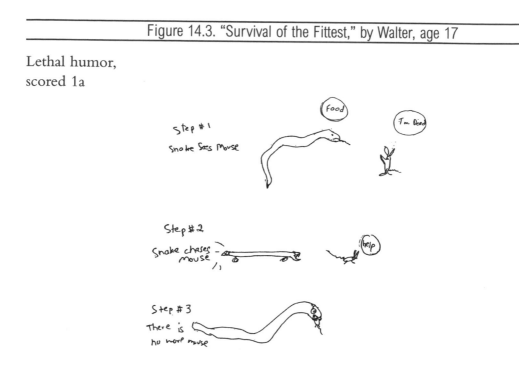

Disparaging Humor

Humorous responses that disparage their subjects but don't kill or theaten to destroy them appear frequently. They also appear in two forms: a mean-spirited kind of humor that ridicules others and a self-disparaging humor that ridicules oneself.

"The Scared Dragon" (figure 14.4), an example of the first form, disparages the dragon. It was the response of a male adolescent in a school for emotionally disturbed students, who also chose the stimulus drawing of a mouse but associated it with the dinosaur and reversed their traditional roles. Although he labels his mouse a "killer," his fantasy is not about killing, but of intimidating a bully.

In another such response, "Panic in a Church," by Max, age 13, the guests are laughing at his ridiculous bride (figure 14.5).

Figure 14.4. "The Sacred Dragon"

Disparaging humor,
scored 2a

Figure 14.5. "Panic in a church"

Disparaging humor,
scored 2a

On the other hand, "I THINK I'M IN TROUBLE" (figure 14.6), by a young woman, identifies the parachutist dangling from a tree as herself.

A previous study of responses to the drawing task found that a group of senior adults used humor more frequently, and expressed more self-disparaging humor than other groups of children, adolescents, and adults (Silver, 1993a; reviewed in chapter 9).

Figure 14.6. "I THINK I'M IN TROUBLE"

Disparaging humor,
scored 2b

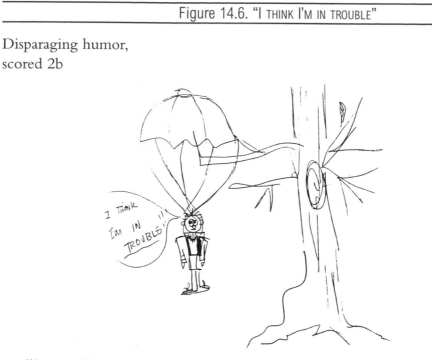

"I AM A PISCES SO WHERE IS THE OTHER FISH" is an example of self-disparaging humor by an older woman (figures 14.7). "Gid-a-up bronco. Says, who?" is an example by an older man (figure 14.8). Both seem to make fun of their own frustrations and invite us to join them in laughing at themselves.

The ability to laugh at oneself is a way of facing and coping with painful situations. It suggests courage and the ability to accept what cannot be changed. Consequently, the scale for rating moderately negative humor also distinguishes between two forms: humor that ridicules others scores 2a; humor that ridicules oneself, 2b.

Figure 14.7. "I AM A PISCES, SO WHERE IS THE OTHER FISH?"

Disparaging humor,
scored 2b

Figure 14.8. "Gid a yup, bronco. Says who?" by an older man

Disparaging humor,
scored 2b

Resilient Humor

In addition, there is a difference between accepting adversity, which is essentially negative, and overcoming adversity, which is essentially positive. Resilient people don't tend to see themselves as passive victims. Instead, they are inclined to take positive action. Responses that reflect resilient humor may be self-disparaging, but they depict positive outcomes, unlike fantasies that do not reveal how painful situations turn out.

To illustrate, "IN THIS COUNTRY A WORM HAS TO FLY" (figure 14.9), was the response of an older man who chose the SD worm and the desert landscape, but gave his worm wings, enabling it to fly over the desert and triumph over its hardships.

Another example, by a male adolescent, is a series of drawings without words. It begins with a mouse about to be crushed by the huge foot of a dinosaur. The mouse struggles to lift the descending foot, causes the dinosaur to fall on its back, and ends with the mouse laughing in triumph (figure 14.10).

Humorous responses that provide (or imply) happy endings, showing losers winning after all, rate 4 points on the humor scale.

Since positive outcomes also may reflect denial of reality, it is important to note and account for the reality that is reflected in wish-fulfilling fantasies.

Figure 14.9. "In this country a worm has to fly"

Resilient humor,
scored 4

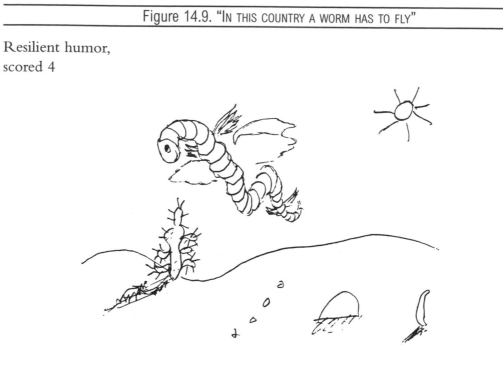

Figure 14.10. "Untitled"

Resilient humor,
scored 4

Ambivalent or Ambiguous Humor

Humorous responses that are unclear, ambiguous, or ambivalent score 3 points on the humor scale, as they do on the Emotional Content scale. To illustrate, "Help!" (figure 14.11) was the response of a 12-year-old boy. When asked what was likely to happen to the parachutist, he replied, "Well, maybe somebody will rescue him."

"The snake and the Mouse" (figure 14.12), the response of an 82-year-old man, is another ambiguous response scoring 3 points. The snake's embrace could be delicious for the snake, but disastrous for the mouse.

Figure 14.11. "Help!"

Ambiguous humor,
scored 3

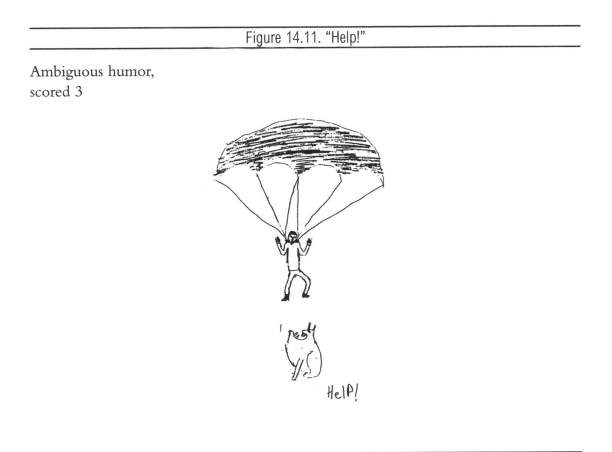

Figure 14.12. "The snake and the Mouse"

Ambiguous humor,
scored 3

Playful Humor

Humor motivated by high spirits or goodwill, which does not seem to have a hidden agenda, seems more positive than humor about hardships to overcome.

For example, "Lyin' in the living room" (figure 14.13), is the playful response of a young woman who chose SD stimulus drawings of a lion and the interior of a room. "Cat Sip or Cat-a-tonic" (figure 14.14), by a young man, is another play on words.

Based on these observations, the form of humor that invites viewers to share the enjoyment of puns or absurdities seems to warrant the most positive rating, 5 points.

A tentative scale for rating humorous responses to the Drawing from Imagination task in the three assessments is presented in the following section.

Figure 14.13. "Lyin' in the living room"

Playful humor,
scored 5

Figure 14.14. "Cat sip or cat-a-tonic"

Playful humor,
scored 5

Table 14.1

Guidelines for Scoring Humor in Responses to the Drawing from Imagination Task

1 point: Lethal humor (strongly negative or aggressive)

Invites viewers to laugh at subjects who are in danger of annihilation.

    a. Suggests pleasure from causing discomfort, suffering, or death.

    b. No suggestion of cruelty or pleasure in causing pain.

2 points: Disparaging humor (moderately negative or aggressive)

Invites viewers to laugh at subjects who are foolish, frightened, frustrated, or unfortunate.

    a. Suggests ridiculing others.

    b. Suggests ridiculing self.

3 points: Ambivalent or ambiguous humor.

    Meaning is unclear, ambiguous, or ambivalent.

4 points: Resilient humor (moderately positive)

    Overcomes problems, relieves anxiety, or achieves safety. The outcome is hopeful or favorable.

5 points: Playful humor (strongly positive)

Invites viewers to share absurdity, amusement, or a play on words.
    It shows no disparagement.

A Study of the Uses of Humor

To collect samples of humorous responses, 888 responses to the Drawing from Imagination task in the three assessments were reexamined. They included responses by 724 children, adolescents, and adults who had no known impairments and 164 children and adolescents with emotional disturbances. The responses that suggested humorous intent were grouped according to age or gender and rated on the 5-point humor scale.

Subjects

The unimpaired subjects included 140 children, ages 9 to 12, in grades 4, 5, and 6, in one private school and 7 public elementary schools in New Jersey, New York, and Pennsylvania. They also included 257 adolescents, ages 13 to 19, in grades 7 to 12, in 10 middle schools and high schools in Minnesota, Nebraska, New York, Ohio, and Pennsylvania, and a class of college freshmen in Nebraska.

The adults included 165 young adults who had responded in college and professional audiences in Idaho, Nebraska, New York, and Wisconsin; and 162 senior adults who lived independently in Florida and New York and had volunteered to take part anonymously while participating in community programs. The children and adolescents with emotional disturbances, ages 9 to 19, attended special programs in Arizona, Florida, Georgia, Montana, New York, and Oregon.

Procedures

Analyses of variance were used by Madeline Altabe, PhD, to compare age and gender groups. In addition, to determine the reliability of the humor scale, two registered art therapists rated 16 humorous responses selected at random.

Results

Eighteen percent of the unimpaired subjects used humor. The humor tended to be negative (68%). Almost twice as many negative responses were disparaging rather than lethal (44% disparaging, 24% lethal), as shown in table 14.2. Approximately one of four was positive (17% used playful humor, 7% resilient humor).

Males produced significantly more humorous responses than females. This gender difference was highly significant (chi square [1] = 37.3, $p. < .01$). In addition, males tended to produce more negative humor than females, as shown in tables 14.3 and 14.4, but this tendency reached only borderline significance (chi square [4] = 7.85, $p < .10$).

Of the 331 male respondents, 24% used humor, compared with 13% of the 393 female respondents. Although both used negative humor to the same degree (67%), more males used lethal humor (26% males, 20% females), whereas more females used disparaging humor (47% females, 41% males), as well as self-disparaging humor (12% of the females, 7% of the males).

No females portrayed cruelty or suffering. The 9 males who did so were adolescents; 3 had emotionally disturbances, 6 were nondisturbed. Eight males had responded to the DAS task, one to the SDT task.

Table 14.2

Age Differences in the Use of Humor in Responses by Children and Adults

Kinds of Humor

Number Using Humor	Age Group	Lethal 1 point	Disparaging 2 points	Ambiguous or Ambivalent 3 points	Resilient 4 points	Playful 5 points
9% 13 (140)	9–12	4 (31%)	5[1]	1	2	1
19% 50 (257)	13–19	18 (36%)	22[2]	1	3	6
21% 35 (165)	20+	6 (17%)	13[3]	5	0	11
19% 31 (162)	65+	3	17[4]	3	4	4
18% (129 of 724)		24% (31)	44%[5] (57)	8% (10)	7% (9)	17% (22)
ED						
8% 13 (164)	9–19	62% 8	31% 4	0	0	8% 1

1. 4 ridiculed others, scored "a"; 1 ridiculed self, scored "b."
2. 20 ridiculed others, scored "a"; 2 ridiculed self, scored "b."
3. 11 ridiculed others, scored "a"; 2 ridiculed self, scored "b."
4. 10 ridiculed others, scored "a"; 7 ridiculed self, scored "b."
5. 45 ridiculed others, scored "a"; 12 ridiculed self, scored "b."

Table 14.3

Humorous Responses by Men and Boys

Score

Number	Age Group	1	2	3	4	5	Total
	9 to12						
61	SDT	1	3	1	0	0	5
19	DAS	1	1a	0	1	0	3
	Ages 13–19						
47	SDT	6	7a 1b	0	1	2	17
16	DAS	3	0	0	1	0	4
	Ages 16–19						
27	SDT	2	3a	0	0	2	7
39	DAS	3	2a	0	1	0	6
	Age 20+						
18	SDT	2	3a	5	0	0	10
27	DAS	1	1a	0	0	0	2
10	SD	1	1a	0	0	2	4
	Age 65+						
17	SDT	1	3a	1	0	1	6
17	DAS	0	1a	1	0	1	3
33	SD	0	2a 5b	1	2	1	11
331		21	33	9	6	9	78 24%
		26%	41%	11%	11%	11%	100%

Table 14.4.

Humorous Responses by Women and Girls
Score

Number	Age	1	2	3	4	5	Total	
	9 to 12							
53	SDT	2	1b	0	1	1	5	
7	DAS	0	0	0	0	0	0	
	13–15							
43	SDT	1	2a	1	0	0	4	
40	DAS	1	1a, 1b	0	0	2	5	
	16–19							
31	SDT	1	1a	0	0	0	2	
14	DAS	1	4a	0	0	0	5	
	20+							
62	SDT	0	6a, 1b	0	0	3	10	
22	DAS	2	0	0	0	3	5	
26	SD	0	1b	0	0	3	4	
	65+							
27	SDT	0	2a	0	0	0	2	
45	DAS	1	1a, 1b	0	1	0	4	
23	SD	1	2a, 1b	0	1	1	5	
393		10	18a, 6b	1	3	13	51	(13%)
		20%	47%	2%	6%	25%	100%	

Although more females than males used playful humor (25% of females, 11% of males), these differences did not reach significance. More males than females used resilient humor (11% of males, 6% of females).

Although the children and adolescents with emotional disturbances produced less humor than the control groups did (8% of those with emotional disturbances, 18% control), 93% of their humorous responses were negative (62% lethal, 31% disparaging), compared with 68% of the control group (24% lethal, 44% disparaging). This difference did not reach significance.

To determine whether the three assessments differed in eliciting negative humor, the ratings of unimpaired respondents were analyzed. Responses to the SD assessment were significantly more positive than responses to the other two assessments (F [2] = 3.79, $p < .05$). The mean score of responses to the SD was higher than the mean score of responses to the DAS and SDT assessments (3.08, 2.18, and 2.39, respectively).

To examine the scale's reliability, two registered art therapists met for approximately 1 hour to discuss and practice rating a variety of response drawings. Subsequently, they rated 16 responses independently, without discussion. Using the Pearson correlation between two sets of ratings, interrater reliability was estimated to be 0.77, suggesting that the humor scale has reliability, but, like the instructions and training, needs further development.

Although these findings are preliminary, they are offered to encourage further study of the humor expressed in responses to the tasks.

Chapter 15

Cross-Cultural Studies

◇   ◇   ◇

This chapter will report the findings of clinicians and educators who used the SDT to assess children and adults in Brazil, Australia, Thailand, and Russia and to assess ethnic differences and similarities within the United States.

Use of the SDT in Brazil

A group of art therapists and psychologists in Brazil standardized the SDT on approximately 2,000 children and adults (Allessandrini, et al., 1998). They also examined responses for possible differences in schooling, gender, and type of school (public or private) and compared the performances of respondents in Brazil and in the United States. In translating the SDT manual into Portuguese, they made an adaptation to Brazilian culture in Predictive Drawing, substituting a soft drink for the ice cream soda, which is not widely consumed in Brazil. After administering the SDT and scoring responses, they developed norms and analyzed results.

Subjects

The subjects included students in elementary and high schools, as well as three groups of adults: Those whose education had been limited to elementary schools were placed in Group 1; those who had attended high school, in Group 2; and those who had attended college, Group 3.

The psychologists and art therapists tested 1,995 subjects in Sao Paulo. The largest city in Brazil, it receives heavy migration from elsewhere in the country and was considered representative of the Brazilian population. The children, ages 5 to 17, included subgroups based on grade, gender, and type of school; the adults, ages 18 to 40, were grouped on the basis of educational background. The testers selected at random 10 girls and 10 boys (or more) from at least three schools in each of 13 subgroups: one school in a central city area, another on the outskirts, and the third in-between. Each subgroup of children and adults included at least 30 subjects.

The adult sample consisted of volunteers who were blue-collar workers and professionals in several companies and educational institutions. They included 196 women and 304 men, ranging in age from 18 to 40 years, with a mean age of 29 and a standard deviation of 8 years.

A team of psychologists and art therapists trained by the authors administered and scored the SDT. The investigators hypothesized that the SDT could measure manifestations of emotion, cognition, and level of development; that cognitive scores would improve with schooling; and that there would be significant emotional content in responses to the Drawing from Imagination task. They used an analysis of variance to determine whether there were significant differences between groups.

Results

The analyses yielded differences in school grade and type of school, increasing with age and grade level in subtest and total scores. The differences were significant at the .001 level of probability. Growth was more pronounced in the early grades. In general, the scores of private school students were higher than the scores of public school students. High school students were not differentiated, either by grade or type of school. The mean scores of adults with limited education were below those of school-age children.

The findings confirmed the dependence of cognitive scores on age and level of education, regardless of gender. No significant gender differences were found, although borderline differences emerged in Predictive Drawing and Drawing from Observation. No differences emerged among high school students, either in grade or in type of school, but college graduates had higher mean scores than high school seniors. In both Brazil and the United States, the trend of growth in mean scores was similar, increasing gradually with grade and age level.

Among adults, analyses of variance confirmed the high correlation of SDT scores with level of education but not with gender. Among Groups 2 and 3, who had 7 to more than 11 years of schooling, nonsignificant gender differences emerged in Predictive Drawing, with superior performances among males. This finding was inconsistent with research findings in Australia, as discussed later in this chapter.

Although the trend of mean scores was similar in both Brazilian and American cultures, the American scores were consistently higher in subtest mean scores and total scores, a finding that was inconsistent with the findings in Russia, as discussed later on.

No significant cultural differences were found in the emotional content of responses to the Drawing from Imagination subtest. In addition, the authors broke down the five SDT ratings of 1 to 5 points, ranging from strongly negative to strongly positive, classifying them into 21 specific items. For example, Brazilian items 1 to 5 included subjects who were sad, isolated, suicidal, dead, or in mortal danger. Items 11 to 13 included ambivalent content, unemotional content, and ambiguous or unclear content. The investigators found more negative than positive ratings and the rate of ambivalence very high.

Similar emotional content was found in the responses of 6th-graders, 12th-graders, and college students. They also shared a high level of ambivalence compared with the other groups. None of the Brazilian 12th-graders responded with strongly negative content. Among 7th- and 8th-graders, however, strongly and moderately negative themes were frequent.

Nonemotional content predominated among Brazilian children from preschool to fourth grade. From fourth to sixth grades, the three neutral categories were more equally balanced, but in the sixth grade, ambivalent content was more prevalent.

The Brazilian investigators found the rate of ambivalence consistently high. They interpreted this as demonstrating a tendency to see both sides of an issue and concluded that the SDT "offers a dynamic and integrated form of evaluating the subject, especially those presenting with learning disabilities," enabling the clinician to understand how the subject thinks and feels and providing guidelines for treatment.

In our studies of students in the United States, the emotional content mean scores of male students, but not of female students, paralleled the Brazilian finding of a tendency toward negative themes. On the other hand, the mean scores of our female students expressed ambiguous, unemotional, and ambivalent themes, paralleling the high rates of ambivalence found among Brazilian respondents of both genders.

To examine interscorer and test–retest reliability, three judges, working independently, scored responses by 32 children selected at random in all grade levels. Results indicated strong interscorer reliability, with correlation coefficients of .94, .95, and .95 in total SDT scores. To examine retest reliability, the team administered the SDT twice to a group of 44 subjects after intervals of 15 to 30 days. Correlation coefficients ranged from .62 to .87, showing reliability.

Use of the SDT in Australia

Glenda Hunter, a graduate student in the master of education program at the University of New England, used the SDT as well as four other assessments, to examine individual and gender differences in Australia (Hunter, 1992).

Her subjects included 65 male and 128 female students, ages 15 to 53. Most of the males were enrolled in the university's engineering and construction apprenticeship courses; the female students, in office education courses.

Procedures

Hunter used the mean ratings of two scorers to assess 11 variables, based on the three SDT subtests: ability to sequence and predict horizontality and verticality (Predictive Drawing); ability to represent spatial relationships in horizontality, verticality, and depth (Drawing from Observation); ability to select, combine, and represent, emotional content, and language abilities, based on titles of responses to the Drawing from Imagination. Hunter also grouped the variables into three components. Component 1 reflected originality in solving problems that were satisfying to the test taker rather than providing a correct solution to a problem. She defined these responses as *unrestricted* spatial thinking or problem solving, which included ability to select, to combine, and to represent.

Component 2 reflected *restricted* spatial thinking—that is, correct solutions to problems of representing spatial relationships in three dimensions and in sequencing. Component 3, which accounted for 11.1% of the variance (eigenvalue = 1.2), reflected ability to conserve and predict by visualizing changes in position while the properties of objects remain the same.

Results

Two multivariate analyses of variance found significant gender differences in restricted and unrestricted spatial thinking or problem solving. The women had higher mean scores in unrestricted spatial thinking, performing better than the male students in the Drawing from Imagination tasks. The women were also superior on restricted tasks, which required defining visual–spatial relationships of objects in height, width, and depth and, to some extent, sequential order.

The contrast of gender, using the multivariate set of DVs, was significant (F [1,150] =5.8, p <.001). The associated univariate F test for Drawing from Imagination was significant (F [1,150] = 13.3, p < .001, Eta 2 = .08). In addition, the associated univariate F test for Drawing from Observation was significant (F [1,150] = 7.7, p < .006, Eta 2 = .05).

Drawing from Imagination accounted for 33.3% of the variance (eigenvalue + 3.7) defined by the variables loading .81 or above (ability to select, combine, represent, and language). The variable projection (emotional content), which loaded .53, was not found significant. Predicting horizontality loaded .73 and predicting verticality loaded .71. Drawing from Observation accounted for 17.6% of the variance (eigenvalue = 1.9) with loadings of .78 or higher (height, width, and depth).

Hunter observed that the findings were consistent with the theory that cognitive skills evident in verbal conventions can also be evident in visual conventions. She also observed that the gender differences found in her study were worthy of consideration in developing course methodologies that may facilitate more effective learning outcomes for these college students.

Use of the SDT in Thailand

Piyachat R. Finney returned to Thailand after graduating from and teaching in the expressive therapies program in the graduate school of Lesley College. In addition to serving as a clinician for 7 years in the United States, she is continuing to practice and teach in Bangkok universities.

Before returning to Thailand, Finney described her use of art therapy assessments with adults in a psychiatric day-care center (1994). She used the SDT for access to her clients' cognitive abilities and use of fantasy, creativity, and therapeutic themes. She observed that newly admitted clients usually felt safe with the SDT, and that it decreased performance anxiety by enabling them to regulate distance and closeness, as well as maintain defenses in the first phase of a relationship. She found the House-Tree-Person assessment useful in the middle phase of treatment and both assessments useful as posttests.

After returning to Thailand, Finney taught university courses in art therapy, family therapy, group therapy, treatment of trauma survivors, and psychodrama for counselors, clinicians, social workers, and psychiatric nurses. She also became a thesis adviser to graduate students.

One of Finney's students at Burapha University, Pornchit Dhanachitsiriphong, translated the SDT and used it in her dissertation to assess the effects of an art program on the emotional and cognitive development of male adolescents in a detention facility, as reported in chapter 5. After the program, the emotional and cognitive scores of the experimental group were significantly higher than the scores of the control group at the .01 level of probability, in each of the eight categories under consideration.

To illustrate, "S," age 19, responded to the Drawing from Imagination task by choosing and simply copying stimulus drawings of a boy and an older man, but drew the man larger than a sad-looking boy. As he explained, his father had been ill and passed away while he was incarcerated. He longed to see his father and wished some other delinquents would feel the same pain. Since this response ranked below the 25th percentile in emotional content and above the 75th percentile in cognitive content, it qualified S for the art program.

Responding again after the art program, S chose the boy, bed, and TV, drawing them in a room with pictures and a clock on the wall, and curtains billowing from an open window. As the art therapist explained, S was thinking about having his own bed and TV, adding that boys in the facility sleep on the floor in hot, poorly ventilated rooms.

The change in his drawings from bleak reality to hopeful fantasy, from 1 to 5 points in emotional content and self-image scores, suggests that it was caused by the intervention of 12 sessions in art therapy and rational emotive therapy over a period of 3 months.

Another adolescent, "K," age 18, whose strongly negative response also qualified him for the art program, chose and copied the dog and cat. He explained that he was reminded of his dog at home and had enjoyed watching dogs and cats fight and throwing a cat to a dog. The therapist added that many boys chose dogs as well as cats because big boys in the detention center had power over smaller boys.

In his second drawing, K chose and copied the boy and the snake and indicated that a snake bit him. The therapist added that a big boy and his friends continually hurt and made fun of K, that he had to be on his guard, was depressed, and wanted revenge.

For his posttest, K chose the boy and dog and indicated that they were playing happily. His response also reflects changes in content and self-image from negative to positive, perhaps reflecting relief from his oppressors or a wish-fulfilling fantasy.

Although the 10 Thai adolescents in the experimental group drew pictures about their own situations or concerns, all but 1 copied the stimulus drawings they chose. The exception was a single drawing that portrayed a male subject with Asian features. These respondents may not have been told that they could alter the stimulus drawings.

The strongly negative responses produced in Thailand do not seem different from strongly negative responses elsewhere. To generalize, however, would require matched samples, larger numbers, and statistical analyses.

Use of the SDT in Russia

Alexander Kopytin (2001), an art therapist in Russia, translated the SDT and conducted a normative study with the assistance of 11 psychologists. They collected samples and administered the tasks, then sent response drawings to Kopytin, who scored the responses with the assistance of a psychologist skilled in scoring and analyzed results with a psychologist skilled in statistical analysis.

Subjects of the normative study included 702 children, adolescents, and adults residing in large cities and small towns in various parts of the Russian Federation and Estonia. The children and adolescents included 350 girls and 294 boys, ages 5 to 19; students in public kindergartens and schools; those in public schools with innovative programs; and students from specialized schools for children and adults with language impairments. The adult sample of 36 women and 22 men ranged in age from 19 to 48 years; 38 had received higher education.

The psychologists administered the tasks individually or in small groups. Most had participated in a training program that included a seminar on the SDT.

Results

As in the United States and Brazil, cognitive scores in Russia increased with age. This growth was considerable but uneven, with the greatest gains in the early school years, then beginning to slow at ages 12 to 13, with adults receiving the highest scores. A surprising finding in both Russia and the United States, was that scores on the Drawing from Imagination and from Observation subtests were lower at ages 17 and 18 than at ages 15 to 16.

These investigators found the scores of Russian and American adults to be the same, but the scores of the Russian children and adolescents were often higher than scores of their American counterparts in Predictive Drawing, Drawing from Observation, and total test scores. On the other hand, American scores were higher on the Drawing from Imagination subtest. They attributed these findings to cultural differences, such as noting that manual skills (Drawing from Observation?) are valued highly in Russia, where children usually are trained to use them early in their lives.

Investigators found no significant difference in the scores of children and adolescents with normal language skills and the scores of adolescents with language impairments, suggesting that the cognitive skills assessed by the SDT are independent of verbal skills.

They found no significant differences among children and adults from various regions of the Russian Federation and Estonia, but they did observe differences between children attending regular public schools and those in schools with innovative programs.

Although they found no differences between the sexes in cognitive content, considerable gender differences emerged in emotional content and self-images. Females had higher, more positive scores in both categories.

In addition, they compared the frequencies of different responses. Although ambiguous, unemotional, and unclear drawings (3 points) predominated, investigators found strongly negative themes three times more frequently among males in emotional content (life-threatening relationships or sad or helpless solitary subjects, scored 1 point).

At the same time, they found strongly positive themes three times more frequently among females (caring relationships or effective/happy solitary subjects, scored 5 points) and moderately positive themes twice as frequently (friendly relationships or fortunate but passive solitary subjects, scoring 4 points).

Positive self-images also predominated among females, suggesting that females identified with powerful, beloved, or effective subjects (5 points) as well as with fortunate but passive subjects (4 points) three times more frequently than males did.

Similar gender differences in emotional content scores were found in the United States, as reported in chapter 4. More than three times as many American males responded with strongly negative themes, scored 1 point (17% of males, 5% of females), and more females than males responded with strongly positive themes, scored 5 points (13% of females, 9% of males) and moderately positive themes (27% of females, 15% of males).

The reverse emerged in self-image scores. More American males than females scored 4 points (18% of males, 12% of females) and 5 points (18% of males, 12% of females), although neutral 3-point scores predominated among both genders (59% of males, 59% of females).

Use of the SDT with Hispanic Students in the United States

In the Miami-Dade County Public School system, one of the largest in the nation, 52.8% of the student population is Hispanic, 33% is African American, and 14.2% is white, non-Hispanic, and other. Approximately 58% of the students do not have English as their primary language, and more than 59% of the district's students are eligible for free and reduced lunch. The system's clinical art therapy department (M-OCPS) provides remedial services and designs appropriate treatment plans to help students with emotional handicaps and severe emotional disturbances. In the school year 2000–2001, the department's chairperson, Dr. Linda Jo Pfeiffer, ATR-BC, added the SDT to its repertoire of art therapy assessments to provide an alternative method of assessing strengths and weaknesses and to provide educators with alternative ways of teaching traditional material.

In a cross-cultural study, the SDT was used to compare a sample of Hispanic students in Miami with a sample of presumably non-Hispanic students elsewhere in the United States. Cheryl Earwood, ATR, an art therapist in the M-OCPS department, administered the SDT to 30 students, ages 14 to 16: 20 boys and 10 girls, from a class in English for Speakers of Other Languages (ESOL). Previously, they had resided in South or Central America, and had been in the United States less than 1 year. Their responses were compared with the responses of 30 students, approximately the same ages, attending public schools in Indiana and Pennsylvania, as well as in suburban and urban New York. The group included 14 girls and 16 boys.

Because cognitive differences tended to diminish or disappear during adolescence in the United States, Russia, and Brazil, this pilot study examined the emotional content and self-image scores of responses to the Drawing from Imagination subtest.

Results

The total scores did not reveal much, but when the scores were examined separately, intriguing differences between groups emerged.

Self-Image Scores

In total self-image scores, 53% of the Hispanic students, compared with 47% of the controls, responded with positive themes; 6%, compared with 13%, responded with negative themes; and 33%, compared with 47%, responded with ambiguous, ambivalent, or unemotional themes.

When positive scores were examined separately, however, substantially more Hispanic students scored 5 points, seeming to identify with subjects who were powerful, loved, destructive, assaultive, or achieving goals (40% of Hispanic students, 27% of controls), as shown in table 15.1. For example, a 14-year-old boy selected (and copied) the stimulus drawing dog and snake, then wrote, "The snake its sleeping, but when it wake up see a dog trying to kill her, she went right away to bit the dog."

Table 15.1

Comparing the SDT Self-Image Scores of 30 Hispanic Adolescents, Ages 14 to 16, in the United States Less Than One Year, with the Scores of 30 Controls

| | Self-Image Scores | | | | |
	1	2	3	4	5
Hispanic Adolescents	3%	10%	33%	13%	40%
Controls	3%	3%	47%	20%	27%

A 15-year-old Hispanic girl selected the girl and the ice cream soda, then wrote, "The girl is going to eat the ice cream. She is very happy for the ice cream because her mom give to her because she is good student."

On the other hand, fewer Hispanic than American adolescents drew moderately positive fantasies, scored 4 points, and seemed to identify with subjects portrayed as fortunate but passive (13% of the Hispanic, 20% of controls).

When negative self-image scores were examined separately, more than three times as many Hispanic students seemed to identify with subjects portrayed as frightened, frustrated, or unfortunate, scored 2 points (10% of Hispanics, 3% of controls), whereas small but equivalent proportions of both groups (3%) seemed to identify with subjects portrayed as sad, isolated, or in mortal danger, scored 1 point.

Emotional Content Scores

In total emotional content scores, proportionally 43% of the Hispanic students, compared with 47% of the controls, responded with negative themes (1 and 2 points); 33%, compared with 34%, responded with positive themes (4 and 5 points); and 23%, compared with 20%, responded with ambiguous, ambivalent, or unemotional themes (3 points).

When the negative scores were examined separately, however, more than twice as many Hispanic students scored 1 point, drawing pictures about violent relationships or sad, isolated individuals (23% of Hispanic students, 10% of controls), as shown in table 15.2. In 2 points, however, the findings reversed: substantially fewer Hispanics than controls drew stressful relationships or unfortunate solitary subjects (20% of Hispanic students, 37% of controls).

Table 15.2

Comparing the SDT Emotional Content Scores of 30 Hispanic Adolescents, ages 14 to 16, in the United States Less Than One Year, with the Scores of 30 Controls

	Emotional Content Scores				
	1	2	3	4	5
Hispanic Adolescents	23%	20%	23%	13%	20%
Controls	10%	37%	20%	17%	17%

When positive scores were examined separately, fewer Hispanic students scored 4 points (13% of Hispanic students, 17% of controls), drawing fantasies about friendly relationships or fortunate solitary subjects, but more scored 5 points, drawing loving relationships or effective solitary subjects (20% of Hispanics, 17% of controls).

Three Art Assessments

Strongly Negative Self-Images

Although their numbers tend to be few, any student who draws a strongly negative self-image warrants attention. For example, a 14-year-old Hispanic girl selected stimulus drawings of the girl and the bed, then drew the girl lying in bed, tears on her cheeks. Her written story: "Someday one girl was crying. I think that actual cry too, because all she's dreams are very difficult and don't feel well for her parents, so she want to leave the house."

Because her response (scored 1 point) suggests that she might be at risk for depression, she was referred for clinical follow-up.

Students who score 5 points on the self-image scale, but 1 point on the emotional content scale, are also of concern. For example, a Hispanic boy who chose stimulus drawings of a snake and an insect drew a sequence of encounters between them. Starting with the snake, his first drawing shows it lying in the grass, the sun shining overhead. His second drawing shows the spider under a cloud. The snake then chases the spider, which leaps into a tree as the snake hits its head against the tree trunk and falls back, with stars circling its head. The snake recovers, jumps to the top of the tree, and in the final scene the spider is lying in the snake's open mouth.

The aggressive humor that characterizes this response suggests a wish-fulfilling fantasy. Previously, his classroom teacher had described his behavior as controlling and often "out of control." She had not asked him to join classmates who had been asked to respond to the drawing task, but was unable to prevent him from joining nevertheless.

Discussion

The finding that 40% of the Hispanic adolescents, compared with 27% of the American adolescents, scored 5 points on the self-image scale suggests that the Hispanic adolescents felt more secure and confident in themselves. Although separated from their native countries less than 1 year, they did not seem to be experiencing acculturation stress, as measured by responses to the SDT. The fact that they resided in Miami, within a large population of Spanish-speaking residents, may have played a critical role.

This finding accords with the findings of two large studies that compared the prevalence of psychiatric disorders among Mexican immigrants and American residents in the United States. One study (Vega et al., 1998) examined 3,012 adults in California, ages 18 to 59, of Mexican origin. These investigators found that 24% had experienced 12 of the *DSM-III-R* disorders, compared with 48.1% of United States–born respondents. They concluded that despite very low education and income levels, Mexican Americans had lower rates of lifetime psychiatric disorders, compared with rates reported for the U.S. population, and that psychiatric morbidity among Mexican Americans is primarily influenced by cultural variance, rather than by socioeconomic status. Mexican immigrants had lifetime rates similar to those of Mexican citizens, whereas rates for Mexican Americans were similar to those in the United States.

The second study (Escobar, 1998) found that immigrants, compared with patients born in the United States, had significantly lower prevalence of depression and post-traumatic stress disorder, despite their lower socioeconomic status.

As Dr. Pfeiffer observed, it may be that an expansive sense of family has contributed to the positive SDT responses of Spanish-speaking students in Miami. Extended families, such as distant cousins and three or four generations may be more likely than small families to engender feelings of security and confidence.

These findings suggest that by widening our circle of shared experiences, we gain mutual support and extend the boundary between "us and them."

Observations

The studies reviewed in this chapter suggest that the SDT is relatively free from cultural bias that favors some and discriminates against others. I am aware of only one cultural adaptation in administering the test: Allessandrini and her associates decided to change the ice-cream soda of the Predictive Drawing subtest into a plain soda, to accord with the Brazilian culture.

In responding to the SDT, however, cultural differences emerged. The cognitive scores of American children were higher than the scores of Brazilian children, but lower than those of the Russian children. Although the Russian investigators found that American children had higher scores in Drawing from Imagination, they also had lower scores in Predictive Drawing, Drawing from Observation, and total scores. On the other hand, in all three countries, cognitive scores improved gradually with age and level of education, with adults receiving the highest scores. No cognitive differences were found among adults in different countries.

No gender differences emerged in the American and Russian studies, but in the Australian study, women had higher scores than men in Drawing from Imagination and Drawing from Observation.

As measured by the emotional content scale, negative themes predominated among males, positive themes among females, in both America and Russia, whereas no significant gender differences were found in Brazil. In self-image, American males had higher (more positive) scores than did American females, whereas the reverse was found in Russia.

How can these cross-cultural differences and similarities be explained, and what do they imply? Do cognitive differences indicate that children in one country are more or less intelligent than children in another country, or are these differences determined by cultural preferences in deciding what children should learn and how they should be taught?

As Kopytin observed, manual skills are valued highly in Russia, where children are trained to develop them early in life. Manual skills and art skills seem valued less highly in American education today, where many elementary and secondary schools have eliminated art from the curriculum.

Perhaps the similarities found across cultures have biological explanations, while the differences have cultural explanations. Although these are speculations, the findings suggest that further investigation with larger populations and additional cultures would be worthwhile.

The following chapter brings this book to a close with concluding observations.

Chapter 16

Concluding Observations

◇   ◇   ◇

The three assessments presented in this book are based on the premise that cognitive skills and emotions can be evident in visual, as well as verbal, conventions and can be expressed and assessed through responses to the stimulus drawing tasks. The studies that were reviewed seem to support the premises. Some were based on individuals or small samples, others on groups large enough for statistical analysis. Correlations are not causations, and even though we cannot generalize from the behavior of individuals or small groups, they provide information that escapes detection in large groups.

It seems there are two kinds of knowledge, objective and subjective. As Fluornoy observed, the scientific intellect analyzes, abstracts, and generalizes, and when it deals with particular objects, dissolves their particularity, but it is just this unique individuality that is the exclusive interest of art (see Allen 1967).

Other observers include both kinds of knowledge. Karl Stern (1965), for example, distinguished between the analytical and the intuitive. The artist's knowledge is intuitive, subjective, and poetic, "an immediate beholding of essences" (p. 42). It can be experienced, but not explained, and is contrary to the scientist's knowledge, acquired through objective analysis. Nevertheless, we can study movement both ways, by floating in the stream ourselves, as well as by timing the passage of a stick past certain points on shore.

Jacob Bronowsky (1973), a scientist at the Salk Institute, suggested that the scientific search for truth and the human search for understanding belong together, that science has a way of formalizing its language so that it can be persuasive and constantly checked, whereas art and literature carry many messages, not one, and speak for our most secret thoughts and feelings.

Robert Sternberg (1997), a psychologist concerned with successful intelligence, cautioned that our schools emphasize analytical intelligence at the expense of developing ability to think. We value students with analytical abilities but often write off those with creative abilities who do not perform well on IQ tests, but who may become highly successful in business, engineering, architecture, or the arts.

We seem to need both subjective and objective knowledge and they seem to converge in art therapy. Without both, the information that became evident in the behavior of an individual, or of small groups with high or low scores, vanishes, eclipsed behind scores of the large groups that statistical analyses require.

The findings of studies reported here seem to indicate that responses to the drawing tasks offer unique opportunities to contribute to knowledge about human behavior and age, gender, or cultural differences and similarities. The responses can provide access to cognitive skills, wishes, concerns, and attitudes toward self and others; opportunities to identify individuals at risk and to enhance the development of all. I hope readers find the assessments useful and will continue to explore the opportunities provided by the visual arts.

Section V

Appendices

Readers are free to reproduce testing materials in the Appendices for their personal use, but not for resale or any other commercial purpose.

Appendix A

The Silver Drawing Test of Cognition and Emotion

◇   ◇   ◇

Drawing What You Predict, What You See, and What You Imagine

Rawley A. Silver, EdD, ATR–BC

Name.................. Age........Sex........Date..............

....

SDT Predictive Drawing

Suppose you took a few sips of a soda, then a few more, and more, until your glass was empty. Can you draw lines in the glasses to show how the soda would look if you gradually drank it all?

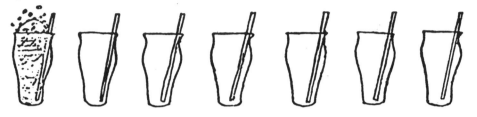

Suppose you tilted a bottle half filled with water. Can you draw lines in the bottles to show how the water would look?

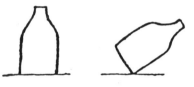

Suppose you put the house on the spot marked x. Can you draw the way it would look?

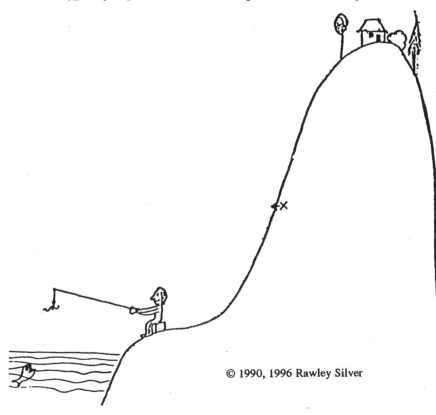

© 1990, 1996 Rawley Silver

SDT Drawing from Observation

Have you ever tried to draw something just the way it looks? Here are some things to draw. Look at them carefully, then draw what you see in the space below.

Drawing What You Imagine

Form A, Silver Drawing Test

Choose two picture ideas and imagine a story - something happening between the pictures your choose.

When you are ready, draw a picture of what you imagine. Show what is happening in your drawing. You can make changes and draw other things too.

When you finish drawing, write a title or story. Tell what is happening and what my happen later on.

Drawing What You Imagine

Form B, Silver Drawing Test

Choose two picture ideas and imagine a story- something happening between the p[ictures you choose.

    When you are ready, draw a picture of what you imagine. Show what is happening in your drawing. You can make changes and draw other things too.

    When you finish drawing, write a title or story. Tell what is happening and what may happen later on.

SDT Layout Sheet

CYLINDER
4½" high
(No. 2 can without label)

CYLINDER
4½" high
(bathroom tissue roller)

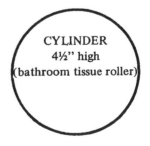

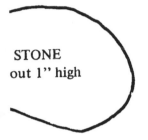

STONE
out 1" high

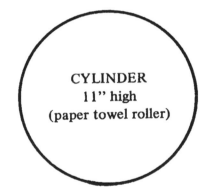

CYLINDER
11" high
(paper towel roller)

SDT Drawing from Imagination

Drawing

Story:_____
_____
_____
_____
_____

<u>Please fill in the blanks below:</u>

First name _____ Sex_____ Age _____ Location (state): _____ Date:_____

Just now I'm feeling _____very happy _____O.K. _____angry _____frightened _____sad

SDT Classroom Record Sheet

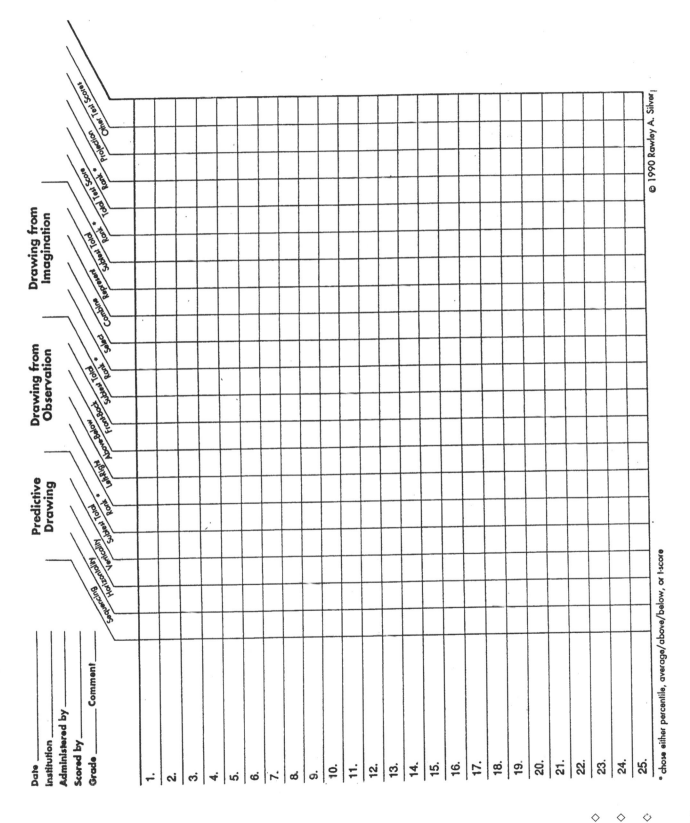

Record Sheet for Response Drawings

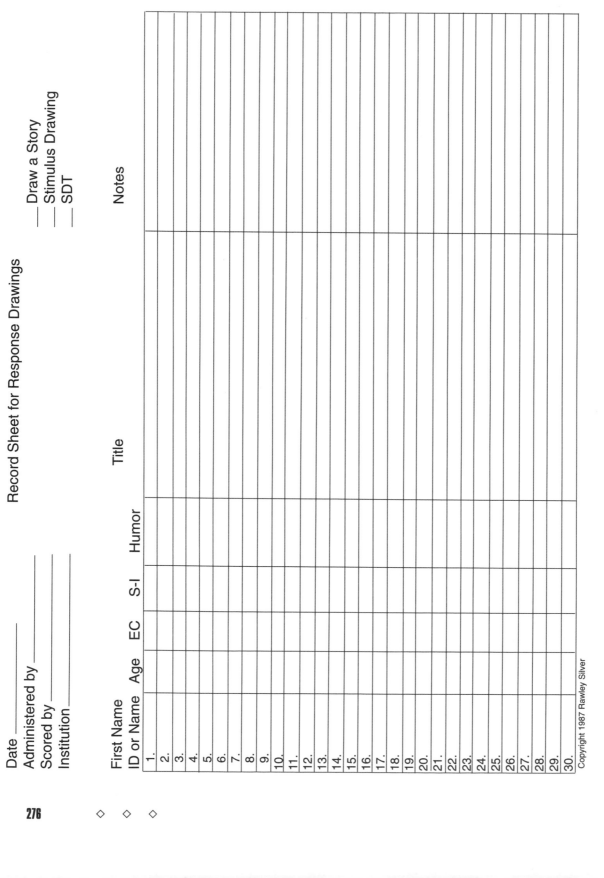

Record Sheet for Response Drawings

Date —————
Administered by —————
Scored by —————
Institution —————

___ Draw a Story
___ Stimulus Drawing
___ SDT

First Name ID or Name	Age	EC	S-I	Humor	Title	Notes
1.						
2.						
3.						
4.						
5.						
6.						
7.						
8.						
9.						
10.						
11.						
12.						
13.						
14.						
15.						
16.						
17.						
18.						
19.						
20.						
21.						
22.						
23.						
24.						
25.						
26.						
27.						
28.						
29.						
30.						

◇ ◇ ◇

Forms for Assessing Individual Responses to the
Silver Drawing Test of Cognition and Emotion (SDT)

Name_____ Age____Sex___ Date_____

School_____Administered by_____

The SDT is designed to assess cognitive development and to screen for emotional problems. The SDT includes three subtests: Predictive Drawing, to assess the ability to sequence and predict changes in the appearance of objects; Drawing from Imagination, to assess the emotional content of responses, as well as assess three cognitive skills and Drawing from Observation to assess concepts of space.

Predictive Drawing Subtest

Predicting a Sequence

____0 points: No sequence representing the soda inside the glass or glasses.
____1 point: Incomplete sequence.
____2 points: Two or more sequences.
____3 points: Descending series of lines with corrections (trial and error).
____4 points: A sequence with unevenly spaced increments but no corrections.
____5 points: A sequence with evenly spaced increments and no corrections (systematic). The sequence does not have to continue to the bottom of the glass.

Predicting Horizontality★

____0 points: No line representing water surface is inside the tilted bottle.
____1 point: Line parallels bottom or sides of tilted bottle (suggesting that the frame of reference is inside the bottle).
____2 points: Line almost parallels bottom or sides of tilted bottle.
____3 points: Line is oblique (suggesting that the frame of reference is external but not related to the table surface).
____4 points: Line seems related to table surface but is not parallel.
____5 points: Line is parallel to table surface within 5 degrees.

Predicting Verticality★

____0 points: No representation of house or, if examinee is younger than 5, the house is inside the mountain.
____1 point: House is approximately perpendicular to the slope.
____2 points: House is neither perpendicular nor vertical but on a slant or upside down.
____3 points: House is vertical but has no support (may be entirely inside the mountain if examinee is older than 5 years).
____4 points: House is vertical but has inadequate support, such as partly inside the mountain.
____5 points: House is vertical, supported by posts, columns, platforms, or other structures.

★ The tasks for predicting horizontality and verticality are adapted from experiments by Piaget and Inhelder (1967).

Drawing from Imagination Subtest

Cognitive Content

ABILITY TO SELECT (the content or message of a drawing)

___0 points.   No evidence of selecting.

___1 point.   *Perceptual level*: single subject, or subjects unrelated in size or placement.

___2 points.   Subjects may be related in size or placement, but there is no interaction.

___3 points.   *Functional level*: concrete, shows what subjects do or what is done to them.

___4 points.   Descriptive, rather than abstract or imaginative.

___5 points.   Conceptual level: imaginative, well-organized idea; implies more than is visible; or shows other ability to deal with abstract ideas.

ABILITY TO COMBINE (the form of the drawing)

___0 points.   Single subject, no spatial relationships.

___1 point.   *Proximity:* Subjects float in space, related only by proximity.

___2 points.   Arrows, dotted lines, or other attempts to show relationships.

___3 points.   *Baseline:* subjects related to one another along a base line (real or implied).

___4 points.   Beyond the baseline level, but much of the drawing area is blank.

___5 points.   Overall coordination: shows depth, or takes into account the entire drawing area, or else includes a series of two or more drawings.

ABILITY TO REPRESENT (concepts and creativity in the form, content, title, or story)

___0 points.   No evidence of representation.

___1 point.   *Imitative*: copies stimulus drawings, or uses stick figures or stereotypes.

___2 points.   Beyond imitation, but drawing or ideas are commonplace.

___3 points.   Restructured: changes or elaborates on stimulus drawings or stereotypes.

___4 points.   Beyond restructuring, moderately original or expressive.

___5 points.   Transformational: highly original, expressive, playful, suggestive, or uses metaphors, puns, jokes, satire, or double meanings.

Emotional Content

___1 point. *Strongly negative themes*: for example,
Solitary subjects portrayed as sad, helpless, isolated, suicidal, dead, or in mortal danger;
Or relationships that are destructive, murderous, or life threatening.

___2 points. *Moderately negative themes*; for example,
Solitary subjects portrayed as frightened, angry, frustrated, dissatisfied, worried, destructive, or unfortunate;
Relationships that are stressful, hostile, or unpleasant.

___3 points. *Neutral themes:* for example,
Ambivalent, both negative and positive;
Unemotional, neither negative nor positive;
Ambiguous or unclear.

___4 points. *Moderately positive themes*: for example,
Solitary subjects portrayed as fortunate but passive, such as watching television or being rescued;
Relationships that are friendly, or pleasant.

___5 points. *Strongly positive themes*: for example,
Solitary subjects portrayed as happy, effective, or achieving goals, active.
Relationships that are caring or loving.

Self-Image

___1 point. *Morbid fantasy*: Respondent seems to identify with a subject portrayed as sad, helpless, isolated, suicidal, dead, or in mortal danger.

___2 points. *Unpleasant fantasy:* Respondent seems to identify with a subject portrayed as frightened, frustrated, or unfortunate.

___3 points. *Ambiguous or ambivalent fantasy:* Unclear or invisible (such as the narrator), or else respondent seems to identify with a subject portrayed as ambivalent or unemotional.

___4 points. *Pleasant fantasy*: Respondent seems to identify with a subject portrayed as fortunate but passive, such as watching television or being rescued.

___5 points. *Wish-fulfilling fantasy*: respondent seems to identify with a subject represented as happy, loved, powerful, admirable, intimidating, destructive, assaultive, or achieving goals.

The Use of Humor

___1 point: *Strongly aggressive humor,* invites viewer to laugh at victim(s) of violence or in life-threatening danger. Suggests desire to punish or overpower.

___2 points. *Moderately aggressive humor,* invites viewer to laugh at someone (may include self) who is suffering, embarrassed, frustrated, ridiculous, or unfortunate.

___3 points. *Unclear or ambivalent use of humor.* Invites viewer to laugh at subject who is both negative and positive, such as both frustrating and endearing, or both ridiculous and dangerous.

___4 points. *Self-disparaging humor,* invites viewer to laugh at subject who seems to be self bualso invites sympathy or admiration (suggests resilience, ability to cope).

___5 points. *Playful humor,* invites viewer to share amusement, absurdity, double meaning, or play on words (no suggestion of hostility, denial, or covert meanings).

Comments or
recommendations_____

_____

_____

_____

_____

_____

_____

_____

_____

Drawing from Observation Task

Sketches of the arrangement are shown below. The front view can serve as the criterion for drawings scored 5 points.

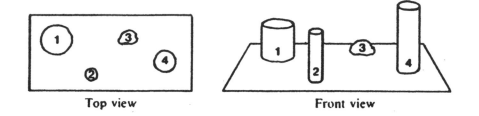

Top view   Front view

When scoring, note that cylinder #1 is the widest, #4 is the tallest, #2 is in the foreground, and the stone, #3, is behind and between #2 and #4.

To examinees seated toward the left, #2 appears farther from #1 and closer to #3.

To examinees seated toward the right, #2 appears farther from #3 and closer to #1.

Horizontal (Left–Right) Relationships

___0 points.   No objects are in the correct left–right order.

___1 point.   Only one object is in the correct left–right order.

___2 points.   Two objects are in the correct left–right order.

___3 points.   Three adjacent objects, or two pairs, are in the correct left–right order.

___4 points.   All four objects are in correct order but not carefully represented.

___5 points.   All horizontal relationships are represented accurately.

Vertical (Above–Below) Relationships

___0 points.   All objects are flat; no representation of height.

___1 point: All objects are about the same height.

___2 points.   Two objects (not necessarily adjacent) are approximately correct in height.

___3 points.   Three objects (not necessarily adjacent) are approximately correct in height.

___4 points.   All four objects are correct in height but not carefully represented.

___5 points.   All vertical relationships are represented accurately.

Relationships in Depth (Front–Back)

___0 points.   No adjacent objects are correctly related in depth.

___1 point.   One object is above or below a base line (drawn or implied), or else front–back relationships are incorrect.

___2 points.   Two objects are approximately correct in front–back relationships (not necessarily adjacent).

___3 points.   Three adjacent objects, or two pairs, are approximately correct.

___4 points.   All front–back relationships are correct but not well represented.

___5 points.   All depth relationships are accurate, and the layout sheet is included.

Appendix B

Draw A Story

◇   ◇   ◇

Draw a Story

Drawing

Story:_____
_____
_____
_____
_____

<u>Please fill in the blanks below:</u>

First name _____ Sex_____ Age _____ Location (state): _____Date:_____
Just now I'm feeling _____very happy _____O.K. _____angry _____frightened _____sad

Draw a Story

Form A

Choose two of these drawings and imagine a story - something happening between the subjects you choose.

When you are ready, draw a picture of what you imagine. Make your drawing tell the story. Show what is happening. Feel free to change these drawings and to add your own ideas.

When you finish drawing, write the story in the place provided.

Draw a Story

Form B

Choose two of these drawings and imagine a story - something happening between the subjects you choose.

When you are ready, draw a picture of what you imagine. Make your drawing tell the story. Show what is happening. Feel free to change these drawings and to add your own ideas.

When you finish drawing, write the story in the place provided.

Form for Assessing the Story Content of Responses to the
Draw-a-Story Task★

Name_____Age____Gender_____Date_____

Location_____Scored by_____

1 point: Strongly Negative, for example,

____ Subjects are sad, isolated, helpless, suicidal, or in mortal danger.
____ Relationships are destructive, murderous, or life-threatening.

2 points: Moderately negative, for example,

____ Subjects are frustrated, fearful, fearsome, or unfortunate.
____ Relationships are stressful or hostile.

3 points: Intermediate level, for example,

____ Subjects or relationships that are both negative and positive, suggesting ambivalence or conflict.
____ Neither negative nor positive, unemotional.
____ Ambiguous or unclear.
____ Subjects or relationships that are unemotional, neither negative nor positive, no feelings expressed toward the subjects or relationships portrayed.

4 points: Moderately Positive, for example,

____ Subjects are fortunate but passive.
____ Relationships are friendly.

5 points: Strongly positive, for example,

____ Subjects are happy or achieving goals.
____ Relationships are caring or loving.

★To evaluate responses for cognitive and creative skills, see *Silver Drawing Test* (1990), pp. 42–43.

Stimulus Drawings and Techniques

◇   ◇   ◇

Form for Assessing the Emotional Content of Principal Subjects and Environments

Name_____**Age**____**Gender**_____**Date**_____

Location_____**Scored by**_____

Principal Subject (s)

_____1 point. *Strongly negative*: for example, subjects are dead, dying, helpless, sad, or in grave danger.

_____2 points. *Moderately negative*: for example, subjects are angry, frustrated, frightened, or suffering.

_____3 points. *Mildly negative*: for example, subjects are dissatisfied or unfortunate.

_____4 points. *Intermediate level*: for example, subjects are ambivalent (both negative and positive) or ambiguous (unclear or neither negative nor positive).

_____5 points. *Mildly positive*: for example, subjects are smiling or enjoying something.

_____6 points. *Moderately positive*: for example, subjects are effective, strong, or fortunate.

_____7 points. *Strongly positive*: for example, subjects are loved, loving, escaping, or overcoming powerful forces.

Environment (including people, objects, and events)

_____1 point. *Strongly negative*: for example, life-threatening situations, dripping knives or smoking guns.

_____2 points. *Moderately negative*: for example, dangerous, frustrating, stressful, or unfortunate situations.

_____3 points. *Mildly negative*: for example, unpleasant activities or scenes, rain, snow, dark clouds, deserts, storms, sunsets, or bare trees.

_____4 points. *Intermediate level*: for example, ambivalent situations (both negative and positive), ambiguous situations (unclear or neither negative nor positive).

_____5 points. *Mildly positive*: for example, pleasant activities or scenes, flowers, fruits, sunrise, or leafy trees.

_____6 points. *Moderately positive*: for example, tasty, friendly, pleasurable, or fortunate situations or events.

_____7 points. *Strongly positive*: for example, loving or deeply gratifying relationships.

Drawing

Story:_____

_____

_____

_____

_____

Please fill in the blanks below:

First name ____ Sex____ Age ____ Location (state): _____Date:_____

Just now I'm feeling ____very happy ____O.K. ____angry ____frightened ____sad

Stimulus Drawing Cards

To remove cards, cut along dotted lines, then cut cards apart.

1. *Group A (People)*

© 1978 Rawley Silver

© 1978 Rawley Silver

©1978 Rawley Silver

©1978 Rawley Silver

© 1978 Rawley Silver

© 1978 Rawley Silver

2. Group A (People)

3. Group A (People)

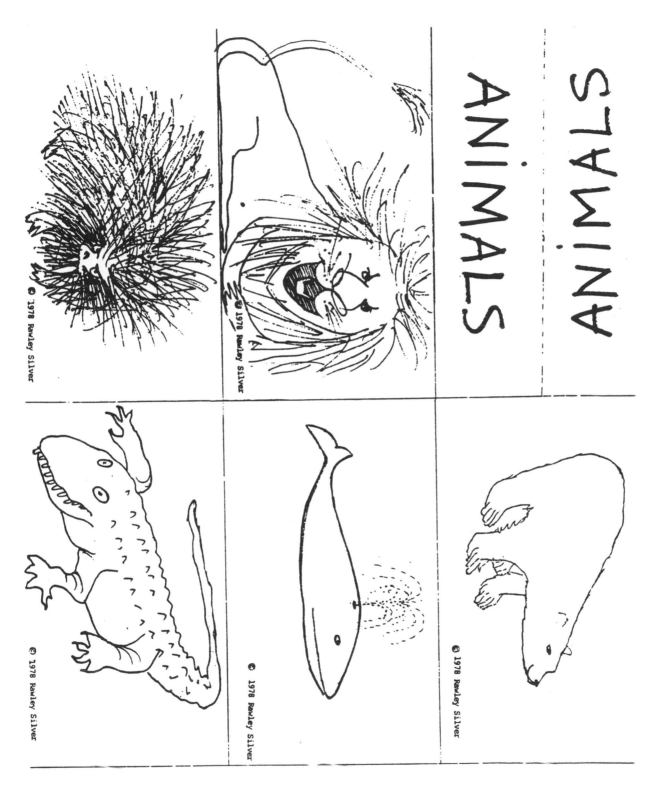

4. Group B (Animals)

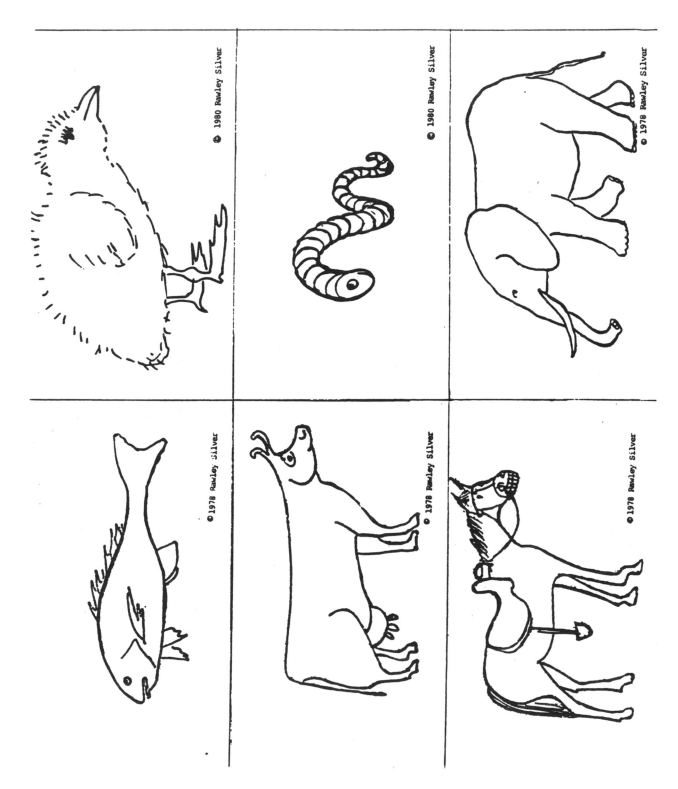

5. Group B (Animals)

6. Group C (Things)

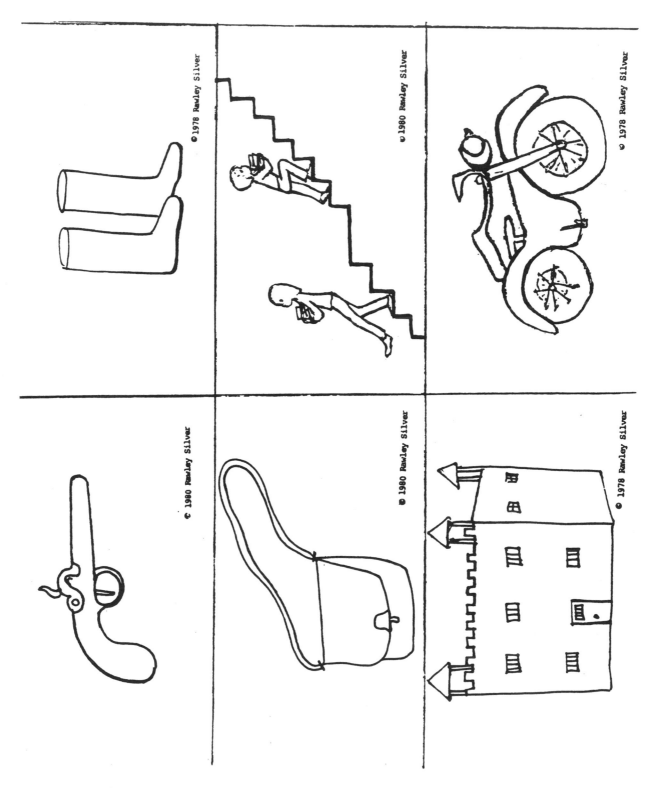

7. Group C (Things)

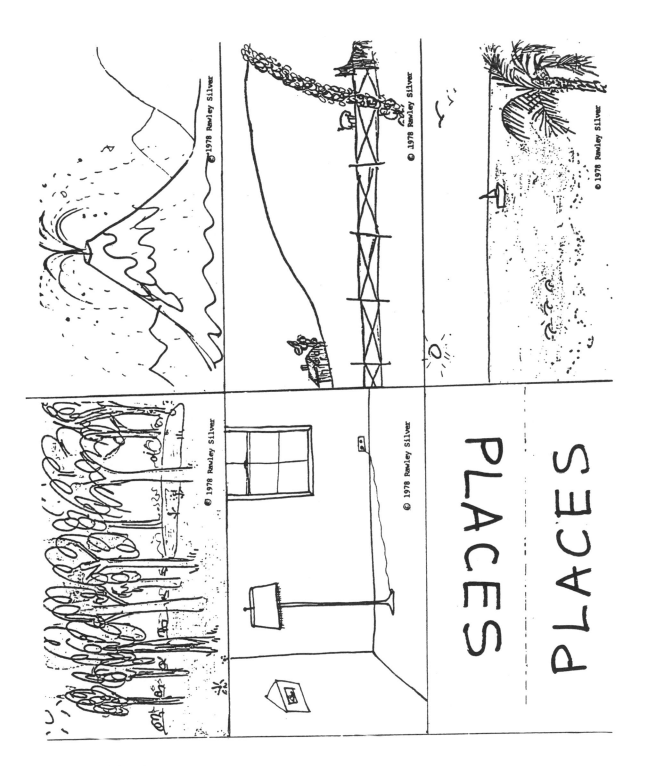

8. Group D (Places)

9. Animals and Places

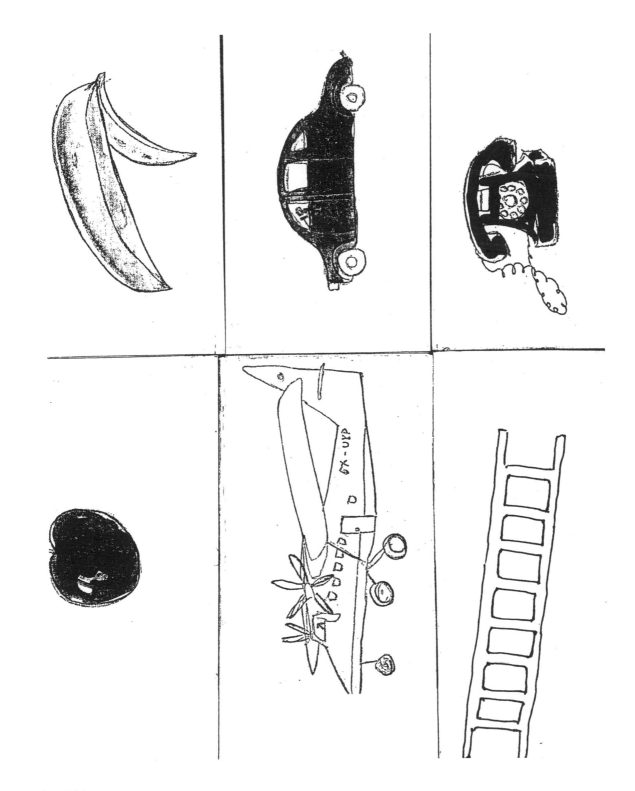

10. Food or Things

References

Allen, G. W. 1995. *William James* (p. 497). New York: Viking.

Allessandrini, C. D., Duarte, J.L., Dupas, M. A., & Bianco, M. F. 1998. SDT: The Brazilian standardization of the Silver drawing test of cognition and emotion. *ARTherapy, Journal of the American Art Therapy Association, 15*(2) 107–115.

American Psychiatric Association. 1994. *Diagnostic criteria from DSM-IV.* Washington, DC. Allen Frances, MD, Chair, Task Force on DSM-IV.

Anderson, V. 2001. *A study of the correlations between the SDT Drawing from Imagination Subtest and the Gates-MacGinitie Reading Comprehension Test with middle school students.* Unpublished master's degree thesis, MCP Hahnemann University, Philadelphia.

Arnheim, R. 1969. *Visual Thinking.* Berkely, CA: University of California Press.

Bannatyne, A. 1971. Language, reading, and learning disabilities. Springfield, IL: Chas C. Thomas.

Beck, A. T. 1978. *Depression inventory.* Philadelphia: Center for Cognitive Therapy.

Blasdel, L. 1997. *Critical thinking skills developed through visual art experiences.* Unpublished master's thesis, Emporia State University, Kansas.

Brenner, C. A. 1974. *Elementary textbook of psychoanalysis.* New York: Anchor.

Brandt, M. 1995. *Visual stories: A comparison study utilizing the Silver art therapy assessment with adolescent sex offenders.* Unpublished master's thesis, Ursuline College, Pepper Pike, Ohio.

Bronowski, J. 1973. *The ascent of man.* Boston: Little, Brown & Co.

Bruner, J. S., Olver, R. R., Greenfield, P. M., Hornsby, J. R., Kenny, H. J., Maccoby, M. et al.

1966. *Studies in cognitive growth.* New York: John Wiley.

Buck, J. N. 1948. The H.T.P. technique, a qualitative and quantitative scoring method. *Journal of Clinical Psychology* (no. 5).

Buber, M. 1961. *Between man and man* (p. 91). Boston: Beacon Press.

Burns, R., & Kaufman, S. H. 1972. *Actions, styles, & symbols in kinetic family drawings.* New York: Brunner/Mazel.

California Achievement Tests. 1957. Monterey, CA: CTB, McGraw-Hill.

Canadian Cognitive Abilities Test. 1970–1990. Scarboro, Ontario: Nelson.

Carrion, F. & Silver, R. Using the Silver Drawing Test in school and hospital. *American Journal of Art Therapy, 30*(2), 36–43.

Cohen, B. M. 1986. *The diagnostic drawing series.* Alexandria, VA: Barry Cohen.

Coffey, C. M. 1995. *Women, major depression, and imagery.* Unpublished master's thesis, Southern Illinois University, Edwardsville, Illinois.

Couch, J. B. 1996. Poster presentation, Annual Conference of the American Art Therapy Association, Philadelphia.

Craig, H., & Gordon, H. 1989. Specialized cognitive function among deaf individuals: Implications for instruction. In Martin, D. S. (Ed.), *Cognition, education, & deafness.* Washington, DC: Gallaudet University Press.

Damasio, A. R. 1994. *Descartes' error.* New York: Putnam.

Dhanachitsiriphong, P. 1999. *The effects of art therapy and rational emotive therapy on cognition and emotional development of male adolescents in Barn Karuna Training School of the Central Observation and Protection Center.* Unpublished master's thesis, Burapha University, Thailand.

Dunn-Snow, P. 1994. Adapting the Silver Draw-a-Story Assessment: Art therapy techniques with children and adolescents. *American Journal of Art Therapy, 33,* 35–36.

Escobar, J. I. 1998. Why are immigrants better off? *Archives of General Psychiatry, 55*(9), 781–782.

Finney, P. 1994. A review of two art assessment tasks in an adult day treatment center. *ARTherapy, 11*(2), 154–156.

Fluornoy, E. 1995. In Allen, G. W. *William James.* New York: Viking.

Gantt, L. & Tabone, C. 1998. *The formal elements art therapy scale: The rating manual.* Morgantown, WV: Gargoyle.

Gardner, H. 1993. *Multiple intelligences.* New York: Basic.

Gates-MacGinitie Reading Comprehension Test, Evaluation 5–6, Form K., 7–9, Form K. 1989. Haska, IL: Riverside.

Gilligan, C., Ward, J. V., Taylor, J. M., & Bardige, B. 1988. *Mapping the moral domain.* Cambridge, MA: Harvard University Press.

Goodenough, F., & Harris, D. B. 1963. *Children's drawings as measures of mental maturity.* New York: Harcourt, Brace & World.

Gordon, H. 1989. In Craig, H., & Gordon, H. Specialized cognitive functions for deaf individuals: Implications for instruction. In Martin, D. S. (Eds), *Cognition, education and deafness.* Washington, DC: Gallaudet University Press.

Hao, Ching. *The spirit of the brush.* 1948. Translated by Shio Sakanishi, PhD. London: John Murray, 50 Albemarle St.

Hayes, K. 1978. *The relationship between drawing ability and reading scores.* Unpublished master's thesis, College of New Rochelle, New York.

Heath, W. 2000. Cancer comics: The humor of the tumor. *ARTherapy: Journal of the American Art Therapy Association, 17*(1), 479.

Henn, K. 1990. *The effects of an integrated arts curriculum on the representation of spatial relationships.* Unpublished master's thesis, Buffalo State College, New York.

Hiscox, A. R. 1990. *An alternative to language-oriented IQ tests for learning-disabled children.* Unpublished master's thesis, College of Notre Dame, Belmont, California.

Hoffman, D. D. 1998. *Visual intelligence: How we create what we see.* New York: Norton.

Hornsby, J. J. 1966. On equivalence. In Bruner et al. (Eds.), *Studies in Cognitive Growth,* (pp. 79–85). New York: John Wiley,.

Horovitz-Darby, E. 1991. Family art therapy within a deaf system. *Arts in Psychotherapy, 18*(3), 254–261.

Horovitz-Darby, E. 1996. Preconference course presentation, 1996 Conference of the American Art Therapy Association, Philadelphia.

Hunter, G. 1992. *An examination of some individual differences in information processing, personality, and motivation with respect to some dimensions of spatial thinking or problem solving in TAFE students.* Unpublished master's thesis, University of New England, Armidale, Australia.

Iowa Test of Basic Skills. 1955–1996. Chicago: Riverside.

Jakobson, R. 1964. Linguistic typology of aphasic impairment. In A. DeReuck and M. O'Conner (Eds.), *Disorder of language.* Boston: Little, Brown.

Jung, C. G. 1974. *Man and his symbols.* New York: Dell.

Kaplan, F. F. 2000. *Art, science, and art therapy.* London: Jessica Kingsley.

Koppitz, E. M. 1968. *Psychological evaluation of children's human figure drawings.* New York: Grune & Stratton.

Kopytin, A. 2001. The Russian standardization of the Silver Drawing Test and the problem of culturally dependent and culturally independent variables of graphic images. *The Healing Art, International Art Therapy Journal , 4*(3), 23–46. (Published in Russian)

Kramer, E. 1971. *Art as therapy with children.* New York: Shocken.

Lachman–Chapin, M. 1987. M. Kohut's theories on narcissism: Implications for art therapy. *American Journal of Art Therapy, 19,* 3–9.

Lambert, C. 1999. *Harvard Magazine* (Sept.–Oct.).

Lampart, M. T. 1960. *The art work of deaf children.* American Annals of the Deaf, 105, 419–423.

Lane, R. D. & Nadel, L. 2000. *Cognitive neuroscience of emotion.* New York: Oxford University Press.

Langer, S. K. 1957. *Problems of art.* New York: Scribner.

Langer, S. K. 1958. *Philosophy in a new key.* New York: Mentor.

Langer, S. K. 1962. *Reflections on art.* Baltimore: Johns Hopkins University Press.

Levick, M. F. 1989. *The Levick Emotional and Cognitive Art Therapy Assessment (LECATA).* Miami: Myra F. Levick.

Ledoux, J. 1996. *The emotional brain.* New York: Touchstone.

Linebaugh, A. J. 1996. *What the school age child perceives in a hospital environment: The DAS instru-*

ment with physically ill children. Unpublished master's thesis, Long Island University, Brookville, New York.

Malchiodi, C. A. 1997. *Breaking the silence.* New York: Brunner/Mazel.

Malchiodi, C. A. 1998. *Understanding children's drawings.* New York: Guilford.

Mango, C. & Richman, J. 1990. Humor and art therapy. *American Journal of Art Therapy, 28,* (May), 111–114.

Marshall, S. B. 1988. *The use of art therapy to foster cognitive skills with learning disabled children.* Unpublished master's thesis, Pratt Institute, School of Arts and Design, Brooklyn, New York.

Martin, D. S., 1991. *Advances in cognition, education, and deafness.* Washington, DC: Gallaudet University.

McGee, M. 1979. Human spatial abilities: Psychometric studies and environmental influences. *Psychological Bulletin, 86*(5), 889–918.

McKnew, H., Cytryn, L., & Yahries, H. 1983. *Why isn't Johnny crying?* New York: Norton.

Metropolitan Reading Instructional Tests. 1960. San Diego: Psychological Corp.

Metropolitan Achievement Test. 1931–1993. San Antonio, TX: Psychological Corporation.

Miller, W. I. 1997. *The anatomy of disgust.* Cambridge, MA: Harvard University Press.

Moir, A., & Jessel, D. 1992. *Brain sex.* New York: Dell.

Moser, J. 1980. *Drawing and painting and learning disabilities.* Unpublished doctoral dissertation, New York University, New York.

Olver, R., & Hornsby, J. R. 1996. On equivalence. In J. S. Bruner et al. (Eds.), *Studies in cognitive growth* (pp. 79–85). New York: John Wiley.

Otis Lennon School Ability Test. 1996–1997. New York: Harcourt-Brace.

Pannunzio, D. M. 1991. *Short-term adjunctive art therapy as a treatment intervention for depressed hospitalized youth.* Unpublished master's thesis, Ursuline College, Pepper Pike, Ohio.

Pfeffer, C. R. 1986. *The suicidal child.* New York: Guilford.

Piaget, J., & Inhelder, B. 1967. *The child's conception of space.* New York: Norton.

Piaget, J. 1970. *Genetic epistemology.* New York: Columbia University Press.

Polio, H. R. & Polio, M. R. 1992. Current research in cognition, education, and deafness: some observations from a different point of view. In Martin, D. S. (Ed.).

Restak, R. M. 1994. *The modular brain.* New York: Scribner.

Pfeffer, C. R. 1986. *The suicidal child.* New York: Guilford.

Rubin, J. A. 1987. *Approaches to art therapy.* New York: Brunner/Mazel.

Rubin, J. A. 1999. *Art Therapy: An introduction.* Philadelphia, Brunner/Mazel.

Rugel, R. P. 1974. WISC Subtest scores of disabled readers, a review. *Journal of Learning Disabilities, 7,* 57–64.

Sandburg, L., Silver, R., & Vilstrup, K. 1984. The stimulus drawing technique with adult psychiatric patients, stroke patients, and adolescents in art therapy. *ARTherapy: Journal of the American Art Therapy Association, 1*(3), 132–140.

Schafer, D., & Fisher, P. 1981. The epidemiology of suicide in children and young adolescents. *Journal of the American Academy of Child Psychiatry, 21,* 545–565.

Schlain, L. 1998. *The alphabet versus the goddess.* New York: Penguin.

Silver, R., & Carrion, F. 1991. Using the Silver Drawing Test in school and hospital. *American Journal of Art Therapy, 30*(2), 36–43.

Silver, R., & Ellison, J. 1995. Identifying and assessing self-images in drawings by delinquent adolescents. *The Arts in Psychotherapy, 22*(4) 339–352. ERIC EJ 545 763.

Silver, R., & Lavin, C. 1977. The role of art in developing and evaluating cognitive skills. *Journal of Learning Disabilities, 10*(7), 416–424.

Silver, R., Boeve, E., Hayes, K., Itzler, J., Lavin, C., O'Brien, J. et al. 1980. *Assessing and developing cognitive skills in handicapped children through art.* National Institution of Education Project # G 79 0081. New York: College of New Rochelle. ERIC ED #209878.

Silver, R. 1962. Potentialities in art education for the deaf. *Eastern Arts Quarterly, 1*(2) 30–38.

Silver, R. 1963. Art for the deaf child—Its potentialities. *Volta Review, 65*(8), 408–413.

Silver, R. 1966. *The role of art in the conceptual thinking, adjustment, and aptitudes of deaf and aphasic children.* Doctoral dissertation, Teacher's College, Columbia University, New York.

Silver, R. 1967. *A demonstration project in art education for deaf and hard of hearing children and adults.* U.S. Office of Education, Bureau of Research, Project #6–8598. ERIC ED# oi3 009.

Silver, R. 1971. The role of art in the cognition, adjustment, transfer, and aptitudes of deaf children. In C. Deussen (Ed.), *Proceedings of the Conference on Art for the Deaf* (pp. 15–26). Los Angeles: Junior Art Center.

Silver, R. 1972. *The transfer of cognition and attitudes of deaf and aphasic children through art.* Springfield, Illinois, Office of the Superintendent of Public Instruction.

Silver, R. 1973. *A study of cognitive skills development through art experiences.* New York: City Board of Education, State Urban Education Project # 147 232 101, ERIC Ed # 084 745, EC 060 575.

Silver, R. 1975a. *Using art to evaluate and develop cognitive skills.* Paper presented at the 1975 AATA Annual Conference, ERIC ED # 116 401, EC 080 793.

Silver, R. 1975b. Children with communication disorders: cognitive and artistic development. *American Journal of Art Therapy, 14*(2), 39–47.

Silver, R. 1975c. Clues to cognitive functioning in the drawings of stroke patients. *American Journal of Art Therapy, 15*(10), 3–8.

Silver, R. 1976a. *Shout in silence: Visual arts and the deaf.* New York: Metropolitan Museum of Art.

Silver, R. 1976b. Using art to evaluate and develop cognitive skills: Children with communication disorders and children with learning disabilities. *American Journal of Art Therapy, 16*(1), 11–19.

Silver, R. 1977a. The question of imagination, originality, and abstract thinking by deaf children. *American Annals of the Deaf, 122*(3), 349–354; ERIC ED # 166 043, EC # 093 422.

Silver, R. 1978. *Developing cognitive and creative skills through art.* Baltimore: University Park Press.

Silver, R. 1979. *Art as language for the handicapped.* Washington, DC: The Smithsonian Institution. Catalogue of an exhibition circulated 1979–1982, ERIC ED # 185 774.

Silver, R. 1982a. *Stimulus drawings and techniques in therapy, development, and assessment.* New York: Trillium.

Silver, R. 1982b. Developing cognitive skills through art. In L. G. Katz (Ed.), *Current topics in early childhood education* (vol. 4, pp. 143–171). Norwood, NJ: Ablex. ERIC ED # 207674.

Silver, R. A. 1983a. Identifying gifted handicapped children through their drawings. *ARTherapy, Journal of the American Art Therapy Association, 1*(10), 40–46. ERIC EJ #295 217.

Silver, R. 1983b. *Silver drawing test of cognition and emotion.* Seattle, WA: Special Child.

Silver, R. 1986. *Stimulus drawings and techniques in therapy, development, and assessment.* New York: Trillium.

Silver, R. 1987a. Sex differences in the emotional content of drawings. *ARTherapy: Journal of the American Art Therapy Association, 4*(2), 67–77.

Silver, R. 1987b. A cognitive approach to art therapy. In Judith Rubin (Ed.), *Approaches to art therapy* (pp 233–250). New York: Brunner/Mazel.

Silver, R. 1988a. Screening children and adolescents for depression through Draw a Story. *American Journal of Art Therapy, 26*(4), 119–124.

Silver, R. 1988b. *Draw a Story: Screening for depression.* Mamaroneck, NY: Ablin.

Silver, R. 1989a. *Developing cognitive and creative skills through art.* Mamaroneck NY: Ablin; ERIC ED # 410 479 209 878.

Silver, R. 1989b. *Stimulus drawings and techniques in therapy, development, and assessment.* New York: Trillium.

Silver, R. 1990. *Silver drawing test of cognition and emotion.* (2nd ed.). Sarasota, FL: Ablin.

Silver, R. 1991. *Stimulus drawings and techniques in therapy, development, and assessment.* (3rd ed.), Sarasota, FL: Ablin.

Silver, R. 1992. Gender differences in drawings, a study of self-images, autonomous subjects, and relationships. *ARTherapy: Journal of the American Art Therapy Association, 9*(2), 85–92.

Silver, R. 1993a, 2000. *Draw a Story: Screening for depression and age or gender differences.* New York: Trillium; Sarasota, FL: Ablin.

Silver, R. 1993b. Age and gender differences expressed through drawings: A study of attitudes toward self and others. *ARTherapy: Journal of the American Art Therapy Association, 10*(3), 159–168; ERIC EJ 502 564.

Silver, R. 1993c. Assessing the emotional content of drawings by older adults. *American Journal of Art Therapy, 32,* 46–52.

Silver, R. 1996a. *Silver drawing test of cognition and emotion.* 3rd ed. Sarasota, FL: Ablin.

Silver, R. 1996b. Sex differences in the solitary and assaultive fantasies of delinquent and non-delinquent adolescents. *Adolescence, 31*(123), 543–552.

Silver, R. 1996c. Gender differences and similarities in the spatial abilities of adolescents. *ARTherapy: Journal of the American ARTherapy Association, 13*(2), 118–120; ERIC EJ 530 390.

Silver, R. 1997a. Sex and age differences in attitudes toward the opposite sex. *ARTherapy: Journal of the American Art Therapy Association, 14*(4), 268–272.

Silver, R. 1997b. *Stimulus drawings & techniques in therapy, development, and assessment (5th ed.).* Sarasota, FL: Ablin.

Silver, R. 1998a. Gender parity and disparity in spatial skills: Comparing horizontal, vertical, and other task performances *ARTherapy: Journal of the American Art Therapy Association 15*(1), 38–46.

Silver, R.1998b. *Updating the Silver drawing test and draw a story manuals.* Sarasota, FL: Ablin.

Silver, R. 1999. Differences among aging and young adults in attitudes and cognition. *ARTherapy: Journal of the American Art Therapy Association, 16*(3), 33–139.

Silver, R. 2000a. *Studies in art therapy, 1962–2000.* Sarasota, FL: Ablin.

Silver, R. 2000b. *Developing cognitive and creative skills through art: Programs for children with communication disorders*. (4th ed.). Lincoln, NE: iuniverse.com. An Author' Guild Backinprint.com edition.

Silver, R. 2001. *Art as language: Access to emotions and cognitive skills*. Philadelphia: Brunner/Routledge.

Sless, D. S. 1981. *Learning and visual communication*. New York: John Wiley.

Smith, M. D. et al., 1977. Intellectual characteristics of school labeled learning disabled children. *Exceptional Child, 4*(6) 352–357.

Sonstroem, A. M. On the conservation of solids. In J. S. Bruner, et al. *Studies in cognitive growth*. New York: John Wiley.

SRA Reading Achievement Test and Survey of Basic Skills Ability. 1978–1987. Monterey, CA; McMillan-McGraw-Hill.

Stern, C. 1965. *The flight from woman*. New York: Noonday.

Sternberg, R. J. 1997. *Successful intelligence*. New York: Plume-Penguin Group.

Tannen, D. 1990. *You just don't understand*. New York: Ballantine.

Tinen, L. 1990. Biological processes in nonverbal communication and their role in the making and interpretation of art. *American Journal of Art Therapy, 29*(8), 9–13.

Torrance, E. P. 1962. *Guiding creative talent*. Englewood Cliffs, NJ: Prentice-Hall.

Torrance, E. P. 1980. Creative intelligence and an agenda for the 80s. *Art Education, 33*(7) 8–14.

Torrance, E. P. 1984. *The Torrance test of creative thinking, figural form A*. Bensonville, IL: Scholastic.

Turner, C. 1993. The Draw a Story in assessment of abuse. Preconference course presentation at the 1993 Conference of the American Art Therapy Association, Atlanta.

Ulman, E. 1987. *Ulman personality assessment procedure*. Montpelier, VT: American Journal of Art Therapy.

Vega, W. A., Kolody, B., Aguilar–Gaxiola, S., Alderete, E., Catalano, R., Caraveo-Anduaga, J. 1998. Lifetime prevalence of DSM-III-R psychiatric disorders among urban and rural Mexican Americans in California. *Archives of General Psychiatry, 55*(9) 771–780.

Vilstrup, K. 1984. See Sandburg, Silver, & Vilstrup. The stimulus drawing technique with adult psychiatric patients, stroke patients, and adolescents in art therapy. *ARTherapy: Journal of the American Art Therapy Association, 1*(13), 132–140.

Wadeson, H. 1980. *Art Psychotherapy*. New York; John Wiley..

Wechsler Adult Intelligence Scale (WAIS). 1971–1991. San Antonio, TX: Psychological Corp.

Wechsler Intelligence Scale for Children (WISC). 1971–1991. San Antonio, TX: Psychological Corp.

Whitehurst, G. 1984. Interrater agreement for journal manuscript reviews. *American Psychologist, 39*, 22–28.

White-Wolff, E. 1991. *Art and sand play in twins*. Unpublished master's degree thesis, Sonoma State University, Rohmert Park, California.

Wilson, M. F. 1990. *Art therapy as an adjunctive treatment modality with depressed hospitalized adolescents*. Unpublished master's degree thesis, Ursuline College, Pepper Pike, Ohio.

Wilson, M. F. 1993. *Assessment of brain injury patients with the Draw-a-Story Instrument*. Preconference course presentation at the 1993 Conference of the American Art Therapy Association, Atlanta.

Winder, B. W. 1962. *Statistical Principles in Experimental Design.* New York: McGraw-Hill.

Witkin, H. A. 1962. *Psychological differentiation.* New York: John Wiley.

Zeki, S. 1999. *Inner vision, an exploration of art and the brain.* Oxford, UK: Oxford University Press.

Zeki, S. 2001. Artistic creativity and the brain. *Science, 5*(293) (July), 51.

Ziv, A. 1984. *Personality and sense of humor.* New York: Springer.

de-Zwart, Sinclair, H. 1969. Developmental psycholinguistics. In D. Elkin and J. H. Flavel (Eds.), *Studies in cognitive development.* London: Oxford University Press.

Index

Allessandrini, 257
Altabe, Madeline, 73, 171, 177, 228
Anderson, 126
Anderson, Victoria, 72
Arnheim, 7
Art education, 70
Art experiences
and language, 21
Art assessments, 1, 5, 8
    and emotional indicators, 6
    and intellectual maturity, 6
    studies of, 9

Bannatyne, 13
Beck Depression Inventory, 161-162
Brandt, Michelle, 183
Bronowsky, Jacob, 259
Bruner, Jerome, 7, 14

California Achievement Test (CAT), 128
Classify
    ability to, 22
Coffey, C. M., 182

Cognitive development, 108–109
Cognitive skills
    and drawing, 7
Combine
    the ability to, 16
Conserve
    the ability to, 17, 22
Couch, Janet Beaujon, 218
Craig, 124
Creativity, 16, 77
Cytryn, 161

Damasio, Antonio, 5
de-Zwart, Sinclair, 7
Deaf children
    artwork of, 19
Depressive illness
    diagnostic criteria for, 161
Depressive patients
    drawings of, 162
Dhanachitsiriphong, Pornchit, 109, 251
    SDT study of, 109
Draw-a-Story Assessment (DAS), 9, 136–140

and abused subjects, 180–181

administering, 134

and adolescent depression, 169

and age and gender differences in attitudes toward self and others, 173–176

and brain-injured clients, 181

and childhood depression, 169

and clinical depression, 164

comparison with SDT, 226–228

comparison with SDT Drawing from Imagination Subtest, 225

comparison with SDT in cognitive content, 229–230

comparison with SDT in emotional content, 229–230

comparison with Stimulus Drawing and Techniques Assessment, 224

and conduct disorders, 176

and depressed adolescents, 182–183

and depressed females, 169

and depressed males, 169

and depressive illness, 163, 165, 167–169

and emotional content of drawings, 162

and emotionally disturbed subjects, 164, 182

and group therapy, 182

and learning disabled subjects, 163–164, 167

and masked depression, 170

rating scale, 135

reliability and validity of, 161

results of, 166–167

scorer reliability, 162–163

scoring of, 141–160, 166

and screening for depression, 133, 164

and self-image, 176–178, 180–181

and self-reporting of depression, 169–170

and sex-offending adolescents, 183

and suicidal adolescents, 182

tasks of, 133–134

test-retest reliability of, 162–163

use of in psychiatric hospital, 182–183

use of with emotionally disturbed and non-disturbed adolescents, 171–173

use of with male adolescent delinquents, 176–177

uses of, 223

Drawing from Imagination Subtest, 3, 6, 25, 70, 72, 94, 125

administering, 44–47

cognitive content scoring, 15–16

comparison with Draw-a-Story, 224–225

comparison with Stimulus Drawing and Techniques Assessment, 223

Emotional projection scale of, 6–7, 14

emotional content scoring, 14

examples of, 51–63, 81

posttest, 84

and reading comprehension, 72

scoring, 44, 48–50, 82–83

Self-image scale of, 7, 14–15

stimulus drawings, 6, 14

uses of, 223

Drawing from Observation Subtest, 3, 18–19, 25, 93, 208

administering, 36

examples of, 39–43

scoring, 37–38, 82–83

Dunn-Snow, Peggy, 182

Earwood, Cheryl, 254

Eating disorders and SDT, 113–114

Ellison, Joanne, 176–177, 228

Emotions and cognition, 5

Finney, Piyachat R., 250–251

Fisher, 162

Fluornoy, 259

Gantt, Linda, 162

Gates-MacGinitie Reading Test, 72

Gilligan, 118

Gordon, 124

Hao, Ching, 5

Hayes, Karen, 70–72

Hearing children
and spatial skills, 124

Hearing impaired
art program for, 20

Hearing impaired children
selecting and combining images and

words of, 125
and spatial skills, 124
Heath, Wende, 231
Henn, 110
SDT study of, 110
Hiscox, 128
SDT study of, 128
Hoffman, Donald, 7–8
Holzman, Eileen McCormick, 198
Horizontality
concept of, 17
Hornsby, 15
Horovitz-Derby, Ellen, 74
Humor
aggressive, 180
ambivalent or ambiguous, 239
disparaging, 234–237
and drawing tasks, 64
function of, 232
in medical treatments, 231–232
in psychiatric in-patients, 231
lethal, 232–234
playful, 240
resilient, 237–238
scoring of for SDT Drawing from
Imagination Subtest, 241
self-disparaging, 227
uses of, 242–246
Hunter, Glenda, 249–250

Inhelder, Barbel, 16–18, 70, 99

Jakobson, Ramon, 15

Kaplan, Frances, 8
Kleinhans, John, 101
Knowledge
kinds of, 259–260
Kopytin, Alexander, 252, 257
Krauss, Beatrice, 197

Lane, Richard, 5
Langer, Suzanne, 7
Language, 21
Language and logic, 7
Language impaired, 20–21
Lavin, Claire, 105–106

Malchoidi, Cathy, 217
Mango, Christine, 231
Marshall, 109
SDT study of, 109
McCormick, Eileen, 84
McGee, 122
McKnew, 161
Metropolitan Reading and Arithmetic Test
(MRAT), 106
Moser, Joy, 69, 76

Nadel, Lynn, 5
National Institute of Education Project
(NIEP), 22–23, 74
administration of, 106
developmental procedures, 106
effectiveness of, 107–108
pre- and posttest scores, 107
test study groups, 106

Otis Lennon Ability Test, 106–107

Pfeffer, 161
Pfeiffer, Dr. Linda Jo, 253, 257
Piaget, Jean, 7, 13–14, 16–18, 20–21, 23, 70,
99, 207
Pollio, 126
Pollio, 126
Predictive Drawing Subtest, 3, 16–18, 25, 70,
92, 124, 208
administering, 26–27
age differences in, 121–122
examples of, 34–36
gender differences in, 121–122
scoring, 28–33, 82–83

Represent
the ability to, 16
Restak, 8
Richman, Joseph, 231

Sandburg, Louise, 217
Schachner, Patricia, 198
Schlain, 8
Select
ability to, 15

Index

Self and others in SDT assessments
  age-related differences in attitudes
    toward, 119–121
  attitudes toward, 118–119
  gender differences in attitudes toward,
    119–121
  older adult attitudes toward, 119
Self-image
  gender differences in, 118
Sequential order
  concept of, 17
Shafer, 162
Silver Drawing Test (SDT), 3, 7, 9
  administering, 25–26
  analysis of, 257–258
  autonomous subject drawings, 118
  cognitive content scales, 85
  and cognitive skills, 75–76
  collection of data, 65
  comparison of Hispanic and American
    adolescent scores, 256
  comparison of use in Russia, Brazil and
    United States, 252
  comparison of use in Russia and United
    States, 253
  comparison to reading test scores, 71–72
  comparison with Draw-a-Story,
    226–228
  comparison with Draw-a-Story in
    cognitive content, 229–230
  comparison with Draw-a-Story in
    emotional content, 229–230
  comparison with Stimulus Drawing and
    Techniques, 227
  and conceptual skills, 77
  correlations with Bender Visual Motor
    Gestalt, 76–77
  correlations with Diagnostic Art Therapy
    Assessment (DATA), 74
  correlations with Draw-A-Man
    Assessment Tool, 77
  correlations with Goodenough-Harris
    Draw-a-Man Test, 76
  correlations with Metropolitan
    Achievement Test (MAT), 73–74
  correlations with SRA Survey of Basic
    Skills Ability, 73

correlations with traditional language-
    oriented tests, 74–75
correlations with Wechsler Adult
    Intelligence Scales (WAIS), 76–77
and creativity, 77
cultural bias, 257–258
cultural comparison between Brazil and
    United States, 248–249
development of, 19–20
and eating disorders, 113–114
emotional content scales, 86–89
field tests of, 20–23
and food attitude associations, 111–114
and gifted children responses, 84
and hearing children, 123–124
and hearing impaired children, 123–124
and learning disabled children, 129
normative data for 1996, 79–80
and opposite sex attitudes, 114–117
overview, 13
process of adding to normative data,
    84–85
and reading disabled children, 129
relationship drawings, 118
relationship with other tests of
    intelligence and achievement, 108
retest reliability, 69–70
scorer reliability, 65–68
and scores of deaf children, 128
and scores of learning disabled children,
    128
and scores of unimpaired children, 128
scoring, 95–96
self-image scales, 86–88, 90–92
subtests of, 13–14
use of by art therapists, 23
use of in Australia, 249–250
use of in Brazil, 247–249
use of in psychiatric day-care center, 251
use of in Russia, 252–253
use of in Thailand, 250–252
use of with U.S. Hispanic students,
    253–256
use with language disorders, 209
and verbal ability, 77
and visual-motor disordered children,
    104–105

◇ ◇ ◇

Spatial skills in SDT assessment
    gender differences in, 122–123, 126
    and hearing children, 123
    and hearing impaired children, 123
State Urban Education Project (SUEP),
    22–23
    administration of, 98–99
    developmental procedures, 98
    goals of, 97
    pre- and posttest scores, 101–104
    results of, 99–101
    test study groups, 97–98
Stern, Karl, 259
Sternberg, Robert, 260
Stimulus drawings, 8
Stimulus Drawings & Techniques (SD), 9, 187
    assessment techniques, 190
    comparison with Draw-a-Story, 224
    comparison with SDT, 227
    comparison with SDT Drawing from
        Imagination Subtest, 223
    developmental techniques, 189
    evaluation scale for cognitive and creative
        skills, 192
    evaluation scale for environment, 191
    evaluation scale for principal subjects, 191
    objectives of, 188–190
    procedures, 188–190
    reliability of, 197–198
    retest reliability of, 198–204
    scorers, 197
    scoring, 193–197
    and SDT, 197
    and SDT Drawing from Imagination
        Subtest, 198
    therapeutic techniques, 188
    use in age and gender difference studies,
        218–220
    use in remediation, 209–215
    use with adults with chronic
        schizophrenia, 217
    use with dementia patients, 218
    use with hearing and language impaired,
        205–208
    use with learning disabled, 213–215
    use in psychiatric hospital with
        adolescents, 216
    use with seniors, 213
    use with sexually abused children, 217
    use with twins, 217
    uses of, 223
Swanson, Joan, 73

Taylor, 118
Torrance, E. Paul, 1–2, 16
Torrance Test of Creative Thinking, 1, 19–20
Turner, Christine, 180–181

Verbal deficiencies and art, 5
Verticality
    concept of, 17–18
Vilstrup, Kristen, 216
Visual art, 15
Visual brain, 15
Visual intelligence, 7–8
Visual-motor disordered children
    and SDT, 104–105

Wadeson, Harriet, 162
Ward, 118
Wechsler Intelligence Scale for Children
(WISC), 13
White-Wolff, 217
Williams, 126
Wilson, Mary, 181–182
Witkin, 7
Woods, 126

Yahracs, 161

Zeki, Semir, 5, 7, 15, 17–18
Ziv, Avner, 232